KT-599-194

BALLETOMANIA

BALLETOMANIA

The Story of an Obsession

BY

ARNOLD L. HASKELL

LONDON

VICTOR GOLLANCZ LTD

14 Henrietta Street Covent Garden

First published September 1934
Second impression September 1934
Third impression October 1934
Fourth impression April 1935
Fifth impression (first cheap edition) September 1936
Sixth impression November 1936
Seventh impression January 1938
Eighth impression April 1940
Ninth impression October 1940
Tenth impression April 1941
Eleventh impression September 1941
Twelfth impression January 1942
Thirteenth impression March 1942
Fourteenth impression July 1942
Fifteenth impression November 1942
Sixteenth impression May 1944
Seventeenth impression January 1946
Eighteenth impression March 1946

Printed in Great Britain by
The Camelot Press Ltd., London and Southampton

DEDICATION

To

LEONIDE MASSINE

Souvenir of a journey of discovery ;
a small return for *Les Présages*, *Choreartium*,
and the rest

A. L. H.

CONTENTS

A PREFATORY NOTE

I HAVE TRIED in the choice of photographs, as in the text, to record the true line of succession from the Maryinsky *ballerinas* through their successors in the Diaghileff Ballet to the reigning stars of to-day, their pupils. The number of photographs assigned to me seemed ample, until I came to make the choice, when it was obvious that everyone could not be fairly represented. I have therefore deliberately concentrated on the young dancers of to-day. There are many works dealing with history, and even with the immediate past, none, as yet, with the present and the future. This pictorial record, therefore, of these fine artists, at the very start of their careers, should in the years to come prove valuable. Will the poses, perhaps, seem a little quaint to the *balletomane* of the 1960's? They are young enough to be shining then, with just a faint dimming of the light. But here they will be for ever young.

In the actual photographs selected, out of the many hundreds I have examined—my own collection comprises well over a thousand—I have not been guided by the idea of getting a fine dancing picture, graceful, aerial and suggestive of motion, as much as of finding something that is truly typical of the performer, and that reveals an aspect of personality. I have carefully avoided everything that has been faked for effect.

The photographs in which the toes are made into small tapering points, barely touching the ground, are an abomination, as are also the many photographs of motion, taken from such a distorted angle that the effect of the elevation is increased to the point of absurdity. The most æthereal dancer has weight, and a foundation of bone and muscle with which to support it. The functions of the old lithograph and the camera are distinct. The main importance of a dancing photograph, and its true beauty, lies in its value as a document, in its ability to fix one instant of beauty from the many that an evening at the ballet affords.

The names of ballets are for the most part in French.

I have adopted no system for transcribing Russian names in English. There are many admirable ones, strictly logical, but all the same they give comical results, after one has been used to certain spellings. The Russians themselves are very haphazard in this respect, sometimes varying from season to season. In any case they can all be easily identified here, and that is all that really matters.

I am grateful to too many people, characters in this book and others, to be able to enumerate them all.

In particular I must thank my good friends Colonel de Basil, whose guest I must have been on over 200 occasions, and Mr. Serge Grigorieff for the many opportunities they have given me for studies on the spot ; also Mme Tchernicheva for allowing me to be an almost permanent onlooker at her inspiring class ; Mr. Warren Zambra for his reading of the proofs and his many valuable suggestions, and that fine photographer and brother *balletomane*, Iris, for the endless trouble he has taken on my behalf.

Finally, Gontcharova and Larionov for letting me reproduce so many of their unpublished sketches and caricatures—and then for giving me the originals.

A. L. H.

LIST OF ILLUSTRATIONS

(*Between pp. 192 and 193*)

ILLUSTRATIONS IN THE TEXT

(from the sketch-books of Gontcharova and Larionov)
The original drawings for their productions

INTRODUCTORY

"*Socrate :* Mais qu'est-ce donc que la danse, et que peuvent dire des pas ?

"*Phèdre :* Oh ! Jouissons encore un peu, naïvement, de ces beaux actes ! . . . A droite, à gauche ; en avant ; en arrière ; et vers le haut et vers le bas, elle semble offrir des présents, des parfums, de l'encens, des baisers, et sa vie elle-même, à tous les points de la sphère, et aux pôles de l'univers. . . ."

PAUL VALÉRY : L'Âme et la Danse

THIS IS IN NO SENSE a history or a complete survey of contemporary ballet. Both the personal angle from which it is written, and the recent rapid developments of this vigorous art make that an impossibility. It is written very definitely from a personal angle, the angle of a man madly, but let us hope not blindly, in love with a certain conception of ballet, and consequently uninterested in, and even hostile to, many other forms of the dance. That conception is, I believe, large enough to cover a very wide ground, and the love intense enough to be critical of everything that bears the name *ballet*, until it has proved itself by a whole series of performances. It is only then that a true perspective can be obtained ; and when a work and a company are both so well known that carmine-coloured nails, objectionable at all times, can in *Les Sylphides*, by cutting off abruptly the fine line of the fingers and substituting bloody stumps, produce a feeling of profound irritation, that the right diagnosis is *balletomania*.

This is the story of an adventure in search of the experience that alone can give the very maximum of pleasure at

a performance, an adventure that has led me into the classrooms of the world to dissect every movement, so that just
as the concert-goer can follow with his score, I can solve
the mysteries of movement with my mental score. It is
cold-blooded perhaps, but when I applaud and shout
I must know why, and if I know the reason first, then I am
completely happy, without the fear that soon, after two or
three performances, I shall be a little ashamed of my
temporary intoxication.

Nothing is more difficult than to express dancing in
words. The actual life of the dancer is so short. What can
the seven-lettered word *Pavlova* mean to those who never
saw her, however many books in her praise are left behind ? Yet how much it can convey to those of us who did,
who can still see *The Dying Swan* on an empty stage, and
relive its thrills, moment by moment, till that final unforgettable tremor, when the ruby brooch seemed to
liquefy into an actual drop of blood from the heart of The
Swan. A drama, a life's experience in two minutes, based
on the classroom *pas de bourrée*, and made up of a simple
sequence of steps. No, analysis cannot be cold-blooded. It
makes the achievement the nobler, Anna Pavlova still
more supreme. Even the work of those dancers still with
us dies as the curtain falls; the performance of each night
remains unique.

I am fond of reading contemporary accounts of some
great dancer of the past, of looking at drawings, old prints
and faded photographs. It was with a thrill that I spoke
to an old lady who had taken lessons from Taglioni herself. She remembered it all so clearly : the apartment in
Paris, the portrait dedicated by Rossini " à la plus légère
des Sylphides," and the rather prim old lady " with arms
so unusually long that one wondered at her poetry." She

was fussily correct in her *tenue*, and took the little girl severely to task one day: "Il ne faut jamais dire 'embétant,' ce n'est pas un mot qu'une jeune fille doit prononcer, dites ennuyeux, mais jamais, jamais ce mot de domestique." That is sentimental, a memory of no real importance, but such sentimental links also serve to keep our art alive when the last farewell has been given. If we are to be cold-blooded, critical, analytical, we must leave space for gossip too. Time can lend dignity to that gossip.

Like the dancer himself, sometimes I shall be gossiping in the wings, sometimes busy on the stage. The actual criticism consists largely of those performances of the last few years that are still alive in repertoire and memory. Thus the reader will be able to relive his own experiences as well as mine, point by point, and names will mean more than just a grouping of letters. There is a risk in this, too. The young dancers of to-day, the Toumanovas, Baronovas, Riabouchinskas, heroines of the latter part of my story, are developing rapidly. Already their charming, gawky rendering of a dance, that suddenly gives one a fresh vision of its meaning, is almost a thing of the past, replaced by a new-found perfection. But, whatever their development and their ultimate goal, they have already coloured their whole period. The new "Baby Ballet," patronised at first, is now assured of its place in history. Massine has guided them and made them dance, Derain, Mirò, Masson and others have dressed and decorated them, Auric has given them melody, and they have interpreted the music of the immortals.

I have tried throughout to give those who are really moulding our art the chance to express themselves, away from the stage itself, as they have done to me in so many after-performance discussions. Sometimes I disagree with the conclusions expressed, sometimes they are difficult to reconcile with one another, but the remarks of a practical man give one a new stimulus that is worth pages of theory.

If this book contains any lesson or theme, or even has continuity, it is that ballet is so much more than just a pleasant evening's entertainment ; that, like music or the drama, it has endless varieties of shades and subtleties not as yet fully understood outside dancing circles, and that the dancer suffers both in pride and pocket from such a lack of understanding. When we consider that there are fewer truly great dancers than virtuosi of the piano or violin, that a Baronova is as amazing in her depth of expression as a Menuhin, and as brilliant and rare a phenomenon, and that there are far fewer choreographers than playwrights, composers or painters, all first cousins, then we can realise that the dancer has still truly to be discovered, even by her most enthusiastic admirers. Ask anyone who has been applauding a great dancer or a good ballet his exact reasons, and the answer will most certainly be vague—something to do with beauty, grace or lightness, a fraction of the truth. His instinct was correct, but he lacked the very necessary framework in which to fit the experience. My adventure has been the construction of such a framework for myself.

The more concrete historical theme is that Michael Fokine gave us the ballet that we know and love, and that has had such a powerful effect on the whole artistic life of the century ; for a time it was lost, bankrupt of ideas and hidden under a mass of literary and æsthetic conceptions, hostile to the dance, and recently Leonide Massine, after many experimental wanderings, has once again made of it a creative force with a future.

Finally, a word addressed to dancers in an attempt to

preserve my future peace of mind. I believe that my many dear friends in ballet will take my criticism, at any rate of themselves, in good part, as they have done in the past, although each article or book has often meant an embarrassing reunion, until little points were straightened out. I have been entirely frank here. Too often in the past I have been tempted to become the propagandist at the expense of the critic, to see my subjects under the best possible light, to explain their virtues, and not to dwell on their faults. At one time there were so few enthusiasts. For me this present book cancels everything that I have ever written on the ballet ; all of that past writing goes into one big bonfire, with perhaps a shadowy company dancing gleefully around it.

No, decidedly this will not be history, but it may well be the very raw material for history in the future.

New York—Paris—London.
1933-1934.

CHAPTER I

BALLETOMANIA

"The dance is of all the arts the one that most influences the soul. Dancing is divine in its nature, and is the gift of God."

PLATO

"Dancing is silent poetry."

SIMONIDES

"Last Saturday night a very lamentable accident took place at Drury Lane Theatre, which has proved fatal to Miss Clara Webster, the dancer."

Illustrated London News, Dec. 21st, 1844

'A most lamentable occurrence happened last night at the Opéra ... Mlle Livry was about to go on to the stage when all at once her skirt took fire. . . ."

Le Constitutionel, Nov. 17th, 1862

"A Russian dancer, N. Simeonov, committed suicide by throwing himself over Niagara Falls."

Mirror, Stop Press, July 6th, 1932

IT IS MY FIRM BELIEF that human society is divided into three distinct castes : Russian dancers, dancers and very ordinary people. This great truth must first have dawned upon me at about the age of six, for I have always been conscious of it. Whether it came direct from my mother, to whom ballet means much, or as a violent reaction from my father, to whom it means boredom, I cannot tell. Probably it requires both to make the complete fanatic. At any rate, now, after many years of close association with dancers, I still believe it firmly. Even a knowledge of their little intrigues and jealousies, which are fully as

pronounced as in the case of writers or lawyers, if not quite
so bitter as with the scientists, cannot make me recant.
And I have suffered much from this failing. How well do
I know the cold, awkward silence that follows a favourable
answer to the challenging, almost threatening, " And what
did you think of X in *Le Lac des Cygnes* ?—No, really ? "
Yet now I can understand and excuse it. When the dancer
is jealous of her rival's performance, she is certainly even
far more jealous of an abstraction than an individual, a
certain *ballerina* X, who represents an absolute standard of
perfection, and it is in her rival that she can see some
aspects of that ideal. She is also jealous of the opportunity
to work and to develop. Later I will have much more to
say about that jealousy, but already in mitigating it I have
revealed myself. It is a symptom. Now I must make clear
my reasons, not merely to others, but, what is more difficult
still, to myself. What in fact is this dancer whom I worship ?
I know that in a country where so many take cricket in a
similar spirit, study its finesses, respect its traditions, and
make heroes of its exponents, sympathy at any rate will
be with me from the very start. For the cricket-lover and
the *balletomane* share many symptoms.

The dancer is perhaps the only true *amateur* in the
theatre to-day, using that word in its finest sense. She lives
definitely for her art, and not for what it can bring. Its
rewards are painfully meagre ; many years of overwork
at a bare living wage, a very generous share of applause
from a small public, a few Press cuttings with her name
misspelt, bouquets, photographs, with the end almost
inevitably a school, and the grind all over again, this time
vicariously. The dancer is also the supreme professional, at
the very other end of the scale from the film actress, who
starts with great physical beauty, is carefully studied, made

up by experts, and lit and photographed from selected angles that are flattering. She is even provided with a carefully planned personality. Her dramatic effects, if any, are not the climax, the gradual working up of a situation; they are merely made to appear so by those real professionals in the film world, the director and editors. The film actress is the true *amateur* of the theatre in the very reverse sense from the dancer. One day a typist, the next day a star, and the reward is great indeed. Puppet as she is, her work may be hard, but the dancer's is harder.[1] This is a chronicle of hard work. The dancer will never cut her rehearsals, but clamour for more, and, when she is not herself dancing, she watches others, in acute discomfort, for she will make every movement inwardly, and suffer with every fault. She has never finished learning. At the height of her triumph she must submit herself to the discipline, and often to the abuse, of her ballet-master. To him she is never " *Madame*," but always the small girl whose *arabesque* lacks perfection or whose elevation is weak. What a mental and physical training, this daily class. Frequently I refresh myself there, and seek new vision. It is the very start of the whole story.

" One . . . two. . . . Un . . . deux. . . . Rass—dva."

No flattering costumes, even if the traditional revealing black dress is no longer enforced, no scenery, no music. Every fault laid bare before the mirror and analysed, the sarcasms of the teacher, the amusement of the other pupils until their turn comes. I have yet to meet the truly conceited dancer—that is, the dancer who really believes in her

---

[1] Joyfully I make exception of Katharine Hepburn. She is one of the rare film actresses who understands movement and gesture, and can use them to maximum advantage. She is almost certainly ballet trained ; every moment of her films suggests that, and reveals a real personality, and not a directorial creation. Watching her provides one of my few theatrical thrills outside of ballet.—A. L. H.

own pathetic little attempts at bluff. There is always something new to be learned, something that X excels in and that she herself lacks. Her mother is there to blow the trumpet and beat the big drum ; every mother's daughter is a genius (more of dancers' mothers, much more, later), but she herself really knows. Dancers are fêted, meet the most interesting people of their day, but they live in a world apart, a world of their own making—classroom, rehearsal, a hurried meal, shoes and tights to darn, and the stage. " There is no time to be gay at all," said a disillusioned girl to me, with visions of champagne and slippers. They think of dancing, dream of dancing. Their values are their own ; they make and break reputations quite apart from popular estimation. And they respect the opinions of their little world above all else. Just recently I have heard an excited Nemchinova after a phenomenal, shrieking, shouting, clapping, flowery success : "And to think that Fokine should have troubled to come to me, and said all those fine things. It is a very great moment in my life." They know that theirs is the responsibility, that they alone are the sole guardians of a great tradition. In practice nothing much is written down, it all lives in the memory. The spirit of the performance of *Giselle* that we enjoy to-night, even if it has been recorded,[1] has been handed down from person to person for close on a hundred years, from country to country, yet only the smallest changes in detail must have crept in since its creation by Carlotta Grisi (1841), whom no dancer living to-day can ever have seen. Pavlova causes a revolution by discarding the ballet skirt in the second act for grave-clothes draperies that enhance her spiritual interpretation, Spessiva again reverts to tradition, but the

[1] Actually its movement is recorded by the Stepanoff system of steno-choregraphy. The cinema as a means of preserving records will soon make such complicated systems obsolete, but it can never render tradition unnecessary.—A. L. H.

spirit and substance remain unchanged. Massine at times forgets his own compositions, so great in number and diverse in feeling, Woizikovski remembers them, and the ballet goes on. The art of the individual dancer may be ephemeral. To-day we do not know how the great Taglioni danced—from the prints and lithographs we can only tell the incorporeal effect that she produced on her contemporaries—but her art is not dead. Some little girl in London, Paris or Milan dances differently because Taglioni once existed. She will carry part of Taglioni with her on to the stage. Already Anna Pavlova, with so much of Taglioni in her, is only an exciting memory, but a memory that is creative, that has made and still is making dancers, who will possess something of her poetry, even some of her technique, and especially that will to serve and to be artists. La Camargo, because of a pardonable vanity in her shapely legs, has given us the conventional ballet skirt, which has altered the whole technique of dancing. Heinel of Stuttgart has left with us the *pirouette*. To-day every ballet performance is a tribute to La Camargo and Heinel. Kchessinska, Trefilova, Preobrajenska and others of whom I will write, are daily giving something of themselves, so that ballet goes on living and growing, if dancers themselves die.

The ballet dancer is the perfect example of the balance between the individual and the group. Her whole aim in life is to shine as a star, a *ballerina assoluta*, yet she subordinates herself to the whole, the ballet. Always she is under rigid, almost military discipline, a discipline that becomes so much a part of herself that, under extraordinary circumstances, a group of excitable, highly strung young girls can act with the courage and presence of mind of a ship's crew.

It happened in Bournemouth, before a packed house, on the last night of the Monte Carlo Ballet Season.

It is the first ballet, *Le Lac des Cygnes*, with its dreamy romantic music, its comfortable old-fashioned scenery, so drab a background to the filmy white swans, princesses under a spell, and the audience is dazed with pleasure, perhaps under that selfsame spell. Danilova, with Eglevsky as her cavalier, is about to begin the great *adagio*, most completely satisfying moment of all, when piercing shrieks are heard. The unusual in something so well known, so ordered and logical, is especially terrifying. After a pause, a white swan runs fluttering on to the stage, her dress and wings in flames, reaching high above her head. So long does this agonised fluttering seem to last that I can recognise Rostova, the beautiful leader of one flock of swans, and take in her whole dazed expression, as the dancers retreat from her in horror, clutching at their billowing tarlatans. But it is too late, already Tarakanova is well alight, isolated now, as the flock retreats still further. Then Grigorieff in mufti, an intruder on this scene of magic, rushes on to the stage, and seizes her in his arms, while Jan Hoyer embraces Rostova and the flames. The orchestra pauses for an instant, but Danilova nods violently. I can hear her say : " Even if the theatre is on fire we *must* go on ; play." The beautiful *adagio* continues. Then a burned but reassuring hand is waved from the wings, the swans troop on again, Morosova stepping automatically into Rostova's place as leader. It has all been a question of a few bars of music, with nothing to show that the tragedies of poor Clara Webster and Emma Livry, burned alive on the stage, have nearly been reproduced before our eyes : an old-fashioned ballet for this old-fashioned tragedy of naked footlights and a dancer's *tutus*.

An old lady, seated next to me, is considerably amazed at my agitation and says : " Well, I thought it was all a part of the show. You never do know in ballet. They *are* so clever nowadays," and half the audience shares the same impression. They have not realised that Rostova, Tarakanova, the company, and perhaps they themselves, owe their lives, not only to the bravery and presence of mind of Grigorieff and Hoyer, who are badly burned, but to this whole conception of discipline on the stage. Not one of those girls realised that the entire theatre was not on fire, yet they backed into the wings, and walked quietly into the street, as if it had all been a part of Petipa's choregraphy, and Danilova, defying the fresh wiles of the magician, added one more performance of this most difficult of rôles to her brilliant record.

Then the last ballet, the complex *Choreartium*. Rostova appears in her rôle, dances especially well, and the only sign of the incident is Hoyer lifting with a heavily bandaged hand. Behind the scenes there is far less excitement than I have known about the destination of a bouquet, so often a sore point. There are some kisses and handclasps, and a much repeated little joke that seems to give general satisfaction . . . " This is *Lac des Cygnes*, but you gave a performance of *L'Oiseau de Feu*." Danilova, too, is promptly dubbed *The Captain*, but that is all. It is Saturday night ; dressing-rooms are hurriedly cleared, and the company goes home. There is a very early start for Birmingham the next morning, supper to be eaten, packing to be done.

Afterwards Rostova told me how she had gone to the stage dressing-room to touch up her make-up and looking in the glass had noticed a whole background of flames. Thinking that it was the theatre and not her own dress, she ran on to the stage to warn the others, and was terrified as

they drew away from her. I saw all that was left of the
dress, that had been set on fire by a candle carelessly left
alight, a small scrap of tarlatanless silk—yet she was un-
touched. Afterwards at the hotel just a simple : " Has
anyone got a French novel to lend me ? I may not sleep
very well to-night," from a pale little girl of seventeen.

Rostova, after her adventure, danced in *Choreartium*
because she was one of a group that needed her help, but
she danced beautifully, because she was an individual who
wished to excel.

This is as much a digression here as it was at the performance that night, but it is all a part of the tradition,
strong and unbreakable.

There are dynasties of dancers, and a true line of
succession. In 1847 Marius Petipa of Marseilles, real
founder of the Russian Ballet, goes to Russia, and is
received with all the warm St. Petersburg hospitality to
the visiting artist. He becomes a Russian, in spite of a
stubborn Marseillais accent. Before his death in 1910, he
composed fifty-four new ballets, mostly in five or six acts,
and was entrusted with the formation of several generations
of dancers. Christian Johannsen of Sweden also comes to
Russia. He is a pupil of the Bournonvilles, who were themselves pupils of the great Vestris ; an unbroken line. Like
all wise teachers, they too learn from their pupils, and the
Russian school is born. To quote Nicolas Legat, whose own
father was a visitor from Scandinavia : " The Russian
school is the French school that the French themselves
have forgotten."

Petipa composed fifty-four ballets. To-day, when we see
those that have survived—*Le Lac des Cygnes* and *Le Mariage
d'Aurore*—Petipa, and all the dancers who have performed
in them, live once again. The line goes on unbroken to our

day. Fokine works with Petipa, Johannsen and Legat, and then founds his modern ballet. Upon leaving Diaghileff, he teaches and produces in London, Paris, New York, Milan, Scandinavia, South America, leaving everywhere not only his own influence but what has gone before. Old *maestro* Cecchetti, a visitor from Italy, and teacher of a thousand dancers the world over, receives his first lesson from Giovanni Lepri, pupil of Carlo Blasis, a founder of the art. All the dancing wisdom of the world meets in Theatre Street before being dispersed once again. One forgetful generation, and ballet would be dead for ever ; but there is no risk of that. It can survive war and revolution.

Kchessinska, flying before the Bolsheviks, daily performs the exercises that might betray her ; the first pre-occupation on safe arrival in France is for a pair of ballet shoes. Nijinsky, a prisoner of war in Hungary, frets himself ill because he cannot dance, plans ballets, and devises an intricate system of notation, born of the stubborn will that ballet must survive.

Diaghileff dies, Pavlova dies asking for her Swan dress, and there is a terrifying silence, but, in all the dancing schools, classes continue, as if there were still something left for which to live. After a few false starts the broken threads are once more gathered together, and our art enjoys a glorious renaissance. The strength of this tradition, this will to survive, is tremendous. In detail, the exact lines that it has followed are of immense interest to the historian. Here I have only tried to convey something of the atmosphere of the thing, that it is so essential to feel, if this story of great dancers and little girls struggling at the *barre*, of the painters and musicians who work for them, and with them as their medium, is to be understood and seen, not merely as a series of disconnected episodes and studies,

which in form, as the experiences of one man, it may well
be, but as a part of one vast structure. The consciousness of
this, that grew in me only after many years, is present with
the youngest dancer, her pride and part of her life. That
is why, when people so often ask me, " What are dancers
really like off the stage ? " I cannot reply with the obvious,
" Oh, just like other people." The old legend of champagne
in a dancer's slipper will die hard, but, if the dancer can be
a Bacchante, there is often much more of the nun in her
outlook. Dancing has had its martyrs. But recently, a man
has died for it. I will write the story of Simeonov, as it was
told me by Michael Fokine.

" ' If you knew how I loved the ballet ' were the last
words written to me by Nicolai Prokofievitch Simeonov,
a few moments before he leapt into the turbulent waters of
the Niagara Falls. Such words may seem strange to the
layman in a suicide letter, but to me they are easy to
understand, for I knew his ideals, his sincerity, his long-
suffering. I knew how he loved the ballet, how he believed
in its necessity. In each one of his letters to me he asks why
ballet, one of the highest, purest, most beautiful achievements in art, must now pass through a long black period of
neglect through a lack of comprehension.

" He was a member of the Russian Ballet in the stormiest
period of its history, in the period of tumbling traditions
and in the struggle for new ideas. He was born in the
classical school, participated in the creation of the new
ballet and went right through into the radical modernist
experiments. The struggle between various tendencies in
the art did not frighten him. He was deeply interested. It
was a sign of vitality. What made him suffer was the
gradual lack of appreciation of ballet in America, the
countless new schools, established without the smallest

foundation in art or knowledge, and their 'slander and persecution' of ballet in the Press. 'These people must surely hate ballet, for it calls for years of study,' is how he explained it.

"Nicolai Simeonov worried—wrote to the newspapers . . . wrote to me, till one day, July 5th, 1932, I received this final tragic letter.

" 'MY DEAR MICHAEL MICHAELOVITCH,—As you see from the enclosed, I am ending my life by suicide. I can no longer bear the slander and persecution of ballet. Maybe my jump into Niagara Falls will sufficiently disturb you and others, and give you the strength to puncture these inflated modernists. . . .

" 'How I am longing for the Bolshoi Theatre, the Arts Theatre and the others . . . there was enthusiasm, here is business.

" 'A more detailed explanation of my death I have mailed to Valerian Svetloff. My heartiest regards to Madame Fokine.

" 'Your N. SIMEONOV.

" 'P.S. I wanted to send you a kiss, but the dead are not interesting. Do you remember Monte Carlo, Paris ? How excited we were, how enthusiastic. What a success. Here everything is asleep.'

"The letter was supplemented by six pages ; two were written on the 30th of September, 1931, and four on the 3rd of October. The September note starts like this :

" 'I am fifty years old and in perfect health. I will have myself examined again, however, in the local hospital. Yet I must end my life by suicide.'

"I received many letters from him between September 1931 and July 1932, but with no reference to his intentions to commit suicide. You will notice, from the very first thoughts of suicide he had himself examined, so that his death should not be attributed to ill health or insanity. Everything was carefully calculated. Again he writes : ' When municipalities and colleges will be interested in the dance even in the same degree as they are at present in Music and the Drama, Ballet will come back into its own.' In his final letter he sent me the programme of his last recital on June 26th, just a few days before his death. He had demonstrated the pupils of his school and had taught them thirty-one dances. What a degree of labour and of love he must have given in teaching them their rôles, designing their costumes and supervising their make-up. He was still full of power and energy.

"I have known Nicolai Simeonov since 1909, the beginning of the Diaghileff Ballet. I knew him as a man of self-respect and integrity, integrity in art and in business, who would protest against injustice however much damage it did to himself.

"I believe that his death for an ideal typifies and corresponds to his whole life."

In a bygone age this death of a man for his ideal of beauty would have been understood and would have given rise to a legend, just as now a man's death for his ideal of speed is understood. To-day the first is but an interesting study in morbid psychology, a few lines in the newspaper. Perhaps the *balletomane* will understand, assuredly the dancer. I like to think of Simeonov as having acted deliberately and in the full possession of his senses, of having believed in something strongly enough to be willing to die to rouse others in its defence. Mistaken or not, does it matter?

Dancers must remember the name of Nicolai Simeonov, who died by drowning on July 5th, 1932.

CHAPTER II

MY DÉBUT AS A *BALLETOMANE*

LA DANSE

" Insensés ennemis d'un Art également,
De l'Avis des Mortels, et bel et innocent,
Craignez-vous vainement la triste Conséquence,
Quand vous ne cessez pas de voir et d'admirer
Ce corps par Dieu formé, qui scait si bien marcher ?
Le Mouvement fait voir la Raison dans la Danse."

From under an old dancing print. 18TH CENTURY

"WHEN did your interest in dancing first begin ? "
I am asked that now almost daily. Unfortunately I cannot answer. My earliest memories
are of the sparkling Genée at the Coliseum, of Nijinsky
leaping out of a window, of Pavlova and Mordkin in the
Bacchanal, Karsavina sadly awaking from her rose-haunted
dream, and of the backcloth of *Thamar*, that has altered
the whole vision of my generation, and made it colour-
conscious.

It seemed as natural for me in those days to know the
names of every member of a *corps de ballet* as it was for my
friends to reel off batting averages and the like. I decorated
a screen with the portraits of dancers cut out of the illustrated papers, and I still have many of the photographs
that hung on my dormitory walls, to the horror of one or
two schoolmasters, who considered it a thoroughly un-
healthy taste. By the age of ten I was completely obsessed.

Now no Russian has ever asked me that question, for the
balletomane has always been a thoroughly Russian product,

and, from what I hear, is to this day, in spite of all the material hardships. With the biggest pull in Government circles, it is necessary to arrange for seats several weeks in advance when Simeonova, the great Maryinsky *ballerina* of to-day, is to dance, just as in the old days when the best seats were a coveted hereditary privilege. Ballet originated at a Court, flourished under an Emperor, but *balletomania* is the privilege of no one class, and is not the artificial exotic thing that some might think.

Perhaps the greatest of all cases of *balletomania* took place in the very midst of the terror itself. It is told by Tamara Karsavina. Her brother, Platon Karsavin, famous historian and philosopher, was thrown into prison with a group of the *intelligentsia* suspected of counter-revolutionary activities. One night he was fetched out of his cell for the customary inquiry, and the particular form of " third degree " must have been something like this :

The Tchekist : Your name ?

The Prisoner : Platon Karsavin.

The Tchekist : Karsavin—any relation to Tamara Karsavina ?

The Prisoner : My sister.

The Tchekist : Your sister ! That is wonderful ! Absolutely my favourite *ballerina*. I find her *Giselle* unsurpassed. . . .

The Prisoner : . . . and her *Lac des Cygnes*.

And so the discussion may have continued until dawn, all political differences forgotten, the prisoner's friends doubtless giving him up for lost. Perhaps he owed his life to that fact, for what *balletomane* could sentence La Karsavina's brother ?

Then there was that prince of ballet enthusiasts, the Baron Dimitri Gunsbourg, who perished in the revolution. It was he who made Diaghileff's first venture possible, when official help was withdrawn, proud and happy to devote his time and fortune to the art. His name must be especially honoured.

To go from the sublime to the ridiculous : Alexander Plestcheeff, in his history of Russian ballet, tells of how a group of St. Petersburg *balletomanes* bought a pair of La Taglioni's slippers for two hundred roubles, had them cooked, prepared with a special sauce and ate them at a banquet. My Russian friends have told me endless stories of the forms that the obsession can assume ; of a certain General (Russian stories are always told about Generals) who was so far gone that he refused to eat out of any plate that was not decorated with some dancing figure. They feared that I might become the same—perhaps there was some risk—but I rapidly began to rationalise my obsession. To-day my best definition of a *balletomane* is, that he is a person who is sad, very sad, on the first night of a season, just because he realises that it is only for a season, and that a first night implies a last night, most exciting and melancholy of events.

My first actual contact with ballet came about through meeting a little girl at a children's party and later through seeing one of the greatest of all *ballerinas*[1] dance in Diaghileff's unforgettable production of the Petipa-Tchaikovsky-Bakst *Sleeping Princess* at the Alhambra, ill-fated adventure that was ten years ahead of its time. The first gave me a human contact, a career to follow, to be interested in and to try to advance ; the second, a deep lasting artistic experience, that made me rationalise all that had gone before, the vivid, confused mass of exciting impressions, and that gave me certain standards. Subsequently the great *ballerina* became my friend just as the little girl. The extremes

[1] I know that the plural should be *ballerine*, but I dislike it.—A. L. H.

met—the beginnings of a career and the triumphant climax. Years later I was to sit with Vera Trefilova, and to hear her enthusiasm about Alicia Markova in one of her own great rôles.

I first heard of the little girl, Alice Marks, through my mother, who often visited Astafieva's studio in the King's Road, Chelsea.

Seraphine Astafieva, a former pupil of the Imperial schools, and for a time a principal in the Diaghileff Ballet, the beautiful protagonist in *Cléopâtre* and *Prince Igor*, was the first Russian to open a school in London, and her classes were a revelation. By her link with the great tradition, her knowledge, enthusiasm and vivid personality, she was beginning to do things with English dancers, and to break down the legend that they were only fit for the *corps de ballet*. I remember seeing a small girl called June there, who was spoken of as *the* coming English dancer, and there was also a boy, Patrick Kay, who seemed to have unusual talent. Astafieva was warm-hearted, quixotic and incredibly untidy, her beautiful legs hidden by the most extraordinary woollen garment—" It is not really dirty, just near-white"—her skirts hitched up round her waist with string or a safety pin, but she was always beautiful to watch and interesting to talk to. She had an inexhaustible storehouse of ballet legend and knowledge. She could and would help everyone save herself, and was, as a result, the constant prey of picturesque but unscrupulous persons. The more fantastic the hard-luck story, the more readily she believed in it, lending her sympathy and always her aid. Her studio was the meeting-place for the most curious " down and outs," as well as the most interesting people of the day, and she mixed them so well that her parties were a certain success. With a little less sympathy and more common sense in her make-up, she could have started almost unaided many of the subsequent English ballet movements. They all owe much to her and to the fine foundation that she gave her pupils. I consider myself one of them. She guided my youthful enthusiasm, and grounded me in the technical foundations of the dance. Since then I have met in nearly every company in the world someone who worked in the studio at that time. No less a person than Diaghileff, highly critical, especially where women were concerned, admired " Sima's " great qualities and confided in her. He often talked of engaging her to take the classes, but feared the trouble that might be caused through having a temperamental teacher for temperamental pupils. To her English girls she gave something of her vitality; with the Russians there might have been explosions. For various reasons I have seen little of her since those days, but I have always retained my admiration and gratitude.

It appears that little Alice Marks had made a highly dramatic entrée into the school. *Madame* had exploded into a voluble outburst of her particular mixture of English and Russian, and the pupils could talk of nothing else for days.

A pretty young woman with a very frail, timid little girl had come to the door during the morning class and asked to see Madame Astafieva.

" I am Astafieva. What you want, dahlink ? "

Everyone was always "darling" to her, including the coalman one morning, to his great amazement and mine. There was a muttered explanation, a silence to gather up strength, and then the explosion.

" You mothers are all alike. You are a *doura*, yes, a *doura*; in English, eediot. You think because little girl can

stand on toe and wobble she just like Pavlova—yes?
You don't know how long it take to make Pavlova, what
work, what tears, what art. You don't know what it mean.
Good-bye."

She promptly slammed the door in their faces. For the
rest of the class she was too indignant to do anything but
deliver a long tirade against all dancing mothers, the
standard tirade I know by heart, and have heard from
every *maître de ballet* in turn. It appears that this particular
mother had handed her a visiting card, with the daring
words " THE MINIATURE PAVLOVA " printed on it, and
was about to explain the merits of her little girl at considerable length.

A few days later Astafieva told me excitedly that she had
a new pupil of quite exceptional promise—Alice Marks, that
selfsame child whom she had turned out and nearly terrified into a fit. Mother and daughter had discussed the
matter on returning home, and had been so moved by the
outburst and its obvious integrity of purpose that they had
destroyed the offending cards, and had decided that
Alicia must learn there and there alone. Incidentally, in
justice to Mrs. Marks, since that first day in the studio
she has been a model " dancing mother," as her speedy
return proves, and has never again risked her daughter's
career.

It was some time before I came to class again. In spite of
Astafieva's commendation, I was strongly prejudiced
against the " wonder child." Although not so long ago,
those were still the days when children did not yet exist in
ballet, outside of charity functions, and when record
numbers of *fouettés* were only for the very experienced, and
then used sparingly. To-day I would have gone out eagerly
in search of new talent, for now I know that there are no

longer any " wonder children," only very young dancers, whose youth is an added quality. It was completely by accident, therefore, that I met her at a Christmas party, where I had gone to play my great rôle of Santa Claus for a young cousin, a fellow pupil at the class, who has since fallen from grace by a passion for tap-dancing to the gramophone and other profanities. As usual, I gravitated towards the first person who was willing to discuss dancing, and the first person was this child, who was very shy, did not quite fit in, and was just as eager to talk dancing as I was. Immediately her whole outlook, her very great earnestness and her ambition, charmed me. The very next day I went to see her dance, and the provoking words " *miniature Pavlova* " no longer seemed quite so fantastic, and more than once I heard Astafieva herself make the comparison. Her legs were like arrows, she danced as if she meant it, and there was nothing of the conventional prettiness of the small child. She was then the complete *ballerina* in miniature. Although at that time English soloists in the Ballet were quite exceptional, and Sokolova's English birth was still a mystery to the general public, I do not think that any of us, who frequented the studio, doubted for one moment that the boy, Pat, and little Alice would make big names, and play their part in the main movement of ballet. Never for one moment did we identify them with pantomime or cabaret, the chief destination of most of the pupils.

I saw a great deal of Alicia and her three mischievous sisters, mischievous doubtless by contrast, for the only naughty thing that she ever seems to have done was to wipe the floor with a face-flannel, and she shuddered as it was told. Once she danced for me at a charity soirée at Cambridge, but my only positive recollections are of a smoky oil-stove in a draughty, hastily improvised dressing-room, and of the babble of a group of charitably minded spinsters, who flocked round her, making motherly sounds.

" Little girl, do you like dancing ? "

" How it must hurt your poor little toes to stand on them."

" You should have been in bed ages ago."

My knowledge of dancing grew with Alice's increasing technique. I watched her constantly in class, analysed her movements, learned with her.

Pat was the first to go, but his is another story. Diaghileff saw the little girl dance, wanted her for his *Sleeping Princess*, and then gave up the idea, fortunately perhaps, on account of the difficulties in getting a labour permit. So she went on learning. Soon family reasons made it essential for her to earn a living. Any other dancing but ballet would have ruined her future. Astafieva reminded Diaghileff of the little girl. He had never had a child in the company before, and the regulations made it necessary for her to be accompanied by a governess. Would he take her and be saddled with all these difficulties ? Georges Balanchine had just been engaged as *maître de ballet*, and a new version of Stravinsky's *Le Chant du Rossignol* was being planned, with décor by Matisse. Perhaps this frail child would do for the rôle of the nightingale ? She was, I think, quietly confident, though she said little. She was still too young to be impressed by the names Stravinsky or Matisse, or to realise the importance of the work. The audition itself was undramatic, in front of Diaghileff, Nijinska and Balanchine. Knowing him, as I now do, I can imagine his helpful sympathy, a sympathy that he showed later to the twelve-year-olds Toumanova and Baronova. Alicia was engaged, and would be taken on at the end of the Coliseum season to be rehearsed and " made " at Monte Carlo, workshop of ballet for so many years. Here at last was a definite, thrilling contact with the thing I loved best. Now I, too, could make my début as a true *balletomane*. There would now be someone from home, someone whose problems mattered, in the very centre of activities. Doubtless then I realised the importance of the engagement far better than she did. I was fully as excited.

The next day she lunched with us in triumph. The immediate problem was to make Alice Marks into a good Russian Ballet citizen, a process of naturalisation I have since seen so many times. It may be hotly attacked but it is not snobbery. She would dance just as well under the name Lizzie Smith, if we wish to be coldly logical, and yet I do not fully believe it.

The adoption of the Russian name is in a way symbolical, signifying the entrance into the fine tradition, that is the living force in ballet, the motive of my first chapter. It is also a gracious compliment to those who made her and gave her the opportunity to shine. When England has a genuine ballet tradition of her own, the name Lizzie Smith may be in great demand.

After a heated discussion and references to Tolstoi and Dostoievski, we settled on the obvious *Markova*, and then watched this English girl gradually growing acclimatised, even to the extent of wrestling with her hair, which had then to be worn in a severe, well-defined manner. Now, with no Diaghileff to protest, dancers are apt to bob it, and the true classical style is worn chiefly by autograph hunters and ballet-struck girls. I remember at

that same luncheon two amazed questions of Alicia's:
" Why does everyone call Diaghileff Sergy Pock ? "
" Who is this man Basket they are always talking
about ? "

In spite of her hour-old name, she was not yet Russian
enough to have heard of patronymics (Sergei *Pavlovitch*),
or of the glory of Russia, Leon Bakst.

Her big ordeal was still to come, when Diaghileff presented his new protégée to the company. She was to dance
for them at a party given by Astafieva at the studio. I was
excited both on her account and mine. To think that at
last I should meet Diaghileff and all the members of that
glorious company ! I was still then more emotional in my
approach than critical, though I had begun to formulate
certain standards, but to this very day I am just as thrilled
at meeting a dancer whose work I admire, and I have yet to
be disillusioned, so perfectly is the character revealed in the
movement. Perhaps in my own excitement I forgot a little
that no more critical or frightening audience could have
been chosen, and that Alicia was not quite thirteen years
old. They were not going to be impressed by any childish
charm. The words " dainty " and " sweet " applied to
dancing, which was a serious business, had no meaning for
them. They too had danced at that age, though not in
public, and some of them had daughters who knew the
classical repertoire, and could perform really well. I had
just seen, at a children's party in the studio, Woizikovski's
little girl, now a promising dancer, aged six, dressed in a
Blue Bird costume, going through all the movements of that
dance, in the grand manner, in an unconscious parody of
her elders. Many people, who have since become my
friends, were there : Lubov Tchernicheva, most beautiful
member of the company ; the severely classical Doubrovska,

looking like a madonna, with a very great sense of humour; and the new dancers but lately from Russia: Tamara Gevergeva, one of the few fine talents that Diaghileff passed by, and who is certainly the richer for it as Tamara Geva of the Ziegfeld Follies; Alexandra Danilova, future *ballerina* of the company; and the piquante, angular Nikitina, a shooting star. There were doubtless many others, but my head was in a whirl, and these in particular held my attention. Dolin was watching anxiously. This studio was his home, he was host, and somehow felt the responsibility. Once during the evening he drew me aside.

" I know you are interested. Well, you see that dark boy over there, romping in the corner. He is going to be a very great dancer, really great. . . . His name ? Serge Lifar."

What a contrast to the children's party, although very much the same games were played, and there was noise, crackers and paper caps. Late in the evening Markova danced. She had chosen the *Valse Caprice*, and was made to improvise, as a still sterner test. She danced with a new-found assurance, and a personality that she was not to show again for many years. Her audience challenged her, and her whole future depended on the result. One could see there something of Pavlova's, and Pavlova herself had recognised it. That combination of strength, precision and apparent fragility proved irresistible.

In an imagined story one would say that the audience was completely carried away, acclaimed her, and gave her an ovation. It was not so. They applauded a little, and I remember Tchernicheva voicing the general verdict : " There is fine material there. She is young, has faults and must first prove herself. She may become one of us in time." It was not grudging, but a very real tribute, worth all the flattery and applause to which she had been used. Now she was truly one of a magnificent group, and Diaghileff was pleased, Dolin relieved, Astafieva radiant.

She left for Monte Carlo in a pea-soup fog, nearly missing the train ; first taste of a life of continual, agitated hurry. The great adventure had begun in earnest.

The story of Markova in the Diaghileff Ballet is the story of a careful, slow preparation under expert hands, preparing for a big chance as *prima ballerina* that would surely have been hers had Diaghileff lived.

" Watch my little English girl," he said in the very last interview he gave to the Press. He genuinely loved " his little English girl " and often told me, " I will do big things for her when she really wakes up."

Her first rôle of importance was the famous *Lac des Cygnes* adagio, in a *divertissement* from that ballet. The costume, the smallest ever made in the studios, was afterwards presented to her with one of his very rare bouquets.

I went to Monte Carlo to follow that season carefully. She was technically almost flawless and Cecchetti had given her a new strength. She had everything that she has now, save personality. Diaghileff never lived to see the mature artist, who has been the corner-stone of all our English endeavours. For him she danced Little Red Riding Hood in *Le Mariage d'Aurore* and much later *L'Oiseau Bleu* in the same ballet with Dolin, her school friend, the Child in *La Boutique Fantasque*, the Nightingale in *Le Chant du Rossignol*, her creation, the *pas de trois* in *Cimarosiana* and *La Chatte*. Each time she showed a frigid perfection that never gave one the impression that some day she could give a really fine performance in *Giselle*. Her story, like that of all dancers, soon became one of ceaseless work, classes, rehearsals, trains and " digs." When that happens there is little more that can be written that is not pure criticism. I heard from her, journeyed to the more accessible places, and was moved by her worries and difficulties. For the first time then I heard of those little jealousies and intrigues. They seemed dreadfully important, but I did not then know the game, the rapid change of friendships, the easy nervous tears, the reconciliations.

So the little English girl, eldest of four sisters, disappears from the story, to be replaced by the dancer.

. . . .

Pat, my other "school" friend, has already told his story in his book, *Divertissement*, but there are many omissions that I can fill in. I have seen him dance more often than anyone, have followed him from the music-hall to the Russian Ballet, and backwards and forwards again. His first ballet costume was confectioned by Astafieva from an old dress of my mother's, who would reward him with a box of chocolates for any difficult technical feat well accomplished.

Pat was the first to leave school for the real world of ballet. He was engaged for a small part in the vast production of *The Sleeping Princess*, that was to have its influence on the outlook of every dancer, if the larger public did not at the time grasp its significance. He is to be found in the programme as Patrikeef ; Dolin was not yet born. There the dancing of Spessiva affected him as deeply as Trefilova's did me. It gave him the ambition to dance with her one day. On his return to the studio we noticed a great difference in him. He worked all day and half the night too, throwing himself down on a couch, exhausted, to sleep. He was no more the " star pupil," contented with himself, struggling for the best place in front of the mirror. In fact, he was now very far from being contented with himself, for he knew what really great dancing meant, and he had a very definite ambition—to rejoin the Russian Ballet as its *premier danseur*, perhaps to partner the divine Spessiva. Now he interested himself in music and prepared his mind as well as his body for the task. He was always studying forms of movement outside the syllabus of work. He would turn cartwheels or walk on his hands. With the aid of Astafieva he adapted these acrobatics to the strictly classical plastique, forcing the points. All this was an unconscious preparation for *Le Train Bleu*, led directly to its creation, and has made it up to the present day his alone. It gave rise to an entirely new type of dancing. But such apparent modernism was always classical in mechanism and feeling. Dolin has always been a classical dancer, even in his famous *Espagnol*. His excursions into the purely romantic *demi-caractère* of such a rôle as Harlequin in *Carnaval*, and *Le Spectre de la Rose*, although extremely well danced, seemed forced and have left me unmoved.

His true début, and the birth of *Anton Dolin*, took place through one of those muddles, with brilliant results, that can only happen to Russians. Suddenly one morning Astafieva found herself talked into putting on a large scale programme, at the Albert Hall of all places, with just the talent available at her studio and a few days in which to arrange dances, improvise costumes, and see to the orchestration of the music. A pupil show, in fact, disguised under the high-sounding name of *The Anglo-Russian Ballet*.

As the programmes were being printed Pat suddenly conceived the idea of disguising himself under a Russian name. " It will be an excellent joke. It is sure to mystify all my friends and annoy some of them intensely. What shall I be ? " He reached for a volume of Tchekov. " Anton,

at any rate, is a good beginning." The rest was not so easy.
Most of the names were difficult to pronounce, and still
more difficult to remember. Someone—it must have been
Astafieva, hit upon Dolin. " It is simple and will look well
in print. I can already hear the public calling out : ' Dolin !
Bravo, Dolin ! ' "

They did the very next night. I still have my programme,
the first signed with the new name.

Much of it was amateurish, and looked more so still in
the vast Albert Hall ; also there was a hitch that nearly
stopped the performance at the last minute, and made a
Russian curtain even later than usual in rising. No one
had remembered that there was an orchestra to be paid
save the orchestra, who wisely insisted on immediate
payment. After a delay and many Russian expletives,
when it seemed that all the hard work had gone for nothing,
a generous friend of ours and of ballet, Nathan Golodetz,
whose beautiful wife was an occasional pupil, came to the
rescue. He may have played a big rôle that night through
ensuring for Dolin that highly spectacular start. Now for
the first time in history there was to be a truly English
premier danseur classique. I must not insist on the word
English without some qualification. It was one of the small
contributory causes of Dolin's leaving the ballet. Well-
meaning admirers, with a misplaced patriotism, started
counting up the number of English dancers, and got it
into their heads that the Russian Ballet was being run by
them, a fact that could not be expected to please Diaghileff, especially as there were only six—Sokolova, Savina,
de Valois, Coxon, Markova and Dolin—in a company of
over forty, with a purely Russian choregraphy. Dolin
himself has always insisted that as an artist he is a Russian,
who owes everything to Russian training and environment.

Time enough to rejoice if, and when, like the Russians themselves *vis à vis* the Italians, we find a genuine and not an accidental individual supremacy.

After the performance we all went back to the studio to talk and wait for the papers, Dolin clutching his first wreath.

The Press was enthusiastic and unanimous. J. T. Grein wrote in the *Daily Sketch* :

" A new dancer, Anton Dolin, carried us away in enthusiasm . . . Dolin is as light as a feather, as graceful as a fawn, as wing-footed as Mercury. I for one believe that Dolin, wholly unaffected, immersed in his art, will ere long be proclaimed the rival and successor of Nijinsky, and, if he remains unspoilt, he may be the greater of the twain, for so far his great work is entirely free of pose."

Not a little surprising, for the performance of a young boy at a pupil display. Astafieva sent the news to Diaghileff and an audition was arranged in Paris. Dolin proceeded to Monte Carlo a year ahead of Alicia.

There were three sequels to this haphazard choice of a name. The first, by no means flattering, an advertisement in the Russian Press stating that a certain family Dolin wished to disclaim all relationship with the dancer of that name; the second, a long, pathetic letter in Russian, which Diaghileff translated. " I lost my son Anton [Dolin] in the early days of the Revolution. I am in despair. In spite of all my efforts I have failed to trace him. Now the news of your triumphs fills me with hope again. Can it be that you are he, and that God in His mercy will give you back to me once more ? "

The third event occurred upon his first appearance in London, when the " Irish dancer," Le Beau Gosse of *Le Train Bleu*, had become the rage. There was a very simple, obvious and straightforward explanation to the name. Pure Irish, of course, and it did the boy credit; for Dolin read Dolan !

Dolin's great rôles are now a part of ballet history, the subject of many accounts in every language, but there are three outstanding performances, that I shall never forget, and that explain his temperament. The first was his own *Hymn to the Sun* at the Albert Hall, that started him; the next *L'Oiseau Bleu* at the Coliseum, the last night of his first London season, that proved quite conclusively that he was no nine days' wonder ; the third, the last performance of *Le Train Bleu* the night he left the Ballet, danced in a violent temper, when, smarting under a sense of injustice, he wished to show Diaghileff and the company the full extent of their loss. It was the very first ballet, and so dramatic in effect that Jean Cocteau, realising that it meant the end of his ballet, left the theatre. Each one of these performances was given under the stress of a strong emotion.

There is no more curious case in ballet than the career of this boy, who might so easily have become a successful public school athlete. Even when we pass over the extraordinary fact that Patrick Kay became so very completely Anton Dolin, he should have ruined his career time and time again through his flirtations with the commercial stage, with banality and bad taste. Few dancers can survive a season of music-hall appearances, certainly no young dancer. I have followed him carefully in the music-hall, and it has hurt me, both for his sake and for the art that he represents, but he has always done the thing supremely well. " If the audience want a little sensation, a little flattery too, then they'll get it," has been the attitude of this dancer, who on the ballet stage can be the embodiment of classical dignity, keeping his audience at a respectful distance. It has become a habit now, after seeing him in some trivial engagement, to talk of him as finished. People began to say so when he left the Ballet for the first time, but his colleagues never did. He has had an enormous share of the approbation of his fellow dancers, the appreciation that alone truly counts, and especially from the many *ballerinas* whose partner he has been. People may talk of the vanity of the male dancer—of course it is monstrous; it is a favourite topic of my own—but as a partner Dolin has always sought to put the *ballerina* in the limelight, and to make of himself a fitting background. The audience can feel the obvious admiration that he has for his partner, and their pleasure grows with his.

" I can dance on my points quite naturally, as you will remember in *Les Facheux*. I have danced for my own amusement all the great *ballerina* parts; that is why, when I am partnering, I can feel and appreciate it so well. I get a real thrill in watching and trying to enhance the effect."

Pat's ready appreciation of fine work reveals the artist. " Quel magnifique collègue," said Lifar to me recently. It was Pat who first drew my attention to him, and who told me with enthusiasm of a newcomer, then unknown— David Lichine.

It is this understanding and an extraordinary adaptability that have saved him from all the worst faults of the virtuoso, faults that are very near to him with his sense of showmanship and his ability to gain extra applause through an effective climax. He has done dreadful things, vapid, meaningless, flashy things ; he knows it, and so far can always recover in time, and in the right surroundings. This adaptability has made him into the complete Russian dancer, as it has only made one other person, Lydia

Sokolova, who can speak Russian, and curse in Russian too, like a *moujik*, when occasion arises. Dolin assimilates with rapidity the atmosphere of an environment. One day he will greet me with :

" Seet down, Arrnold, I weel be weeth you in just meenute."

" Are you raving mad, Pat ? "

" No, why ? "

" That stage Russian."

" Oh, I hadn't noticed it. I've just been speaking with Boris for the last hour."

I have heard him speak Anglo-French, Anglo-Spanish at a *corrida*, and tolerable American. It is decidedly not a pose ; his whole career proves that. It is the very thing that has made him a *premier danseur classique* or a cabaret artist as the occasion demands. His book, *Divertissement*, shows this, with its extraordinary enthusiasm at being included in a Royal Command music-hall performance, with acrobats and sea-lions. In anyone else, especially a Russian, this would have meant a desertion of serious work, while with him it merely implied that he was a different person temporarily, doing a different job with whole-hearted enthusiasm, and doing it well. Apathy is his only enemy.

Dolin may have done everything possible to damage his name with the casual ballet public, which may even bear him a slight grudge for not being born a Russian, but, when not lazy, he is a very great dancer and a considerable artist, who has influenced his whole period.

Now perhaps there is to be a new career, another essay in adaptability. After a performance in *Ballerina*, where I heard him speak his first lines on the stage, and was duly shocked :

" Soon I may give up dancing altogether and try to

become an actor. I don't want people to say about me : ' You should have seen him when he was young '—it has made me suffer too much for others. I know quite well that the big name I made had something to do with my youth and freshness. As Le Beau Gosse in *Le Train Bleu* I created a new type of dancing. It was the one Diaghileff ballet that was never revived for anyone else. That is something to remember, and I don't wish people to forget it by leaving it too far behind."

There is one memory that he will never forget ; Diaghileff made his last public appearance at a party in Pat's studio after the *première* of *Le Bal,* all differences between them forgotten.

There are many fine years before him as a dancer, if he joins some established troupe under strong discipline, and works as he did in the past. To remain at the top is almost harder than to arrive. On the first night of the Monte Carlo Ballet, most wonderful of nights, he was still the fine Anton Dolin, because the company demanded it of him. The casual appearance must finally ruin him, so that he is right in his resolve, if he has the strength to keep to it. I have yet to meet the dancer who has.

These, then, were my fellow pupils.

CHAPTER III

THE LESSONS OF *THE SLEEPING PRINCESS*

" Will the young folk ever see anything so charming, anything so classic, anything like Taglioni ? "

THACKERAY : *Pendennis*

" A smile should hover about a dancer's lips like a bird flutters about a rose, but it does not require to be fixed on those lips under penalty of mis-shaping them."

THÉOPHILE GAUTIER

" ... Une simple préparation de Mme Trefilova, quelque cinquième position de départ, en son équilibre immobile, nous ravit par la composition parfaite et désinvolte, par l'harmonie simple et logique des courbes et des droites."

ANDRÉ LEVINSON : *La Danse au Théâtre*

PARALLEL with my emotional unreasoning passion for ballet, and my interest in my friends, came an experience that made me pause, take stock and really " discover " ballet, just as it had made Pat, on the other side of the footlights, feel less pleased with himself, and revise his standards.

During the season of 1921, *The Sleeping Princess* was presented at the Alhambra, the most important event since the first coming of the Russians in 1909. Its failure altered the whole course of ballet, kept Diaghileff from London for many years, and made him bitter and disappointed.

" I was always years ahead of my time," he said, " but this time too many years."

Yet this ultra-modern experiment, so much ahead of its time in Western Europe, was one of the great Petipa ballets, originally produced at the Maryinsky Theatre in 1890, with Carlotta Brianza, the Wicked Fairy of the 1929 revival, as the Princess Aurora, Paul Gerdt as the Prince Charming, and the beautiful Marie Petipa as the Lilac Fairy. It rapidly became an established success, and every great *ballerina* is associated with it, especially Mathilde Kchessinska, who took it from the Italians, and first proved the Russian worth. It is replete with magnificent dances ; one fragment of it alone makes the brilliant *Le Mariage d'Aurore* ; one dance even, *L'Oiseau Bleu*, the acid test of the classical dancer, the success of any virtuoso programme to-day.

Diaghileff decided to put this on in lavish fashion, with new costumes and décor by Leon Bakst, to transfer Theatre Street to Leicester Square. Nor had he neglected his usual calculated precautions in preparing the public mind. There was the obvious danger that Tchaikovsky, the one great composer of " ballet music," might not prove popular with his typical " *dernier cri* " audience. Tchaikovsky therefore must be sponsored by one of their idols, someone who was himself above suspicion and perfectly secure in position. A commendatory letter from Stravinsky, who had himself re-orchestrated some of the music, appeared in the programme:

" . . . It is a great satisfaction to me as a musician to see produced a work of so direct a character at a time when so many people, who are neither simple, nor naïve, nor spontaneous, seek in their art simplicity, ' poverty ' and spontaneity.

" Tchaikovsky in his very nature possessed these gifts to the fullest extent. Tchaikovsky possessed the power of melody, centre of gravity in every symphony, opera or ballet composed by him. It is absolutely indifferent to me that the quality of his melody was sometimes unequal. The fact is that he was a creator of *melody*, which is an extremely rare and precious gift. Among us, Glinka, too, possessed it, and not to the same degree, those others.

" And that is something that is not German. The Germans manufactured, and manufactured music with themes and *leitmotif*, which they substituted for melodies.

" Tchaikovsky's music, which does not appear specifically Russian to everybody, is often more profoundly Russian than music which has long since been awarded the facile label of Muscovite picturesqueness.

" . . . The convincing example of Tchaikovsky's great power is, beyond all doubt, the ballet of *The Sleeping Princess*."

This interesting letter should have secured a success in certain circles, but Tchaikovsky was apparently still out in the dark. In this very theatre, twelve years later, *Les Présages* to Tchaikovsky's fifth symphony was a sensational success, repeated throughout the long season, which it had made possible, and Diaghileff himself, on his return, could fill his house with Tchaikovsky's *Mariage d'Aurore*, and *Le Lac des Cygnes* scarcely missed a performance.

Perhaps the greatest attraction of all lay in the quality of the dancers.

THE PRINCESS AURORA ...... Vera Trefilova	}	on
Olga Spessiva		alternate
Lubov Egorova		nights

THE LILAC FAIRY .... Lydia Lopokova.
THE OTHER FAIRIES : Felia Doubrovska, Lydia
Sokolova, Bronislava Nijinska, Ludmila Schollar,
Vera Nemchinova, Lubov Tchernicheva and
Carlotta Brianza.
THEIR PAGES : L. Woizikovski, N. Zvereff, N.
Kremneff, T. Slavinsky, A. Wilzak, E. Addison,
S. Idzikovski.
THE PRINCE CHARMING .... Pierre Vladimiroff.

I do not say that we shall never see such an *ensemble*
again; such rash statements contradict my whole attitude,
and infuriate me in others, but this once I am very much
tempted.

In this programme there are the names of two Russian
prima ballerinas, Vera Trefilova and Olga Spessiva (under
her true name of Spessivtseva then). *Prima ballerina*, much
abused words to-day, when it is a commonplace to read of
Madame Smithova, former *ballerina* of the Imperial
Theatres, to be deceived, and to enjoy the deception.

Actually, even in Russia, the home of ballet, the *ballerina*
was a rarity. It was as definite and as official a rank as
that of General, with the very important difference that
Generals abounded ("no wedding is complete without
its General"), while there were only five *ballerinas* of the
Maryinsky at any one time, five in an Empire !

Actually the Russian life of the Russian Ballet is a very
brief but brilliant period, within the experience of many.
At first there is the fixed belief that only the Italians can
dance, and the major rôles are created for them. Legnani,
the Italian, causes a sensation with her thirty-two *fouettés*;
Kchessinska a still greater one, in which patriotic fervour

is mixed, by being the first Russian to do the same thing.
All this is recent history, but a few weeks ago I saw a ten-
year-old, still a Russian, turn fifty faultless ones.

Of our times then there are but five *ballerinas* : Kchessinska, Preobrajenska, Trefilova, Pavlova, and Karsavina.[1]
I have known them all. Each one is an exceptional personality. Alas, I have never seen Kchessinska, the *ballerina
assoluta*, dance, though the impression of her in class,
demonstrating to her pupils, is quite unforgettable. Without hesitation I would say that her arm movements are the
most beautiful that I have ever seen. On that evidence
alone—and the rest is hearsay—I must place her among the
very few supreme artists of movement. Round that lightness, those supple, expressive arms and wrists, that beautifully poised head with its indescribable smile, I have built
for myself a whole ballet. Previously Kchessinska meant to
me the dancer who had first raised Russian Ballet to
Italian technical standards, the transition stage between
Russia and Italy, as hard and as brilliant as the diamonds
round her neck. People blindly praised the wrong thing. I
have not seen the technique, I can imagine it, but I have
seen the poetry that so many missed and cannot imagine.
Again I thought of Kchessinska as an important personage
in history . . . " Lenin in occupation of Kchessinska's
palace ! " Now she is *the* dancer, whom I have never seen
dance, but only sketch in a movement lightly.

Each one of these five women had to be an impeccable
virtuoso, with an ear above the average, and a faultless
line. Each must combine the grace of France with the
strength and precision of Italy, and all must add something
positive to the living tradition of the dance. I would say

[1] Egorova was a courtesy *ballerina* on retirement, Spessiva in early Soviet
days.—A. L. H.

that the age of such artists was over had not Kchessinska herself indignantly contradicted me. In any case, the new dancer must find her greatness in another direction ; to-day the whole machinery is different, and the *balletomane*, who demands perfection and can recognise it, is at the moment scarce.

There is one point especially that each one of these dancers has in common : she is *classical*. That word must be thoroughly understood, because it is probably used more frequently than any other in any conversation on dancing. It is necessary to know the classical in the study of every branch of art. In the present case too it is so frequently confused with so-called Greek dancing. I once defined it in a small monograph on the art of Vera Trefilova, the very first results of this *Sleeping Princess*. I will repeat it, as it has been accepted by those who have seen the greatest per- formances of the type, and it is essentially a question of quality and not of period. Such definitions and elaborations may appear dull, but they are in reality tremendously exciting and of practical use in appreciation. *Ballet suffers from its tacit acceptance as something beautiful*. No art has become more difficult to understand, just because it is immediately pleasing and there is so little opportunity to follow it to its sources. " Classicism, very freely translated, means pure dancing that is based on the five positions, that produces long graceful lines, that is neither acrobatic, violent nor lacking in dignity ; the *classical* dancer, the dancer of perfect build and technique, who has sought no short cuts to proficiency, and who can hold her audience *by her movements alone, with no extraneous literary conception to divert them* ; the *classical* ballet, ballet that is designed first and last for the maximum exploitation of the dancer's gifts, physical and artistic."

The classical dancer has a very definite system, built up by years of study, and it is only when that system has become second nature that she is ready to be seen by the public. There is absolutely no possibility of bluff in such work. I have seen one dancer, generally considered technically brilliant, dismally exposed in *Le Lac des Cygnes*. The opponent of classicism and therefore of ballet itself, invariably raises the point that steps such as the *pirouette*, *fouetté*, *pas de bourré* are monotonous and meaningless, and that the intelligent public requires something more. Of course, they are monotonous and meaningless when performed by a nonentity, but, apart from the sheer beauty of line that fine movement gives, the classical dance, to be true, must be full of character. These much-maligned steps, for which Simeonov died, are merely like the musical notes, limited in number, in themselves nothing. The effect depends upon how they are combined and executed. It is this *classicism* that is helping the dancer to express herself, that leaves her so gloriously free, if only she is big enough. No mediocrity can exist in the true classical ballet without an exposure that the most untrained audience could feel. The classical ballet in theory is flawless, in practice usually full of those faults that Michael Fokine revealed and banished, but the classical dancer is truly flawless, both in theory and practice, and it was she he used to carry out his reforms.

By *classicism* so far I have meant *school*, but it can also mean temperament. Vera Trefilova has the true classical temperament, as well as the training. If Pavlova is the Poussin of the dance, Trefilova is the Ingres. It was that very reason that made her performance of *The Sleeping Princess* so full of meaning, and that opened up so many new avenues for exploration. It was just because Olga

Spessiva, the other great " discovery " of the season, danced the rôle with more evident warmth, and so placed something extra between the crystal purity of the rôle and myself, the something that made her *Giselle* a triumph, that it was Trefilova who moved me, and whom I shall always identify with the rôle. As each dancer had her partisans, and fierce argument persists to this day, the lesson was made all the clearer. It was impossible any more to see a ballet or a dancer with the same eyes, not so much because one compared them to her, but because her logical, classical conception of the dance, logical but not cold, or so cold that it burned, made things gradually clear.

At the time I was not conscious of this; all I realised was that I wanted to stand up on my chair and shout, which I most certainly did. No *balletomane* ever knew the meaning of restraint, and his infernal din is the dancer's main reward.

During this season my main interest was still centred on the dancer as an artist; ballet itself was unexplored. My many hours in the studio with Pat and Alicia had already given me a sound technical background. I believe that I understood Diaghileff's motives for this return to classicism. It was just to focus once again the attention on the dancer, so as to free ballet from the complications of décor, music and literature, all with an æsthetic axe to grind, that were strangling it to such an extent that puppets might well have taken the place of human beings with no loss at all. In fact, Gorno's Italian Marionettes, one of my first outside lessons, provided a complete substitute for the post-1921 ballet in a parody that was revealing. *The Sleeping Princess* proved conclusively that only when choreography exploited to the full the artistic and physical capabilities of the dancer could it take its place among the other arts.

It is strictly logical to demand that a particular medium be put to its most effective use. Diaghileff had made the ballet the artistic force it was, apart from his own quite exceptional gifts, because of the Maryinsky in the background to provide the essential material, which had sent his own name and those of Bakst, Stravinsky and others across the civilised world. It was now necessary to call a halt before ballet was too definitely committed to modern artistic activity, much of it ephemeral, and to return to the great Maryinsky principle, taking from it only what was best. Moreover, there was not much time to be lost, for the source of supply was being rapidly cut off. Such a pause would give him the time to realise what was definitely worth while in the contemporary movement and what new lines could be followed, for eventually new lines must be evolved if the art is to live. This whole nomadic existence, the feverish chase after new Parisian gods, was stimulating only up to a point, but now saturation had been reached. Diaghileff carefully trained his audience for each new development, but now it had run away from him in its desire for novelty. It could be tickled only by unusual décor or music, a scandal, a name or an idea, but the dancer, the start and the very *raison d'être* of the whole thing, was no longer understood.

This return to classicism was also in the main trend of the artistic development that had acclaimed Ingres as a great master again, not for the subject matter of his vast historic canvases, but for their line and composition. In ballet, it is the dancers who provide the line, the " *dessin* " which is " *la probité de l'art*," and the subject, the fairy-tale or legend, could be accepted or ignored according to individual taste. Such ballet was not old-fashioned; in its essentials it was timeless. This throwing of the onus on to the dancer once more, giving her the main responsibility of boring or enchanting an audience, provided the possibility of producing dancers who were great personalities, great artists and great performers. Vera Nemchinova, who was one of the few great dancers formed from within the company, and who saved it at a critical period, was purely the result of the opportunity to dance in such works. And just as the dancers themselves are best trained in the school of Petipa, so are the spectators. The dancer is fully revealed.

From that season I found certain standards of criticism from which I have never had to depart. They have added to my enjoyment a thousandfold, by giving me the thrill of watching developing talent with more system and certitude than when I assisted emotionally at the birth of Dolin and Markova, taking so much for granted that I could only verify later.

The very first consideration is physical beauty, face as well as body, the perfection of the instrument. There can be no question here of being charitably minded, just, decent people. Mary may be possessed of immense dramatic talent, have a fine musical ear, and a truly infinite capacity for hard work, but if she squints or her legs are unshapely then she is out of place in ballet. Yes, the squint counts. A Russian *balletomane*—I believe he was a General again— once said, " Show me a girl's face, and I will tell you whether she can dance." He may have expressed himself too positively. Had he put it, " Show me her face, and I will tell you if she cannot dance," I would have been with him every time. Twinkling legs alone are not enough. A fine head, well set on the shoulders, a smile that is a smile and not a grin, marks of the Russian *ballerina*, make one wish to look further and judge the dancer as a whole. So many Italian dancers have been ruined through concentrating exclusively on the legs. Beauty, fortunately, is a wide term that must be elastic enough to include the deep classical beauty of Karsavina or Toumanova, the ethereal of Pavlova, the radiant smile of Kchessinska, the wit and elegance of Preobrajenska, the romantic languor of Spessiva, the sparkle of Lopokova, the soul of Baronova.

Ballet dancing is the maximum exploitation of physical beauty in motion. In thinking of the various companies I have known well, I cannot remember one highly trained Russian dancer who was plain; I can think of a number who are exceedingly beautiful in a subtle, non-Hollywood way, for the classical system properly understood trains every portion of the body, from the tips of the toes to the chignon. It gives direction to every movement and gesture. It is organised beauty.

Another point that I would include here is natural grace. To many, grace and dancing are synonymous. This is by no means the case. The purely technical, non-artist dancer is usually clumsy. Faulty training can destroy natural grace, while the soundest training can only create the semblance of it.

Once we have satisfied ourselves about the instrument, bearing in mind the more obvious fact that Kreisler himself is helpless on a cigar box, the next consideration is technique.

Sound technique should be taken for granted. If it is stressed even favourably, there is usually something very much wrong with the performer. The words " a technical dancer " are definitely insulting. Trefilova's technique is faultless. It would never occur to me to bring that up as a point in her favour. There are so many other interesting points to talk about. There is but one stage in the dancer's life when it is relevant, the first few years. It is a characteristic of the young dancer to say, " My turns were perfect to-night," just as it is characteristic of the non-subtle audience to applaud those turns especially loudly, as if they did not belong to the whole. There are obviously degrees of technique : Kchessinska may have had more than Karsavina; but the good technique is the one that is not noticed by dancer or public, and that leaves her free to express the choregrapher's intention and her own personality. Karsavina once told me that the dancer's personality developed with her technique, a fact that I have repeatedly verified. I do not believe in the performer who has immense personality and little technique. In the concert hall she would not be tolerated for a moment. People are always a little too indulgent to dancers.

Technique has developed enormously of late, a fact that must be borne in mind. Just as Kchessinska, when already famous, discovered the Italian secret of thirty-two *fouettés*, so have the smallest pupils to-day found the way to the almost endless *fouetté*, neatly, easily. It is now a definite part of the repertoire, and cannot any more be condemned as an unworthy acrobatic feat. Modern choregraphy has used it with immense effect in such ballets as *Cotillon*, *Concurrence*, *Beau Danube* and *Jeux d'Enfants*, just on account of the fact that Baronova and Toumanova can perform it with ease and grace, with no undue concentration, so that, with it, they can express something definite. This increase in technical resources gives the choregrapher a richer vocabulary, without having to resort to distortion for his effects.

Technique means freedom for dancer and choregrapher,

c

while in so-called " free dancing " the performer is shackled by the difficulty of moving, the choregrapher by the paucity of resources at his command.

So far we are on easy ground. Physical beauty and technique can be measured to a degree not only by the expert but by their effect on an audience, in spite of subtle differences of opinion. The great difficulty arises when it comes to a discussion of dramatic ability, temperament and personality, all three of which are so closely bound up with the question of technique. The dancer who is beautiful and well trained, with nothing much else besides, can hold a certain type of audience through sheer pleasure in her line. There is an endless fascination in watching ballet that depends on line alone, and that is devoid of dramatic content.

A Russian physicist-artist has been undertaking some research on æsthetics, communicated in a paper to the French Académie des Sciences, that illustrates this vividly. He has based his whole theory on optics, the line of least resistance for the eye, and has carried out a lengthy series of experiments, his subjects looking at pictures and dancing while the movements of their eyes are measured on sensitised paper attached to a drum. He has already demonstrated the truth of many artistic adages. He has found that two closely parallel lines in a composition are disturbing, because the eye travels from one to the other rapidly and is wearied, while in the case of parallel lines far apart the eye travels comfortably down the path in the middle. The experiments that interested me specially, and that I followed with care, were just those relating to pure dance technique. According to his experiments, the line of least resistance, his line of beauty, is a long, slow curve that the eye can follow at ease and caress. But if this stands alone, or is repeated indefinitely, it becomes monotonous, and some contrast is essential. According to this, the *arabesque* is the perfect pose, with its long, sloping line from finger-tips to toes, with its inner strong contrasting angles formed by the legs and the arms. Whether this can be demonstrated scientifically or not, it is a plausible theory with exciting possibilities.

Technique is exact. In strict theory there is one way, and one way alone, of making a given movement correctly ; but in fact the exactitude is only approximate and not mathematical, the human elements, both physical and mental, play their part. " Cet art," says Levinson, speaking of the classicism of Trefilova, " tend vers la formule géometrique, mais, au moment suprême, la brise et s'en évade," a perfect summing up. Only the highly trained spectator can gauge the exact departure from the theoretical standard, though at times an audience can sense it. It is just that fraction of difference that reveals the individual. Dancing is so subtle that six *ballerinas* will perform the same *enchainement* in an almost identical manner, and yet create an entirely different impression, and I am talking of a simple sequence of steps here and not of intricate rôles where the atmosphere and facial expression are indicated. It is these little differences in execution that underlie personality, and when they become conscious they are the whole basis of acting or " mime."

The combination of steps in *L'Oiseau Bleu* for instance, from that same *Sleeping Princess* that is responsible for all this, are a straightforward sequence that might be set in any advanced classroom. But for the "bird-flight," "bird-landing " idea to be suggested a special attack is needed. This is the first conscious process of mime. *L'Oiseau Bleu* is not in reality an animal study, and it has no story that develops and comes to a climax like Fokine's *Dying Swan*, where the whole of mime becomes more obvious, and further from its roots. Balletic acting, basis of all acting, has endless degrees of intensity. First, it is a question of attack, scarcely removed from mechanical technique; next, it becomes a question of atmosphere, as in the famous *Sylphides*, the most difficult problem that can confront the dancer, and where countless fine performers have failed. In movement it is simple, well within reach of the inter-mediate pupil. It is a question of expression, face and body combined. The only indication the dancer receives is in the music, the scenery, and the few words of the theme; sylphs in a wood at night. What a test of sensibility and mimetic power, this suite of dances that is so much a com-plete ballet. The average dancer half closes her eyes and looks just tired or bored, others grin, but they grin sheep-ishly to indicate romance; the merely technical dancer does it in a hard, sparkling manner. All are wrong. It is a dream, something brief and fleeting, a little sad perhaps, a land-scape by Corot. There are definite moments for which to look; in the Valse there is none of the tempo of the classical *adagio*; she must float up to him, float down to the ground again, without the feeling of a ballet lift. There is a true tender expression of love, as he draws her to him by wing tips, that is echoed in the climax, where she beckons gently, and he responds in an eager leap. One can only write of how it should not be done, which is how it is usually done, but there are so many ways that are true. Pavlova was poetry itself; Karsavina a little warmer and more human; while among the new dancers all shine, the true measure of their artistry: Toumanova is infinitely sad, with a nostalgia for the world beyond the park, tragically moving; Riabouchinska like gossamer, truly a brush-stroke by Corot; Baronova, my own ideal, joyful, yet a little wistful, profiting from the few moonlit hours in the enchanted garden. A memorable *ensemble*.

In *Giselle*, great test for the classical dancer, the problem is the reverse. The subject matter is very clearly indicated by a complex scenario, while the banal, tuneful music has nothing whatsoever to do with it, and is a definite emotional handicap. When the curtain rises on the village romp the word *quaint* is in one's mind; if it descends with that impression remaining, the *ballerina* has failed ; yet it is ninety per cent conventional gesture to indifferent musical accompaniment, with but ten per cent remaining for individual interpretation. It is that ten per cent that can make it great ; without it the first act is intolerable barn-storming, first cousin to *Maria Marten*, the second act a mere succession of technical exercises. There is an added difficulty, between the acts a total change of atmosphere ; act one is the body, act two the spirit. The story belongs to the great romantic period, the romanticism of sighing swains and midnight graveyards, of kilts and Walter Scott, Willis, werewolves and the Brocken, very different from the later less robust romanticism of a Fokine ballet, though Gautier inspired both *Giselle* and *Le Spectre de la Rose*. It is the difference between Devéria and Bakst.

The betrayed maiden goes mad and finds a suicide's grave. In her madness she repeats the dance she loved when she was still care-free. In the second act she rises from the grave a Willi, temptress of young men, and so meets her repentant betrayer.

It is obvious, from this brief description, that there can be no average *Giselle*. The sentiment and the music and story drag it down to the level of a genteel magazine illustration of the period. Olga Spessiva is an outstanding

Giselle. Pavlova showed more fire and exaltation; Spessiva played with tenderness and melancholy, reaching her climax in the scene of madness. Recently Markova has become the only English Giselle in a beautifully balanced performance, with a well executed mad scene, and a more spiritual second act than I could ever have believed possible in anyone whose technical brilliance has at times intruded into the dream of *Les Sylphides*. But in the second act no one can approach the unearthly quality that was Pavlova's. She remains above comparison.

Le Lac des Cygnes, too, is conventional, and does not call for obvious acting. Like *The Sleeping Princess*, it is purely classical; Trefilova's, Spessiva's, Nemchinova's, Baronova's, Markova's. Yet, in the version now played, it has its one big moment of drama, when the Princess Swan defends her huddled flock from the hunters, with arms outstretched protective and regal ; a gesture that singled out Trefilova and Spessiva from the many who can dance this superbly. The male rôle in this ballet has always interested me as a problem in mime; it is usually pathetically comical. The dancer must believe in it or fail—a difficult task, as in so many versions his variation is cut, denying him any of the dignity of a dancer. Dolin excels as the gallant partner, Lifar through his beautiful walk, while Lichine tackles it too impetuously and fails.

Fokine revolutionises this, mime and dancing become one, as even in the past the great dancer had tried to make them. New problems arise of the type we have already discussed in *Les Sylphides*. In *Le Spectre de la Rose*, gem of the new romanticism, each rôle calls for consummate acting; the woman stands as a complete contrast to the male virtuoso, who must combine both tenderness and strength, great tenderness, for every movement of the arms, that is generally made into a meaningless weaving motion, is a caress. The supreme moment, though, belongs to her. It is not the spectacular leap out of the window, but the girl's gradual awakening, where disappointment and happiness are mixed, small sublime moment in ballet, invariably marred by the applause at the leap. Of all those who have danced this, but one has fully succeeded—Tamara Karsavina. She has made it her own for ever.

These then are but a few of the problems that ballet acting sets, and that is why without the ability to mime the dancer is uninteresting. " Tous nos mouvements sont purement automatiques et ne signifient rien, si la face demeure muette en quelque sorte et si elle ne les anime et ne les vivifie," said Noverre (1759), most of whose precepts were forgotten until Fokine took command.

Another attribute that the dancer requires is a sensitive musical ear, which is a rarity amongst the rank and file, for mime has included the appreciation of music, since it is so often the music that gives the only real indication of the atmosphere. A musical ear, developed to an unusual degree by a study of the piano, gave Sokolova her first big chance with Stravinsky's *Sacre du Printemps* and Ravel's *Daphnis et Chloé*, then so difficult for the dancer to grasp. I have actually seen dancers at rehearsal consulting slips of paper on which the tempo was marked, a method not calculated to give a convincing performance. There are such delicate shades of rhythm that, while it might be impossible to accuse an artist of being " out of time," she has clearly not fully sensed the measure, or is worried by it—just the fraction of difference that distinguishes the best from the second best. The much debated *fouetté* is dancing when it is in perfect sympathy with the music, a stupid *tour de force* when it is not.

This is a great chunk of undiluted criticism, but it is the result of a deep artistic experience gained during that one season, and it is doubtless a part of the message that Diaghileff had to convey, and that was not then received. Whether it will be received now, or has already passed into common experience, it is a vital part of my story ; the fanatic grown rational, the lover more ardent than ever, but no longer blind. Henceforward every performance becomes a series of studies with the first thrill in no wise impaired, but with the hundredth thrill that counts the most of all. When the " babies " came with *Présages*, *Choreartium* and Massine's new choregraphy, I was ready to fit them into my scheme of things, and to shout " Bravo " with conviction.

CHAPTER IV

MONTE CARLO—PARIS, 1925

" Nous commençons à devenir des gens très bien, à avoir des relations très chic, très pourries, très ballet russe."

Le Bois Sacré : DE FLERS ET CAILLAVET, 1910

MONTE CARLO, winter headquarters of the ballet, a paradise for both dancer and *balletomane* ; the little town itself like the carefully planned décor of a not too modern artist, the toy army of uniformed sweepers and attendants perfect walkers-on in a *ballet bouffe*, and in the very centre the actual theatre, a stage on a stage, ideal in size, the right compromise between grandeur and intimacy. What a saving of energy for the permanently overworked dancers ; no bus, tube or tram, at the worst a walk up the steep flight of steps to Beausoleil, where most of them had flats. It was quite unnecessary ever to fix a rendezvous, impossible not to stumble across dancers in all places ; shops, cinemas, cafés and kiosks, everywhere they were known by sight and record. When one of them quietly arranged to have flowers sent to herself at every performance, we knew of it within the hour and laughed, and sometimes we knew of bouquets from genuine admirers before the recipient. After morning rehearsal the terrace was a veritable news exchange. The occupation of the town was complete. Mothers, aunts, children, all were gathered there to be with their " family genius " and breadwinner some portion of the year, when theatrical

" digs " could be forgotten and the full privileges of housekeeping enjoyed. This was home. Only the gaming-rooms were strictly taboo, and on the rare occasions when dancers had penetrated in disguise, they had come away minus the next month's salary, which meant confronting a stern Grigorieff for an advance, which he did not encourage. The artists of the ballet were employees of the State, and once during that season, when two of them went on strike, they found themselves infringing an imposing by-law, No. X, and had to answer to the Government as well as to Diaghileff. They were promptly deported and no one followed their example.

Chief sign of the occupation was the flock of camp followers, hair sleeked back in severe classical style, complete with ballet shoes and mother, waiting. There was that queer individual, too, who followed the ballet around, in the hopes that the conductor would be suddenly indisposed and that he would be summoned to take his place. He had evidently been reading many biographies. His chance never came, but he himself was an institution.

Cecchetti was fully established in his classroom in a cellar of the Casino, giving his daily class to the company, and also numerous private lessons, throwing his little cane at favoured pupils, whose proud privilege it was to replace it when it broke. He spoke in an extraordinary language of his own devising, compound of many that marked his triumphal progress through Europe : " Quandé la giammbé il va en avante, la tête il va toujours dé la même côté dé où qu'il va la giammbé, ma quandé la giammbé il va en arrière——" etc., very rapidly. I still have it humming in my ears.

It was his pleasure constantly to rail against the horrors and infamies of modern choregraphy, not unnatural in someone who had danced in a ballet of Katti Lanner's devising in the Empire of the '90's, ten years after he had danced Petipa's *Oiseau Bleu* for the first time. He said to Diaghileff himself of Nijinsky's *Sacre du Printemps*: "I think the whole thing has been done by four idiots. First : M. Stravinsky, who wrote the music. Second : N. Roerich, who designed the scenery and costumes. Third : M. Nijinsky, who composed the dances. Fourth: M. Diaghileff, who wasted his money on it."[1] He was there to repair the ravages of that choregraphy on his pupils. He was already over 80, but still leapt into the air, bouncing like the little rubber ball to which the *Times* critic, forty years previously, had compared him. Nor was this his last job, for at the end of the season he was summoned to the Scala, Milan, to take charge of the instruction.

He was born in the dressing-room of an Italian theatre, died while in the service of an Italian theatre. His wife, Josephine, kindly and patient, who would interpret and soften his ravings to bewildered pupils, was there by his side. Both still danced that season, *Maestro* miming brilliantly as the shopkeeper in *La Boutique Fantasque*, Josephine, the duenna of *Les Dames de Bonne Humeur*, wearing a period wig over her own, both narrowly missing coming off during one performance. Cecchetti, in whose experience almost the entire history of ballet lay, but one generation removed from Vestris, dancing in a Massine ballet, and rubbing shoulders with " Les cinq," Picasso and Braque ! It was a rare privilege to have watched his classes, to have been even so remotely a pupil. He was surrounded by young girls of every nationality – private pupils, willing to pay any price to get into the ballet, thrilled already at this first contact. It was as such a

<hr>

[1] Quoted from *Enrico Cecchetti*, a memoir by Cyril W. Beaumont.

camp-follower pupil of *Maestro's* that Romola Nijinska worked her way into the ballet and won her husband from Diaghileff.

Naturally I found it impossible to stay away from this Mecca. The pilgrimage was indispensable. Here was the opportunity to watch the laboratory at work, and to take up friendships constantly interrupted by the hurry and bustle of Paris and London. The seasons were always given in two portions, with a middle period " out " to put new works into rehearsal. Then the dancers were comparatively free, with six hours' work instead of nine, except some of the non-principals, who were loaned to dance in the opera ballets. It was a chance to earn extra money, especially in the wire-flying ballets, which were considered a little dangerous. Also, under the kindly supervision of Raoul Gunsbourg, instead of Diaghileff, it need not be taken too seriously. There at once one could realise what dancing for Diaghileff meant. Gunsbourg nursed his artists, had cumbersome scenery shifted to suit their movements, while with Diaghileff everything had to be just so, a complete picture in which every element was carefully balanced, and the dancers were clearly just one of the elements.

I arrived straight from the station at the theatre where the first matinée was in progress, meeting Diaghileff on the steps. " How is Sima [Astafieva] ? Is she coming ? I have invited her specially to see Dolin and Markova. I am angry. I have just missed *Les Sylphides*, my favourite ballet, for the first time in years. I hope it was danced well. Why couldn't someone have told me what time it began ? " In that mood, someone would surely catch it.

1925. His last truly brilliant year, just before the transition period and the gradual waning ; Nemchinova and

Dolin at the very top of their form, physically and temperamentally ideal partners, dancing in nearly every ballet; Tchernicheva contributing the finish and perfection of the early years; Doubrovska, about to be discovered as the perfect instrument for modernist experiment; Sokolova, most Russian and biggest personality of them all, favoured artist of the great man himself; Leon Woizikovski, always superb, retaining his position through sheer merit, with every change of régime, generous colleague, ready to pass on his experience to the new arrival; and Serge Grigorieff, the backbone, with every ballet and lighting cue in his head, a big Russian Bear but a hundred per cent efficient. There was young Serge Lifar at the very beginning; he had recently made a success of his first important rôle, the shopkeeper's assistant in *La Boutique Fantasque*, and was rehearsing for his first creation in *Zéphir et Flore*; Markova just thirteen, in socks, but learning her very own Stravinsky ballet, and dancing *Le Lac des Cygnes adagio*; and Nikitina and Danilova, the great hopes, whose fate was then being decided at the Hôtel de Paris, where Diaghileff sat with his cabinet; Poulenc and Auric, Boris Kochno, Picasso, Stravinsky, Pruna, Dukelsky and Edwin Evans.

Evans was musical adviser, and, during the London season, intermediary between Diaghileff and any disgruntled member of the company. No wittier nor more kindly person could have been chosen for so arduous a task, and he looked the rôle. Diaghileff, with no sense of time, would ring him up almost regularly at three o'clock in the morning to discuss some new idea. It was only when Evans suggested that there might be very good reasons why this was inconvenient that Diaghileff gave it up. Any idea so simple as the desire for a good night's rest could not appeal to him. It was understood that no petty annoyance

should be allowed to get past Evans, but one day during a
season at the Coliseum an angry principal proved too
much for him, and marched straight into the lion's den,
staggering under a load of posters and handbills of a size
that only the Coliseum could use.

" Look here, and here, and here "—dumping them down
on Diaghileff's desk—" it is disgraceful. I am a star and my
name is here in very small print and under X's, who has
never danced any leading rôles. What is going to be done
about it ? "

" This is interesting. I have never seen so many posters.
I didn't even know that we had them. Tell me, how did you
get hold of them ? Who gave them to you ? "

" My husband."

" Your husband ? It's a pity, a great pity, that he
couldn't give you any other signs of his affection."

It was in Monte Carlo that I began a form of entertainment that has ever since given me the keenest pleasure ; listening to Edwin Evans discourse on every con-
ceivable subject, from finance—and he was once the
editor of a city journal—to music. He is always better
informed than the next man, always magnificently witty.
His knowledge of cookery and his discourses are a joy.
I believe that he is prouder of having been recognised in
France as one of the few English gourmets than of his
vast European reputation as a music critic. That year at
Monte Carlo he was the only English member of the
cabinet, and one of its most active.

Diaghileff's boast at the Paris *première* that season, " If
the theatre burned down to-night all the artistic talent of
Europe would perish," was fully justified.

The members of the company of that year alone have
played the leading rôle in the whole world of ballet,

providing *prima ballerinas* for the de Basil Company, the Kovno opera, the Vic-Wells, also the *maîtres de ballet* for those theatres, the choregrapher and *premier danseur* of the Paris opera, the *premier danseur* of the Opéra Comique, and the founder of the American Academy of the Dance. This is an incomplete list. It honours Diaghileff as nothing else could.

My first *formal* meeting with Alexandra Danilova, after the Astafieva party, was in one of those irritating intervals that the French are so fond of having between the reels of a film, in this case *The Orphans of the Storm*, where I had gone with Dolin. He was wearing, I remember, a tie of many bright colours and intricate design that I rudely criticised. " Well, it must be all right, it was designed for me by Picasso." That shut me up completely; then he went on :

" Look, just four rows away in front of us is Danilova— there, you can just see the back of her head. She's divinely beautiful, and a really fine artist. Big things are being planned for her," then a wild yell across four rows of heads :

" Shoura—SHOURA, turn round a minute. I want Haskell to see you. I've just told him you're very beautiful. There, I thought you wouldn't be disappointed. It's all right, *galoupchik*, he's seen you—you can turn round again."

Every afternoon after rehearsal we met at Rumpel-mayer's, Pat going from tray to tray, sampling the choco-lates, commenting on them, and offering them to Alicia, towards whom he was very much " the heavy father."

" Send that child home to bed at once, she's worn out " ; or on one occasion, when she was proudly displaying a new rabbit-wool jumper, " So they're dressing the child in furs now. Perfectly ridiculous."

He looked after her wonderfully, like an elder brother who had been in the school a few terms longer.

It was precisely this schoolboy attitude that irritated Diaghileff so profoundly, and that was the beginning of their quarrel. He had no understanding of the English character. For him, a day's outing on the river was an absurdity, and tennis or a picnic with friends the limit of vulgarity. He expected his favoured artists to live at " high pitch " the whole time; the first essential, entire subservience to his will, to discuss artistic topics and to visit museums with him. A visit to a museum with Diaghileff was inspiring, but utterly exhausting. His great pleasure was in the reactions of his companion, and it was difficult, with his expectant gaze fixed upon one, to react sincerely or intelligently, especially during three hours. He could not sympathise with Pat's very natural desire to escape with less intellectual friends, and complained to me bitterly on many occasions about the English and all their ways. He never failed to bring in his great sore point, the river party, as being the very height of imbecility, and the dangers of draughts and open windows.

Nemchinova joined our little company, practising her English on me when she could.

" My foots is all bloody," was one of her very first efforts.

One day I nearly ruined the whole future of ballet by taking her, Savina and Alicia out in a motor-boat. It was very rough, but they egged me on, and we only just reached the shore in safety, all of us very green. The only casualty was a black coat of Vera Savina's. She had sat on a bag of peppermint creams.

The great event of the season that occupied everyone's time and attention was the preparation of Massine's *Zéphir et Flore*, the vehicle for Lifar's rise to stardom. He had been working with Cecchetti almost the entire day, and, together with rehearsals, I counted on occasions ten hours. We never saw him at all. This also was to be Alice Nikitina's first big chance. I can never remember having seen anyone who promised more. Angular, a trifle gawky, piquante, everything that she did had a strong personal quality; her very faults were the making of future virtues. Unfortunately she has not lived up to that promise. Her failure was due to an attempt to make her into a *ballerina* quickly and artificially. The Nikitina boom strangled all her immense talent, the faults, that should and could have become virtues, became glaring faults—hard arms in *Les Sylphides* and the like. One could clearly foresee that her lack of technical strength would result in continual small accidents. Less haste would have made Alice Nikitina into something unique. I hear that now she has discovered a charming voice, and in that way a second chance. I am glad, for so genuine an artist should not be lost. Perhaps here at last is a Mimi who will know how to sing and die, or a Salome who can sing and dance.

Diaghileff was amazed at his good fortune. That season he was a truly happy man, with Nikitina, Lifar and Dukelsky, whose total ages only amounted to sixty. Lifar alone has lived up to, and exceeded, that early promise. Nikitina was forced, and Dukelsky has led a " double life " as a composer of ballets and as a writer of popular melody for Ziegfeld and others, under the name of Vernon Dukes, which has since become the better known of the two.

From the very first this ballet was dogged by ill luck. I remember the first dress rehearsal. It began at nine o'clock and at two we were still sitting there when it was cut short by the first accident. Every detail in each one of the acts was attended to by Diaghileff himself, and one could only be amazed at his immense practical knowledge. The lighting was his great speciality, and some of the effects would take hours to set. He could mix colours like paint on a canvas, and was revealing to us bit by bit all the richness of Braque's fine décor.

Meanwhile the dancers went on and on, while he criticised and called for repeats. The first *contretemps* was the inevitable one with the orchestra.

" I am sorry, Monsieur Diaghileff, I can do nothing more. The members of the orchestra say that it is well past their time and refuse to stay."

" They are artists and not factory hands. Tell them that they can have ten minutes' rest "—looking at his watch; " then they must come back to their places, and play till we have finished, perhaps another four hours, perhaps more. I intend to finish."

In ten minutes' time they were back, and it began again, movement by movement, another two hours of it, until suddenly Lifar crumpled up and fell. In turning he had touched one of the dancers, and both ankles, tired from overwork, were badly strained. The theatre was cleared in an instant, Diaghileff in tears. " It was too good, too beautiful to last. I thought the great days had returned again and now this perfection has been spoiled. I should not have boasted; it is my fault." He was intensely superstitious.

The *première* in Monte Carlo was put off and the company left for Barcelona. Nemchinova alone remained behind with an acute attack of mumps, unpoetical malady that had made her usually beautiful *Lac des Cygnes* into something grotesque, yet she had been forced to dance, to the horror of the rest of the company.

In Spain, Lifar's ankles showed no signs of mending. He was helpless in bed and the doctor talked of six weeks at least. " I am sorry," Diaghileff told him, " but by my contract I must give the *première* in Paris next week. It will not be the same thing but someone else will have to dance it, and I will make it up to you later."

But Lifar was determined, saw the end of his career before the beginning, and talked of suicide. He was ready on the night, performed admirably, but in dreadful pain, with the doctor waiting anxiously in the wings. The day before and the day after he could not walk, but that night he danced. Diaghileff in his joy inscribed a present to him : " Au plus jeune parmi les premiers, et au premier parmi les jeunes."

I have seen such feats of will power, that are inexplicable to doctors even, on many occasions, with Sokolova, Toumanova, and Lifar himself, once again, in London. Just before *Lac des Cygnes* he was practising an *entrechat* in the wings, and, leaping too high, his head hit an iron staircase with great force ; he was half stunned, but when his cue came, he went on to dance, the blood trickling from under his wig. Afterwards the wig was removed with great difficulty and he was laid up for some time, swathed in bandages.[1]

Lifar's mishap was not the end of the *Zéphir et Flore* ill luck. Nikitina was injured during one of the first Paris performances, and Danilova took her place, a new partner for the still inexperienced boy. Finally Dolin, the third important member of the cast, left, Tcherkas taking his place.

This ballet did not enjoy a long life or deserve it. To-day

[1] On February 6th, 1934, day of the Paris *revolution*, Lifar suffered from another blow on the head, a non-theatrical accident this time. Returning quietly from the Opéra, he was hit and stunned. Fortunately the blow was not serious.—A. L. H.

it would not bear revival, but it played an important part in discovering Lifar. I had once more assisted at the beginnings of a new talent, and a photograph that I have of that date is inscribed : " To one who assisted at the birth of my art." This is another case, the most important, where Diaghileff did not see the magnificent progress of the artist in whom he so greatly believed. His Lifar was still technically unformed.

The last week of that Monte Carlo season I fell madly in love and became engaged. Mutual enthusiasm seemed a sufficient reason. It was immediately after a performance of *Thamar*, and we had met on the Terrace that very same afternoon. Then the Ballet left, we saw them off at the station together, and when the train disappeared through the toy tunnel, everything suddenly changed. Things seemed different, we both regretted it, did not quite like to admit it or to put it into words, and the parting was a horrible anti-climax.

The Ballet did things like that to one. Gambling was not the only or the worst madness of the season. It was sometimes difficult to know what was real, what was illusion. The dancers were saved by their work, their tired muscles, *Maestro's* curses ; we, quite helpless, living their dreams without effort. In London or Paris escape was possible ; in Monte Carlo, 1925, all was pure ballet magic.

. . . .

Paris that season saw the first revival of *Les Biches*, most perfect of all the " decadent " ballets, and a landmark in history. It remains unique, a satirical literary subject that is told perfectly in movement alone, a modern *Sylphides*, the sylphs still there, an elegant house of pleasure substituted for the woods. It is at the same time a keen analysis of contemporary womanhood in its reactions to the male, represented by the three disturbing athletes, who enter into the women's lives, from the flamboyancy of the hostess to the indifference of two friends who ignore them completely in their very own love duet. It is vicious, exceedingly so, but never in any way vulgar. It does not intrude itself. If you ignore its meaning, which it is easy to do when it is disguised as the *House Party*, it can still remain a thing of beauty. This avoidance of the obvious is especially noticeable in Nijinska's own dance, "The Rag Mazurka," where the character must be vulgar. It is a perfect interpretation, but never the real thing. Here, as in the classicism that inspired it, the whole responsibility rests with the dancers. The dancer who excels in *Le Lac des Cygnes* can excel in this. Who can ever forget Vera Nemchinova?

"L'entrée de Nemchinova est proprement sublime. Lorsque cette petite dame sort de la coulisse, sur ses pointes, avec de longues jambes, un justaucorps trop court, la main droite gantée en blanc, mise près de la joue comme pour un salut militaire, mon cœur bat plus vite ou s'arrête de battre. En suite, un goût sans fléchissement combine les pas classiques et les gestes neufs."

When such an experienced *balletomane* as the poet-artist, Jean Cocteau, can write in this manner of a dancer in her rôle, the choreographer has obviously succeeded. Here is modern ballet at its peak. *Les Biches*, too, demonstrates better than anything else Diaghileff's skilful choice of collaborators. Nijinska, Poulenc and Laurencin are one, each interpreting the same thought in his own particular medium.

Nijinska's whole influence on dancing has been of first

class importance. The only successful woman choregrapher in history, great sister of a great brother, she has understood the systematic development of the male dancer. Dolin owes much to her, his first *maître de ballet*, and pays constant tribute to her inspiration; Lifar started as a conscious artist under her régime,[1] as did Lichine in the Ida Rubinstein ballets. Each one bears the unmistakable stamp of her influence. As a dancer she has few equals. She is apart from ordinary standards. She has much of the strength and elevation of her brother, his own particular attack. She is also the only ugly dancer to find fame, ugly but never in any sense plain. There was no incongruity in her assuming the rôle of the Lilac Fairy, her movement and expression were so in keeping with Perrault's tale.

Her *Noces* too was revived at that time. Another truly literary subject treated plastically, another landmark, the return to Russia of the Russian Ballet. When Diaghileff left Russia far behind, as he was bound to do, he lost at any rate one important asset, the sympathetic and complete understanding of his interpreters. *Petrouchka* could move them and the audience because it was the story of Russia and the universal story of a man's soul. *Noces* too, because it was the life of a Russian woman, counterpart to *Petrouchka*, and an aspect of a universal institution, marriage. The further the origins of the Ballet were left behind, the less moving could be the performances. While *Les Matelots*, a novelty that season, a modern non-Russian ballet, was easily understandable as broad knockabout pantomime, it was rather much to expect a Russian choregrapher and dancers to enter into such a purely local joke as the elaborate Victorian *The Triumph of Neptune*. The

---

[1] He was a pupil of hers in Russia first, and in that way first joined the Ballet.—A. L. H.

Swedish Ballet as a dancing force was lost through forgetting its origins too long, and becoming the plaything of French artists, for the exploitation of temporary and localised experiment. Diaghileff never made that mistake for long. *Les Noces* and later *Le Pas d'Acier* were healthy signs that the ballet could flirt with Western Europe and remember where its roots lay.

At this time in Paris I saw much of the Russian painter and decorative artist, Constantine Korovin. He was a link with the theatre of the past, and had done hundreds of costumes and décors for the Imperial theatres, specialising in Russian costume. His set for *Russlan and Ludmila*, a fine baronial hall, was used by Diaghileff for the *divertissement Festin* in the very first programme. This and the dear old set for *Lac des Cygnes*, dignified through age and travel, was their only link. I had been introduced to him with a view to induce him to write down the part he had played in, and all that he knew of that vanished epoch of Russian art, as brief and brilliant, as the literature, music and ballet of the epoch, but quite unknown to us, where it did not touch the stage. Although our only common language was a rather shaky French, helped out by Russian and gesticulation, Korovin was so fine a storyteller and an actor that it was possible to catch every word he said, although nearly always impossible to reproduce it in black and white, so rapidly did the stories succeed one another, so much did their point depend upon some vocal inflection, some mime or gesture. Our project of recording the conversations was soon given up, but my enthusiasm for things Russian had touched him, and he decided to adopt me, and to pilot me round the Russian colony. Korovin is a magnificent-looking man, deeply impressive, like many of the actors he had magnificently dressed in the make-up of a Boyar, tall, white-bearded. He talks ceaselessly, studying his audience with care, leaving no effect to chance; everything else however is left to take its own course. He is generous to a fault, untidy—I had to wade through piles of drawings and canvases to greet him—and rarely by any chance keeps an appointment in time. There were many points of resemblance between him and my first Russian friend, Astafieva.

One morning, at the beginning of our friendship, he turned up at my flat early. For once he seemed in a hurry.

" We go to see Chaliapine—now—right away. I have fixed everything; he expects you. Hurry, I have a taxi outside."

" But, Constantine Alexandrovitch, I am in pyjamas; I cannot possibly go like this."

" Pyjamas ? Yes. What does it matter ? We are artists; you love our art. Chaliapine will understand; he understands everything. Anyhow, what do clothes matter ? "
He burst into song in his favourite imitation of Chaliapine. The argument was irresistible and the taxi was ticking in agreement. I went to the interview in a makeshift costume, more and more embarrassed as butler passed us on to secretary and so on through the big Trocadero flat. Korovin was right; costume did not seem to matter in the slightest, as we talked to the representative Russian artist, almost the one man who made the convention of opera possible. He showed us a gallery full of portraits of himself in various rôles, a unique collection of work by the leading Russian artists, all inspired by the man in front of us. He should have been conceited—insufferably so—but he was not. " We great artists are never self-satisfied," he told me, and I believed him. His pleasure at being world-famous

was so naïve and so genuine, it was of the same quality as
that of the little *coryphée* in her first rôle, and he had had
a full quarter century in which to get used to it. He discussed the pictures naturally and impersonally as if they
had really represented Boris Godounov, Don Quixote or a
mad old miller.

I visited many other museums and galleries with
Korovin. Extraordinary and unsettling experiences. In
front of any picture that thrilled him, he would suddenly
burst into song in a rich bass voice—opera, Russian song,
or tsigane, always music that seemed to bear a close
relationship to the picture. I had to pacify an occasional
guardian.

" Voyons, monsieur, on ne chante pas ici."

But for the most part they seemed to enjoy and understand his enthusiasm. An academician himself, he would
enthuse about Picasso. He was a magnificent connoisseur
of painting and literally savoured it like fine cooking.

" Ça ce tableau—ça c'est quelque chose. Ah, ça, vrai
peinture. Regardez, là et là et là," and he saluted it,
kissing the tips of his fingers.

One day I took a young English painter to see him, and
the meeting was a complete success. Korovin admired the
young man's work, saluted it impressively and then kissed
him exuberantly on both cheeks. This *accolade* terrified
my friend, and I had the greatest difficulty in restraining
him as he rushed for the door. " The old codger's crazy.
I'm going to get out of here quickly."

He admired intensely the new ballet of Diaghileff,
although he was so much a product of an earlier period.
Starting with the somewhat revolutionary upheaval set
into motion by the *Mir Isskoustva*, he had been left behind,
frittering away his fine talent. Alexandre Benois writes of

this " great and delicate talent, rather unbalanced, reaching at many things, but completing nothing. Korovin is by nature the absolute negation of everything balanced, moderate and dully conventional." The only big décor of his that we have seen, Pavlova's *Don Quixote*, was a serious disappointment; he cannot be judged by that. When we met he was engaged on new costumes for *Prince Igor*, which the de Basil Opera, parent of the new ballet, was doing, and painting a portrait of the beautiful Vera Fokina. In his studio I had my first conversations with Fokine, saddened by the recent choregraphic developments, especially disgusted by *Les Matelots*, which shocked me too at the time, although now I greatly enjoy it as the frolic it is, properly situated in Massine's creations, and not considered as *the* important *première* of the season. With all the fuss of its presentation forgotten, it survives to-day, and is well worth its place on the programme.

For me the great treat arranged by Korovin was my meeting with Vera Trefilova, and the *doyen* of ballet critics, Valerian Svetloff, whose career I so greatly envied. His flat had been a gathering-place after first nights where every movement would be fought over and analysed. In his *Ballet Contemporain* he was the first to recognise the successful revolt of Fokine. To-day, old, bent and white-bearded, the ballet is still his great love. He has survived Anna Pavlova, whom he discovered, worshipped and celebrated in a large critical volume. Our common interest has banished the years, and he has followed my fight for classicism with encouragement. Svetloff, taking his place in the theatre to-day, gives every performance the grand manner.

I had worshipped Trefilova for four years, measured other dancers by her, and knew her every little movement by heart. I had already written about her at length, so that we met almost as old friends. At once she remembered the timid youth who had haunted the Alhambra corridors, under pretext of seeing Dolin, too impressed to speak to her. At this very meeting I was struck unconscious through her, but she does not know of it yet.

"You admire my dancing. Will you do me a great service? I hate drinking, but my host will be offended if I refuse. Please drink it all up for me, quietly."

I did so, and my own too. Korovin kept on pouring it out, vodka, wine, brandy. Thank goodness Trefilova left early that night. I could just see her to the door. I came to myself early the next morning, stiff and cold, being shaken by an angry *gendarme*. I had been sleeping on a pile of stones in the Champs Élysées.

Trefilova is quiet, deliberate, calm and infinitely methodical. She always answers letters promptly. Yet she is as typically Russian as the other better-known type of Astafieva or Korovin, made so popular by literature. The sense of reserve power that is so great a feature of her dancing is there in life. Knowing her calm manner, I once told her how remarkable it was that she never suffered stage fright before her important rôles. "But I do, absolute agonies, only it is nobody's business. I keep it to myself. Many times at the Maryinsky I felt like resigning before a performance, and finishing with it all. Only one never does such things."

Trefilova was never in love with the stage, and when she retired, early on in her career, to a happy married life, she did so with joy and intended it to be for ever. The death of her husband destroyed that dream, and her return was a struggle. With quiet determination she worked until she was as flawless as ever. With her infinite sense of balance, mental as well as physical, and her common sense, Trefilova has never known jealousy or intrigue. Her admiration for her very greatest rival, Anna Pavlova, appointed *ballerina* the same day, was intense and unstinting. Trefilova sees in the success of one person the success of Russian art as a whole. When staying with me after the death of Anna Pavlova, I took her to visit Ivy House. We could not find it, and I had to ask a policeman to direct us to " where Pavlova had lived." Trefilova was crying. " To think that even a policeman knows where Pavlova, my school friend and the glory of our Russian stage, lived. It is beautiful." That was one of the rare occasions when she showed her emotions to others. Perhaps never very happy, Trefilova accepts the inevitable, and is quietly content. She does not live in the past, but understands the present. She teaches her beloved art to others. The Trefilova I know as a private person is the same that I have loved and admired on the stage.

Recovered from my Monte Carlo madness, I became engaged again, this time for good. To a Russian, of course, but not to a dancer. Immediately all my friends asked what company she was in, what rôles she had performed. But I knew dancers too well already, by then, to marry one. Immediately I would have become a partisan, forced to take every little tiff as a personal affront, waiting nightly in the wings for the inevitable scene. I would have been cut off from ballet as the property of *the* dancer. There are a few dancers I love, none with whom I have been in love. I believe myself to be immune.

My wife has suffered during each ballet season. Engagements have been cancelled, and furious acquaintances have had to be pacified. They have not always understood that it is quite impossible to miss a performance.

As a Russian she can diagnose the malady. It comes
from her country, and has made me love all that is
Russian, and understand many things. She loves ballet,
too, a little less intensely ; about twenty times a season. Still,
for nearly ten years now she has been infinitely patient,
and I hope that I am grateful.

CHAPTER V

ANNA PAVLOVA

" Mademoiselle Pavlova est à la danse ce qu'un Racine est à la poésie,
un Poussin à la peinture, un Gluck à la musique."

J. L. VAUDOYER

" L'art de la danse nous delivre de notre propre nature ; et c'est le
sentiment de cette délivrance qui nous procure de la joie, cette joie
distribuée par Anna Pavlova à une grande partie de notre planète."

HEINRICH MANN

" She dances no longer ; she flies."

NESTOR ROQUEPLAN on Léontine Beaugrand, 1867.

" O Earth, weigh gently upon me, I trod so lightly upon thee."

GREEK EPITAPH

SEEING ANNA PAVLOVA is one of my very earliest
memories, and throughout her London and Paris
seasons I rarely missed a performance. My reactions
to her dancing were so emotional that it is only now when
the beauty of her work has ceased, and there is no possibility of seeing her again, that I can rationalise my feelings,
but still I cannot quite fit her into my scheme of things.
Anna Pavlova has always been the great exception to every
carefully laid down artistic principle, the individual who
triumphed over the theory.

Physically she was remarkable ; her long, perfectly pro-
portioned arms accentuated the large noble movements of
the Russian school, while her well-modelled legs, her strong
slender ankles and her highly developed instep gave to her
points a unique beauty. Her face was not beautiful ; it was

more than that. It could assume beauty at will ; so that
there was not one Pavlova, but many ; a gypsy, a dying
delirious woman, a coquette. It was this unusual ability
to live each rôle convincingly that made so trivial a sketch
as *Christmas* into something so much more than a charming
period piece *à la Chauve Souris*. Again and again she rose
superior to her material. What she had to say was so highly
concentrated that she never wasted time with frills and
embellishments. It is this concentration that is one of her
chief characteristics.

When she died, following Diaghileff so closely, there died
not only a sublime artist, but a totally different conception
of ballet that no one less great than Pavlova could have
supported throughout the years of rapidly changing
artistic fashion, when yesterday's novelty was old-fashioned
and even ridiculous to-day. That was the mark of her
greatness, the most thorough tribute that could be paid
her.

When one went to a Diaghileff performance it was to
see ballet, to a Pavlova performance, as the very name
implies, to see one woman dance. It was a dance concert,
a glorious *divertissement*, under a slender, unconvincing
disguise, but that one woman could convert a *divertissement*
into a whole drama. When one lived the performance over
again it may possibly have seemed a supreme waste of
genius, if under the spell one could think at all clearly,
but it was not, for her *points* were strong enough to bear it
all. Her public was not the Diaghileff public, the latter were
wrong. She had so very much to give to the highly sophisticated, provided they were true dance lovers, as much as a
whole evening of fine music, fine décor and fine dancing.
It was different when Diaghileff died. Ballet of his type did
not die with him. Genius he may have been, inspiration

he surely had, but ballet of his conception was founded on
something logical, on the close collaboration of certain
artists. To-day and to-morrow such a thing can continue.
It will be of the same kind, differing only in quality.
Pavlova's ballet died with her. It was as ephemeral as the
many rôles she interpreted so feelingly : the Dying Swan, the
Californian Poppy or the Dragonfly. Pavlova was indeed
supreme when representing the life of some frail, beautiful
thing, her own great strength completely veiled. I once
wrote of her : " In the Swan this whole aspect of Pavlova's
art is summed up. I have seen a similar dance interpreted
by Trefilova, *The Black Swan*, and the difference in spirit
taught me a great deal about both artists ; with Trefilova
it was some amazing aristocratic creature that ceased the
making of bewilderingly beautiful movement, while with
Pavlova, the reaching out as if to struggle for flight, the
final quiver, the shudder throughout the whole body and
then repose, meant real death. It was the more poetical,
certainly the more pathetic of the two, if not the more
dramatically effective."

In *The Dragonfly* and *The Californian Poppy* she made the
dance more intense and joyful, because there was always
the suggestion that death was near at hand to put an end
to movement, a conscious suggestion which she seized
upon in her own *Autumn Leaves*, a simple ballet in which
she managed to convey a whole philosophy. Without her
I doubt whether it could ever have existed. It would have
given an impression of intense sentimentality, and Pavlova
had too much true sentiment ever to approach the sentimental. It is that cheating of death for an instant, but with
the certainty that there was no old age to come, that made
the study of youth in *La Fille Mal Gardée*, a ballet conventional enough in every respect, into a personal triumph.

Always she rose above her material. No one has ever shown youth on the stage with such purity. *Chopiniana* is another exceptional Pavlova ballet, even in the inferior version she adopted. Composer and dancer are in such absolute sympathy. Here she is as little tangible as a figure lightly sketched on a canvas with but a flick of the brush.

These are none of them questions of definite interpretative acting. It is in *Giselle* that she reveals herself as a powerful dramatic actress. It is her greatest rôle, as it must be with every *ballerina* who does not fail, and it reveals in her a totally new aspect. Again the quality we notice is pathos, but not the gentle pathos of *The Swan* or *Autumn Leaves*, something incomprehensible and irresistibly strong, too strong by far for tears. The impression made by Pavlova during the mad scene literally made one shudder. It was subtle, very restrained, yet everyone in the theatre could feel it and suffered. The other Giselles that I have seen have not nearly approached this point, and to have seen her in it was to gain a new conception of her genius. For all my *balletomania* the word *genius* is one that I fear to use; with Pavlova there can be no other word. Talent is so manifestly ridiculous. She took ordinary material and made of it something extraordinary. We have seen for a season " The Pavlova Ballet " without her ; pathetic spectacle of good dancers waiting for someone to come and make them dance, or for La Pavlova herself to make us forget our little rules of good and bad choregraphy. She was almost her whole life associated with mediocrity—in music, décor and by comparison in the company in which she danced— but she herself was never anything but great. Her genius defies analysis, for on careful consideration a whole group of negatives make one astounding, unmistakable positive— her genius.

D

There is the Maryinsky Ballet, the Diaghileff Ballet; there was Anna Pavlova.

In spite of the fact that Pavlova, the name, is a household word that means dancing, she herself has never been truly understood save by her fellow artists. No one yet has given a complete and accurate portrait of her, either as an artist or as a woman. Perhaps it is a part of her quality that no one can. I lay no claim to do so. I knew her scarcely at all— our meetings were five or six at the most; but on those occasions we discussed some interesting points, and the vision I have of her is far more plausible, concrete and certainly flattering than the inevitable talk of her love of animals and flowers and her meetings with royalty. Such stories create a certain glamour, but Pavlova above all had no need of anything so artificial. Her glamour was blinding even to her intimates. I have questioned many members of her company. They could feel much, but tell me nothing. In spite of their being on the same side of the curtain, in a position to see and suffer from her little tantrums, or to benefit by her impulsive generosity, she was always, to them as well, the supreme artist with an invisible barrier of footlights between her and them.

The first time that I met her was on the stage at Covent Garden. I arrived early, and took up a position in the wings to watch the *Bacchanal*. From my novel and notoriously unflattering angle there was no loss of illusion, but a positive gain. It became almost unbearably exciting and real, and it was with the greatest difficulty that I could restrain myself from cheering, and making " noises off." Added to the glories of the dance itself, one could feel her contact with the audience as a definite, concrete thing, a feeling that I have never experienced to that degree before. Excitement, the sense of her immense power, made

Pavlova young and vital.[1] Even when the curtain fell for the first time, while the applause continued, she still belonged body and soul to her audience ; in that beautiful bow, so much a part of her performance, she dedicated herself to them, then, when the curtain went down for the last time, the anthem played, and all echoes of the applause had died down, the contact was suddenly broken, and an immediate transformation took place. A tired middle-aged woman, with only the figure of a very young girl, stood before me, the smallest on a crowded stage, instead of the one, the dominating figure. It was a transformation, a shock even, but not a disillusionment. It made her performance all the greater, and it explained something too. No one has ever reacted to an audience to the same degree as Pavlova. Then she spoke :

" So you are a *balletomane*? Are you on my side or Diaghileff's ? "

It was a quite unanswerable question, but it was perfectly clear what she meant. I was on her side at that moment, so to speak, because against all reason she had compelled me to be. I gave a halting conventional reply, and, without waiting for a fuller explanation, she went on :

" Please don't tell me I danced *The Swan* well to-night. I know quite well I didn't. One is not a machine. I wasn't in the right mood. Yet the audience applauds just the same. It is kind of them, but so difficult for me, so bad for an artist. In Russia the slightest shade of difference would be noted and commented on. All the time we had to make a great effort. Here my applause does not vary. I am grateful of course, but it was not so good to-night. I know."

She was dissatisfied. That is a picture that every dancer

[1] " Vous avez une ambition dévorante et vos yeux insatiables voudraient embrasser plus de succès qu'il n'y en a sur cette terre," said Sarah Bernhardt to Anna Pavlova.

will recognise. Pavlova may have been, must have been, exceptionally self-centred, in a sense almost ruthless in pursuit of her ambition—her whole career proves that—but, she was also intensely self-critical, laying bare those little faults that others could no longer see. She could not be deceived by an easy success, was incapable of ever resorting to bluff. When she said, " I danced well to-night," it was true. Pavlova was above any criticism but her own.

She died while she could still produce perfection; only the Pavlova of ten years before was her bitter rival. In dying she averted a terrible tragedy—the tragedy of the *ballerinas* in *Grand Hotel* or *Ballerina*. She often talked of settling down quietly at Ivy House, of concentrating on her sculpture or taking up some new career, sometimes even with great conviction. Once she even flirted with the idea of starting a hotel. She could never have done any of these things. Her look of nostalgia when the curtain went down that night, convinced me. To retire was impossible, to continue with diminished powers equally so.

During her final visit to London I met her at a Sunshine Matinée. She greatly admired the Rambert Ballet, then a new organisation, in *Capriol Suite*, and saw in Frederick Ashton a possible new choregrapher for herself. There was talk of a new repertoire, of ballets by Ashton and Balanchine, that were modern but not " modernist." Then and there I arranged a visit to the studio, so that she could watch some works in rehearsal. She was both critical and enthusiastic, asked to see *Capriol* again, and admired Diana Gould in *Leda* so much that she wished to engage her for a tour. That was Pavlova's one link with the Ballet Club, a precious memory.

I saw her but once again, at Golders Green, more magnificently alive and real than any one of us, her admiring audience. Wisely she had pruned her dances of their greater technicalities, and was showing a restricted repertoire, in which she was still perfection. With her the technique was always so completely natural that it defied discernment. She was alone among the great dancers in never being applauded for any one technical feat. There was none of the hanging knee, the first signs of departing strength, no hint of tragedy. It is from others that I heard how very tired she was.

The news of her death reached me in a cold, empty theatre, during a lighting rehearsal of the Camargo Society. I broke the news to her old friend, partner and professor, Legat. It seemed so very difficult to believe, especially when heard in a theatre at a ballet rehearsal. Gradually the entire committee turned up and we held an informal meeting on the spot. Some suggested cancelling the performance, but that would have meant the ruin of the society. We were heavily committed, and finances, as always, were precarious. Then the idea occurred to Stephen Thomas and myself of playing the music of *The Swan*, with curtains raised on the empty stage. Someone objected, " It wouldn't do at all. Quite lacking in dignity. Too theatrical by far," which aroused from Lydia Lopokova, in her earnest, carefully enunciated Anglo-Russian :

" A good idea, we will do it. We are *theatrical*, so was Pavlova. It is a word of praise; besides, she would have understood and liked it."

It was the most vivid item of the whole programme. This memory of perfection completely put the living performance in the shade ; but it was at the orchestra rehearsal that it was the most impressive, before just a few people, her friends and true admirers, in the intimate workshop atmosphere of the theatre.

These verses by Dermot Spence were sent to me after the performance.

> *A moment's pause before the show goes on,*
> *A minute's breath before we turn the page :*
> *The dying flutter of an unseen Swan,*
> *The weeping music and the empty stage . . .*
>
> *We have lost something more than twinkling feet :*
> *More than a dancer perished when you died.*
> *This was a life untarnished and complete.*
> *And so we stand, in sorrow and in pride.*
>
> *Surely you went as those the Gods love, young,*
> *Before the sceptre trembled, or the crown,*
> *Lifted by listless fingers, fell among*
> *The gay pretenders toasted by the Town.*
>
> *. . . an empty stage . . . and yet the whole house sees*
> *In the blue limelight more than vacant air :*
> *A whispered hint of shadow draperies—*
> *And surely Pavlova is dancing there.*

Since then this idea has occurred to many, and I have seen it carried out in a morbid manner, with a shifting lime.

Many are the uses to which Pavlova's name will be put. There is even talk of a film of her life. How can such a thing be ? What was her life but her art—*Giselle*, *The Swan* and the rest ? Who dares dance them in her name ?

Pavlova's name will be put to many uses for long years to come, for it is now synonymous with the dance. Every new talent that arises will be called a " second Pavlova " by her well-meaning admirers, who in that way will promptly and effectively damn her for ever. I must have

seen over a score of such "second Pavlovas" during the
last few years, and I could not see that any of them bore
the slightest resemblance to her namesake. If Pavlova
herself had been called a "second Zucchi," when she
made her glorious début, we should never have heard
of her to-day. It was perfectly safe to compare her to
Taglioni, for by then Taglioni was but a shade that
stood for something ethereal, but that could be assigned no
positive personality.

Our new star may well have some of those things that
were Pavlova's, but she must have something to give that is
essentially her own.

Will it be possible for such a reputation to be made
at the present day ? That is the way I carefully phrase my
query, for I have great enough faith in the art to believe
that even such a talent as was Pavlova's can be repeated in
quantity but not in quality.

The whole conception of the ballet to-day seems to be
against it ; a one-act affair lasting from twenty minutes to
an hour at most with a variety of parts rather than one
central one. If the dancer makes anything of a name, and
is at all discussed, it is usually in a definite character rôle
and not as herself at all. Aesthetically this may be an
advantage, but it does prevent her from attaining her full
stature as an individual.

At the present day in England ballet is becoming more
and more understood, while the dancer herself is almost
completely anonymous. She is said to dance " charmingly,"
" brilliantly " or " lightly," but she is never appreciated
critically, and never taken to task ; that is the tragedy.

During the Covent Garden season of 1934 a *ballerina*
was compared by three newspaper writers to Don Bradman, much to my disgust and hers—and perhaps

Bradman's ! It was obviously intended as praise, very
great praise, since Bradman was piling on runs, and in
very high favour at the time. Not only did it mean nothing,
but it revealed how fully the dancer is misunderstood by
the very people whose duty it is to interpret her to others.
The ballet is rich enough as an art for some comparison
or some terms of praise to be found from within it.

Another factor that will prevent the dancer from
equalling her elders as a personality is the fact that to-day
she is enormously overworked. In the great period of the
Imperial Ballet, out of which Pavlova herself was born,
nightly performances were an unheard of thing, and the
prominent dancer could go into training for her rôle much
as the opera singer or the instrumentalist. This gave not
only a physical repose, but also full time in which to work
upon an interpretation, and there were always those on
hand who could guide the young dancer.

Igor Stravinsky told me only recently that in Russia
alone was the dancer regarded as a serious artist, the
equal of any virtuoso of piano or violin. This spirit still
exists to-day, but the too frequent appearance must
damage the young dancer both in fact and in the eyes of
the public.

To-day, in her spare time, when she gets any of it, the
dancer is thrown almost exclusively into the society of
her mother, and, all things considered, it is the mothers
who really have the greatest influence, and who are
ultimately the deciding factor between success and failure,
not by their political moves, generally of a clumsy nature,
but by their influence at home. They know, they have
become experts in dancing. Unfortunately they can rarely
be impersonal, and the young dancer is carrying her
mother's opinions on to the stage with her, as well as the

shoes and tights that her mother has darned. A dancer will
become as great as her mother allows her to be, provided
of course that she herself has the essentials.

In Russia in the palmy days of the Imperial Ballet the
State took on the task of mothering the dancers. Each
one received the same education, but personality did not
suffer. Or did it? It may have been a question of the
survival of the fittest, the triumph of a few exceptional
individuals, with the rest as just a decorative pattern in
the background. To-day we have the interplay of personalities struggling to develop; that, as well as lack of
adequate rehearsal time, makes a *corps de ballet* ragged, a
fault that has been found with all young companies
recently. It is inherent in the present system, because the
dancer beginning to develop as an individual cannot
express herself in a group. Again, with the new system as
with the old, the exceptional personality will triumph,
with the difference that in Russia the fight was almost
decided from school days, now it goes on in front of us
daily on the stage.

With the very young, personality develops rapidly,
technique develops and especially stage presence. People
say, "How fickle you are; once again you have changed
your opinion." Ridiculous people, as if it were an opinion
about some inanimate stationary thing. The dancer
develops from season to season, the critic does too, although
there are many, including Diaghileff himself, who say that
critics alone never learn. Perhaps they are right, though
such remarks are usually made by dancers, when you have
not praised them sufficiently. Dancers in fact are for the
most part exceedingly bad critics about the art of others,
unless they have attained the heights and are secure. That
is right, and as it should be; they must needs be thoroughly

self-centred if they are to accomplish. But if only they were indignant when I criticise them, and not when I praise others !

In a sense the path of the great Maryinsky dancers was more direct aesthetically than that of the dancer of to-day. She had a definite mission to accomplish. The following from Prince Wolkonsky will show what the ballet was like before such a dancer as Pavlova came on the scene :

"The first time I went to the Ballet I was a child, and it was to see the *Fisherman and the Naiad*. I liked the fairy side of the performance, I liked the *corps de ballet*, but frankly I disliked the soloists. Even in those early days I felt shocked at their affectation, and the technique, which was stressed to an almost acrobatic extent, left me quite cold. I could neither grasp the difficulty nor the charm of it, so tremendously did the 'untruth' of it offend me. It was true to no convention, illogical, absurd, unnecessary. You will understand something of it when you compare early theatrical photos with those of to-day.

"Even at the beginning of my directorship, although by then great creative dancers had emerged, the atmosphere was much the same. I remember a new production of *Tannhäuser*. The dances in the first act, the bacchanal in the Venus grotto, had been staged by the great Petipa himself. At the dress rehearsal I was horrified, it was just tip-toe, tip-toe, tip-toe, the whole time. The nymphs were *ballerinas*, never forgot it themselves and never let the audience forget it. Think of it, during that wonderful accord which an invisible chorus sings behind the scenes, we saw three *ballerinas* cross the plateau on their points, grinning sweetly to the enraptured audience.

" I gave orders for the scene to be changed but, even if there had been time, nobody could understand in the slightest what I wanted. The dancers had elicited applause, how could there possibly be anything wrong ? "

Tannhäuser bacchanal *sur les pointes,* hand on heart, lover's sighs, that is the atmosphere from which Kchessinska, Trefilova, and then Pavlova emerged, and it was their task to take ballet away from the lumber-room, to dust away its cobwebs, and to give to Fokine and Diaghileff an instrument with which they could work. By Wolkonsky's statement we can measure what these great *ballerinas* accomplished. But now that the battle has been so handsomely won, in what direction can the new *ballerina* develop ?

Only by the fullest expression of her own individuality, through which she will be expressing her age. Individuality is a thing that can be developed in the classroom itself. Kchessinska, artist of tremendous personality, who saw the gifts of Nijinsky and Karsavina before anyone else, and who went out of her way to develop them, believes strongly in the systematic development of personality. She dances continually to demonstrate, but her pupils do not imitate her ; they are not allowed to.

One day I sat in a class watching a classical Mazurka, interpreted by five artist pupils, among the finest dancers of to-day, each one of different physique and temperament.

" That is splendid," said their teacher excitedly, " each one does it in an entirely different manner, and each one is perfectly right."

She stressed a very great truth in dancing, and a little-understood one, that *if there are thousands of ways of doing a thing wrongly there are also thousands of ways of doing it rightly.* She corrected each one, but for the inconsistencies in each *individual* version, and not by some imaginary mathematical standard, or by what she herself or Pavlova would have done.

It is because they are so essentially themselves that to-day I sing the praises of Baronova, Riabouchinska and Toumanova. Because they have never sought to imitate their elders, they can be truly said to have understood those things for which Pavlova stood, and those things from which she, more than anyone, freed the dance. Her name will live, because she was one, unique, unrepeatable, and that too will be the sole condition of their future fame.

CHAPTER VI

SERGE DIAGHILEFF

" Il ne faut à la Danse qu'un beau modèle, un homme de génie, et les
Ballets changeront de caractère."

NOVERRE

" Par la mort de Serge de Diaghileff et la dispersion des aériens génies,
la main du sort vient d'effacer les fresques étincelantes qui recouv-
raient le morne univers."

COMTESSE DE NOAILLES

" The Exhibition of Decorative Art is a tribute to the Diaghileff era."

FRENCH PRESS, May 1927

EVEN DURING Diaghileff's lifetime a legend surrounded him, which has now grown to such
enormous dimensions that it has become impossible to see the real man, or to form a correct estimate
of his achievement, and that of his many brilliant collaborators. His work and vast knowledge drew him into so
many different circles that each person, almost, has a
distorted picture of his particular Diaghileff, coloured
through distance—pictures that it is generally impossible
to reconcile. I have attempted this sketch of him from
innumerable conversations with his collaborators, friends
and enemies, members of his company, and also from my
personal knowledge. I knew him but slightly, and he disliked me from the moment that I began criticising the
Ballet, though he agreed with so many of the conclusions
I reached. He was always intolerant of any independent
criticism, and on one occasion, it is said, visited Levinson's

editor, demanding his instant dismissal. I had an intense admiration for him, and he was the only person of whom I have ever been a little frightened. This distance has given me the possibility of gaining a true perspective ; so over-powering was his personality that anyone at all intimate with him would naturally have coloured views. " I could never talk to him without feeling like crying, and many others were the same," said a usually well-balanced member of his company to me. That makes an approach very difficult. We are immediately on an emotional plane, and it is his intellect that it is valuable to assess.

It is first necessary to destroy some of this legend that gets between us and him. The best known portrait, now, is that by Romola Nijinsky,[1] and it is all the more mis-leading through being on so many points nearly accurate, and always highly plausible. It is of course only natural that the wife of Nijinsky should see in Diaghileff the brilliant villain of the Middle Ages ; *her* Diaghileff must have assumed some of those aspects, but it cannot be allowed to persist in its entirety as a true portrait. I could balance it with as many clearly established acts of goodness, that would, by substituting Santa Claus for Cesare Borgia, form a portrait equally misleading.

We must first admit his abnormal views on love, an undisputed fact. He had only once, early in life, tried normal relations with a woman, and the occasion must have been unfortunate. It left him with a deep disgust, amount-ing to terror. He had never forgotten the incident, and talked of it at times. However, women played a large part in his life. Because of these views, he could meet them as equals, select them for their intelligence, and admire their beauty, coldly, as if they were museum exhibits.

---

[1] *Nijinsky*, by Romola Nijinsky (Gollancz, 1933).

Women were attracted by him, and helped him from the very start. Some of the most remarkable women of the day were his allies, and made his triumphs possible. His deep loves made of him a lonely man, certain to be constantly disillusioned and disappointed, deliriously happy at one moment, dejected the next. He was only attracted by the virile, normal man, who was certain with maturity to attract and be attracted by the opposite sex, and to prefer the company of some witless little girl to the brilliant Sergei Pavlovitch : situations that one could not expect him to accept. Once that fact is admitted and understood, without condoning it in any way, it is not difficult to imagine his feelings on receiving the brief and unexpected telegraphic announcement of Nijinsky's marriage. To Sergei Pavlovitch, it was obviously quite impossible to retain him in the company, to work and to remain in daily contact with him and the intruder, his wife. The dismissal of him at once was no beginning of a dark mediæval plot to wipe him out of existence, but merely the very normal reaction of a very abnormal man. Once one admits this conception of love—and it has never been disputed—what other course was open to him ? Also there was much more in it. It had its idealistic aspect.

Nijinsky as a choregrapher was Diaghileff's own creation, and it was through the opportunities that Diaghileff gave him, the careful nursing, the development of his personality, and the all-important intellectual contacts, that he could compose. Nijinsky was famous in Russia first, but in the old repertoire, and without Sergei Pavlovitch his fame would have remained local—just that of another brilliant dancer among brilliant dancers. Diaghileff must certainly have realised, aside from any feelings of jealousy, that however much Nijinsky was now living the normal life of a normal man, those opportunities would cease and his whole dream of creation would be shattered. Nijinsky was exceptionally receptive material, but needed the constant stimulation that Diaghileff alone could provide. When he left Diaghileff he immediately deteriorated as a dancer, and his choregraphy also failed, in the opinion of many. Another point that must have weighed with him was the fact —and the whole company knew it—that Nijinsky was highly strung and unbalanced from the very beginning, and that he needed the most extraordinary care and a total freedom from responsibility, a care that Diaghileff had always given him. It would be tragic to see him grow worse before his very eyes, without the means or the right to try to save him.

There is no suggestion that Diaghileff seduced him. Nijinsky was not a child. He had an enormous respect and admiration for him, and profited both materially and as an artist from the friendship. As events proved, his one hope of sanity lay in remaining with Diaghileff. While his desire to marry was natural, it must not be looked upon as an escape from some ogre, from an entirely unmitigated evil. The balance between the two men was, up to this point, very even ; materially Nijinsky had certainly gained the most.

Such a separation, therefore, is not only understandable ; anything else was quite out of the question. Then came the demand for the payment of arrears of salary—the first unfriendly act, and from the other side. To a man already suffering, this must have been a heavy blow. It is certain from all sources of evidence that Diaghileff was scrupulously honest ; strangely avaricious in small things, generous, even lavish, in large. Many dancers, during the war and after, remained with him for years without ever having felt the need for a signed contract. For at least two of his dancers he deposited money in the bank in addition to their generous salaries, as some compensation for having taken them away from the guaranteed livelihood of the Maryinsky. This was done without any compulsion. Another dancer, who had refused his advances, he offered to send to a sanatorium in Switzerland, when he was threatened with tuberculosis. When it came to a reckoning between him and Nijinsky, he had looked after all Nijinsky's personal needs, had gratified his slightest wish, and had made him many costly presents. It must surely have been tacitly understood that the large salary was but a " paper " one, for the sake of appearances and publicity. Diaghileff could not stoop to reckon up all these favours, and here at any rate Nijinsky and his wife were the aggressors. A woman older and more experienced than the headstrong young girl, Romola, who knew so clearly what she wanted, and pursued it through so many difficulties, would have persuaded him to leave matters alone instead of taking the lead. She clearly felt her power, and there was a certain thrill even in the duel with her defeated rival—this great man whom her husband still worshipped. Between the two, Nijinsky, sighing for peace and the opportunity to serve his art, must have been both mystified and unhappy.

As to the tale of subsequent persecutions, one cannot for a moment believe them : they are altogether too fantastic and out of keeping with the whole of Diaghileff's known character. Once his dreams had been shattered he would have been bitter and disillusioned, but he would have let so painful a subject alone. Subsequent stories show this to have been the case. Many times disappointed, he still retained a friendship on a non-emotional basis when the other party made it possible. It was while they were still

with him that he fought tooth and nail to retain their
affections, was jealous to the extent of having them
shadowed by detectives day and night, and adopted all
the petty tricks that jealousy inspires even in the greatest
minds.

The charge that Fokine sought to prevent Nijinsky
appearing in *Le Spectre de la Rose* in London, or that
Diaghileff even tried to influence him to do so, is indignantly denied by Fokine. One cannot conceive of these men
as joint conspirators. Neither does it show any plot, that
Bakst refused to collaborate with Nijinsky in his efforts to
rival Diaghileff. Bakst, as a loyal and grateful friend, must
have resented the whole thing, and held back not through
fear or compulsion, as is suggested by Madame Nijinsky,
but through common decency. The notion that Diaghileff
incited two men to drive Nijinsky mad, by putting vaguely
pseudo-Tolstoyan ideas into his head, is the most fantastic
of all. Nijinsky himself was already unbalanced, obviously
sought the company of other unstable men, and one of these
" conspirators " died insane a little time later. The other,
whom I know well, was young, impressionable, and soon
threw off such ideas, which must have come at one time
or another to so many adolescent Russians, who can ill
digest so rich a literature. Also there is not a doubt that, at
the time, he had an axe to grind, and enjoyed his influence over Nijinsky. It was not for nothing that he was
called " Nijinsky's Rasputin " by the rest of the company.
The thing undoubtedly happened as Romola Nijinsky
describes it, but quite spontaneously and without the
knowledge of Diaghileff, who, when he heard of it, strongly
disapproved.[1]

---

[1] He never quite forgave the unfortunate stage manager of the tour, who was
quite powerless to intervene.—A. L. H.

I have investigated, too, the story of the attempt on his life. It was just one of those frightening episodes that, in spite of all precautions, occur from time to time on the stage. The object fell just behind Nijinsky and in front of Leon Woizikovski, for whom it might equally well have been intended. I have myself witnessed almost the identical thing—the falling of a huge weight from the flies. Nijinsky may have been unpopular—all successful dancers are; it is part of the game—but the game does not include murder.

We know that, throughout Nijinsky's unfortunate malady, Diaghileff showed, not remorse, but a very natural solicitude. He could be remorseless in pursuit of his aims, extremely jealous and quite capable of strong hatred—every fault and quality in him was exaggerated—but this aimless vendetta is entirely out of keeping with his essentially creative character, and is not supported by anything more than the vague conjectures of a loving imaginative wife and her delicate husband. Diaghileff had his petty side, but it was shown by such things as making it indirectly difficult for someone he did not like to remain in the company, through passport troubles and the like, but he never pursued them or tried to damage their livelihood.

Nijinsky's own action in keeping Diaghileff away from the American tour, and assuming responsibilities for which he was so obviously unfitted, must certainly have damaged the artistic results of the entire enterprise, and jeopardised its very existence. The ballet could live perfectly well without Nijinsky, as events have proved, but without Diaghileff it was aimless. In this whole unpleasant episode Diaghileff showed the very greatest magnanimity. It was his ballet and he need not have consented to the tour. He wished for its success, and it was Nijinsky himself who selected the artists, omitting Grigorieff, whose help would have been invaluable. Apart from any sentiment, Diaghileff would never have tried to bring about a costly failure; it would have been cheaper to put his foot down from the very start.

In this whole story of the friendship and enmity of these two men, once the unfortunate basis, that made it delicate from the very start, has been admitted, it is clear that Diaghileff was more hurt than hurting.

His *manie des grandeurs*, another important part of the legend, certainly existed, and with some justification. His superiority was felt and admitted by others, who were themselves by no means toadies. He shone in any company, and it was not unnatural to play up to it at times. On one occasion he told me, after some trouble in the company, " I can get rid of all these people and have just as good a Ballet within three weeks. Dancers will pay to say they have been with me." Perhaps this was not strictly accurate at the time, 1925, but it was near enough to the truth. I had heard many of the offers that he turned down.

In one case a very large sum of money was offered him to " star " a young dancer whom he admired, but did not yet think ripe for such responsibility. He badly needed the money, but refused without hesitation, and felt himself insulted. He never forgave her. He had largely made the present company, the Maryinsky supply was exhausted, and he could form others, if not in three weeks, then within the year. On another occasion, at supper, I heard him reprimand one of his dancers for eating peas with a knife. "But, Sergei Pavlovitch, you are doing precisely the same thing." " I can, because I am Diaghileff " ; which was true, and is a very old story that has always been true.

Lydia Sokolova has told me that apart from England, where each dancer has always had groups of friends and admirers, they always danced for Diaghileff and for Diaghileff alone. I have often heard them debating earnestly, when he had gone on one of his trips, as to what train he would take. " Ah, the 8.30, then he will have dinner at once and won't be there for the first ballet," in a tone of relief. His presence made an enormous and obvious difference to the whole quality of the performance. He noticed every single detail of dancing, make-up and costume, from the placing of a safety-pin, and his opinions would reach the dancers via Grigorieff day by day, often in the form of a fine. Diaghileff had a hyper-sensitive eye. One of his *bêtes noires* was a big head. " I have a big head and there isn't going to be another one in the company." He was on that account most particular about the style of hairdressing. Another saying of his was : " There is nothing uglier in the world than a woman's thighs," and he never permitted the short revealing classical *tutu*, except in boyishly slim figures, such as Alice Nikitina's in *Zéphir et Flore*.

This fact, of Diaghileff as an *audience*, can give us a first positive clue to his character; it reveals, and is explained by, his heredity. Ballet in Russia first took root through the nobles having private troupes of their own, brought over from the Continent or composed of their own serfs, performing not for profit but for their amusement and that of their guests. Diaghileff by breeding was such a nobleman. However much a showman he was, educating and cultivating his public, this precedent persisted, and was a part of him. He was Diaghileff the autocrat, and never in any sense an impresario, though he could and did outdistance them all at their own game. His Ballet danced for him,

for his gratification and his greater glory. Everyone in the
theatre worked for him, even carpenters and electricians.
On some occasions the dancers would leave the theatre in
the evening, and find him still seated there the next morning, worn out, with deep bags under his eyes, surrounded
by the technical staff. They earned big sums in overtime,
but for no one else would they ever have done the same
thing. He graciously shared his pleasure with the public,
and with him pleasure largely consisted in watching the
reactions of others to anything that moved him deeply.
That is the essential picture that one must have first of all.
Otherwise the position of the man who was not an impresario, and neither dancer, painter nor musician, but
who influenced all three for a quarter of a century, is
impossible to understand. We can think of him as a Lorenzo
the Magnificent, never a dilettante, but an artist in
appreciation, and, in many interpretations of the word,
a fully creative mind.

Our view of Diaghileff as a creator depends largely upon
the particular period in his career. One of the very best
studies is that of A. Benois, his first mentor, and col-
laborator of the early days. He tells how Diaghileff, the
young provincial, of good county family, joined their little
circle of artists, sponsored by his cousin Filosofov, and of
the impressions he made, beginning as the timid outsider
on sufferance, and soon becoming the dominating force.
One episode he recalls in particular, the sudden interruption during a picnic of a long abstract discussion on
Wagner :

    " Lying as I was on my back, looking at the clouds,
    I could not see what was happening. . . . Serge took
    advantage of this to creep up to me, seize hold of me

and start pummelling me, laughing heartily all the while. Never before had such a thing happened in our group. We were all quiet and well brought up . . . real mother's boys. . . . Also I soon felt that big Serge was much stronger than I, and that, although the eldest, I risked a humiliating defeat. I had recourse to a ruse, screaming lustily so as to persuade him that he had broken my arm. He was impressed, released me with regret at having been unable to follow up his advantage and even helped me to get up, which I did, groaning and rubbing my arm energetically.

" This childish scene has remained fixed in my memory with extraordinary vividness and I think that the reason for it is that suddenly I had a vision of the true nature of Serge, the nature of a fighter. Although we soon became fast friends long before any collaboration, a sort of fight was always mixed up in our relationship, which gave our friendship a particular zest."[1]

Diaghileff, the fighter, was to overcome all the difficulties and intrigues of the twenty-five years that surrounded his venture. Only a fighter and an absolute autocrat could have succeeded. Diaghileff was born a dictator, but that rare thing, the dictator of discrimination and intelligence.

" Only one thing," says Benois, " was lacking in that generation of Russian artists who contributed to the creation of all these fine artistic manifestations—it was just that, the will to create, that same will to create that Diaghileff possessed to the full."[2]

In the years immediately before the ballet, Diaghileff shows magnificent scholarship in a monograph on the

1 and 2 A. Benois, *La Revue Musicale*, December 1st, 1930.

Russian painter Levitzsky. He dabbles in music, tries his voice as a singer, and is dissuaded by Rimsky-Korsakov from composing, after a first effort had been heard. That is the end of dilettantism. Then comes the organisation of art exhibitions, the editing of a review and the sponsoring of a whole new movement. This means fighting and diplomacy. The young provincial has found himself. The first few years of the ballet are an exploitation of that will, but it is still clearly the Fokine ballet, and we are told that the only suggestion he ever made to Fokine was during a rehearsal of *L'Oiseau de Feu*, when he pointed out that the heart was on the left side. Fokine is fully justified in all that he says: the real Diaghileff was still to appear.

It is with the ripening of the Nijinsky friendship that we first see him. The results of that friendship had deprived him of a permanent headquarters, and had made him almost an outlaw. Now he had to rely from season to season entirely on his diplomatic skill. Nijinsky, as an artist, was the result of the opportunities provided for him by Diaghileff, who did not create his ballets or ever claim to do so, but who surrounded him with the necessary ingredients and waited.[1] When Nijinsky left him, he was immediately ready with Massine, a truly brilliant mind, who profited by the opportunities to the full, and soon found his own direction.

Then Diaghileff was ready to enhance those creations. Forsaking for ever ready-made music, and the décor of those artists who had started out with him, he commenced the Diaghileff Ballet, and it is of this second period, the Massine period, that he was proudest. Choregraphy, music,

[1] In all the discussions I had with him, never once did he lay claim to a creation or even to ideas that I knew had come from him. His autocracy and leadership were understood things; it pleased him to be generous; it was the prerogative of being a Tsar.—A. L. H.

décor, all must be commissioned, and the result must show no gaps, and, however bad any of his rare failures may have been, there never was a gap. Much subsequent ballet has been more important, but there have always been some flaws in its presentation, one of the partners struggling to express something different. While it is quite clear that Diaghileff himself was a man of few ideas or direct suggestions, he could inspire ideas in his *entourage*, and then act. He himself never laid claim to ideas and avoided personal publicity. Never on any occasion did he appear on the stage. All the extravagant claims were made by his over-enthusiastic admirers.

" What exactly do I do ? Well, you can say that I superintend the lighting," was his invariable reply. He could play with light like an artist mixing paint on his canvas, and patiently persisted until the crease in the old drop curtain of *Petrouchka* was completely washed away.

It is not true, either, to go to the other extreme and to believe the jibe that painters admired his knowledge of music, musicians his knowledge of painting. " If you placed twenty scores before him, he would pick out the best, and give his reasons, too," Auric told me, while Larionov used the identical phrase to describe his knowledge of painting. I have seen him interrupt an orchestra rehearsal to make some criticism, when Stravinsky himself was conducting, and the suggestion was readily accepted. If he appeared to interfere but little in the actual choreography, it was because he had picked his men with the greatest care, and had influenced their whole minds and manner of thinking, previously. He did not just commission a work as a mere financial transaction. His collaborators stayed with him months at a time at Monte Carlo, and he actually watched the work in progress, criticising it bit by bit. The greatest artists of the day listened to his criticism with respect.

" Creative ? " says Larionov, one of his brilliant collaborators. " In one respect at any rate, admirably so. He created his audiences. For months ahead, before each new departure he arranged for inspired talk to circulate in the salons, and listened carefully to opinions. Even the head waiter in a restaurant was worth influencing. This preliminary ' provocation ' was part of a deliberate system."

Did he always believe in his own works ? At times that is a little doubtful. Once when I asked him what he really thought of a new ballet, he replied : " I cannot tell yet. I haven't read the papers." A *boutade*, of course, but ever since the scandal over *L'Après-midi d'un Faune* he realised the full value of controversy and enjoyed it. It meant a fight. Such a work as *Romeo et Juliette* was boosted far above its merits, through the demonstration and quarrel amongst the *surréalistes*, which Diaghileff definitely anticipated, if he did not foster it. His own personal taste in music was for melody, and in Switzerland, during the war, Stravinsky teased him for his excessive admiration for Tchaikovsky. Stravinsky subsequently revised his opinions ; Diaghileff remained firm, though publicly for a time he left Tchaikovsky far behind.

His taste in dancing was for classicism, though he could admire something totally different. I remember his urging me to see the acrobatics of the Gertrude Hoffman girls. This was a superficial momentary interest of a man whom everything interested. Olga Spessiva was his favoured *ballerina*. He said of her : " Olga Spessiva and Anna Pavlova are like two halves of an apple, but the Spessiva half has been in the sun." Unjust, of course, but he never could forgive Pavlova for having made a success away from his influence. The Maryinsky *ballerinas* he admired whole-heartedly, and could talk for hours about Kchessinska, her art, charm and intelligence. He was far less of a revolutionary than Fokine, though the results associated with him were so much more extreme. The failure of *The Sleeping Princess* affected him more than people can know. It was a return to his own taste, and its rejection in the nature of a personal rebuff. Other failures he could talk of light-heartedly, as " successful failures " or the reverse. His deliberate policy after that, in his own words, shortly before his death, was to sicken the public gradually with the grotesque, and the " *dernier cri*," until he had educated them sufficiently to return to the purity of classicism. Both his choregraphers of the ultra-modern period were themselves sickened, and longing for the return. When he died this was fully planned. Dolin was engaged, Lifar nearly ready, and his beloved Spessiva waiting. Often, too, he tried to induce Kchessinska to return to the stage. The change of direction, which took place after his death, was in a sense due to him. Lifar danced *Giselle* and *L'Oiseau Bleu* with Spessiva; to see this would have given him the greatest joy. Massine discovered the new symphonic classicism.

All this shows clearly that Diaghileff could not initiate artistic movements without years of preparation ; he seized them at their birth, and showed them to the public at large. The era 1909-1929 was the Diaghileff era, because he crystallised what was going on, and not because he actually created it. This does not detract from him; it puts his genius on another plane, and at the same time allows full credit to his collaborators.

Diaghileff has been called, by many, an excellent business man, and if the keeping alive of an expensive company for so long deserves the description, he was, though in point of detail the artist plus nobleman in him always won. *The Sleeping Princess* would have needed a record run to meet its expenses. Each costume in one brief scene cost over £50. Others have profited by this lavishness, for to-day the original costumes are still being worn in *Petrouchka*, *Prince Igor* and *Le Chapeau Tricorne*, still in admirable condition. Not a penny would be spared either on entertaining or on the smallest detail once an idea had entered into his head. He had no fixed home and very few personal wants. Only in the last few years he collected books, chiefly Pouschkiniana, that followed him round in crates. The unique collection of pictures that he formed was all given away. He collected deliberately for others. He paid a friend's doctor's bill in the finest Baksts I have ever seen. His business ability would be more correctly summed up as infectious personal charm and enthusiasm. I can never conceive of his balancing a budget or attempting to do so. If his guarantors lost their money, as they invariably did, they found the results well worth the expenditure, and were ready to lose and gain once more, the next year.

" Enfin, en 1913, pour la saison inaugurale des Champs Élysées, il me tint la dragée haute et me fit payer ses spectacles un demi-million ! Cette folie, que je n'avais pas le droit de ne pas commettre, permit la création du *Sacre*, mais coûta la vie à ma direction."

A remarkable statement from even so enlightened a theatrical manager as Gabriel Astruc.

Often in small expenses he was close. I have seen him haggling with a chauffeur in Monte Carlo over two francs, and at times his dinner-jacket was sadly frayed. Every penny went into his dreams. He handled millions, and died poor.

For so brilliant a man, Diaghileff was strangely superstitious. When a black cat crossed his path I have known him go ten minutes out of his way to take another route, and on one occasion, at the Prince's Theatre, when a black cat jumped on the stage during a rehearsal of *Le Sacre du Printemps*, he was first frantic and then resigned and miserable. Incidentally that season was one of his rare failures. A hat on the table meant sorrow; a hat on the bed, death. He was also frightened of being photographed. He needed much persuading, and considered it most unlucky. There are few photographs of him, scarcely any that are posed.

Strangely enough, this fighter, who could face a moral situation with heroism, was a physical coward. He was terrified of the idea of pain in himself or in others. Once at the Savoy, when a small boil in his mouth required lancing, he shrieked so hysterically at the sight of the instrument that the doctor had to abandon his attempt. It was agony for him to cross the Channel, especially as a gypsy had once predicted that he would meet death on the water. He loathed the very sight of a vast expanse of water, and would remain locked in his cabin ; while at times he waited days for a favourable crossing, letting the company go on ahead. It can be imagined how much he suffered during a war-time crossing to the United States, when there was actual danger. Day and night he wore his life-saving jacket. Once during ship's drill, not satisfied with standing by his station, he clambered into the lifeboat, and was snapped in that undignified position. Then later, when, in a fog, the sirens blew, after shivering in his cabin, he rushed on deck prepared for the worst, but the journey was over, and they were well past the Statue of Liberty.

These anecdotes of weakness are not told to detract from a great man; they are an indisputable part of a true portrait, that must take all such things into account.

His relations with the company are interesting. With a few exceptions none of them knew him. He did not suffer fools gladly, politely, or at all, except where his affections were engaged, and if they were not unusually clever or talented, then they were—just dancers. For their part they admired him: it almost amounted to worship; but at the same time they were thoroughly scared. The fear of secessions on an important scale played a large part in these relations. He was constantly on the look-out, and no one was allowed to assume too much power. It was not a question of megalomania, but of solid common sense. Where he recognised brains or unusual talent—and he was always generous in recognising intelligence in others—there was no service he would not render. He once told Lydia Sokolova, " Remember I am your friend; if ever for any reason you need me, I will come. You can always rely on my help. Consider me as a father." These were not just words. When she was so dangerously ill in Paris, he brought his own surgeon for her, and, on the tour that followed, cabled every few hours. He was frantic and asked the company to pray for her. That is an aspect of him that is little known, but it is very much a part of him, the true friend.

He was always, except with his special favourites, where he was blind, able to separate the individual he liked from the artist who served him. It was quite impossible to ask him for rôles, equally impossible to drop a rôle that had grown wearisome. He disliked intensely any fishing for praise. One artist after an unexpected triumph in a difficult rôle went up to him expectantly. " Not at all bad," he told her, " but let us hope you will do it much better next time."

He kept a careful eye on the company's morals from an æsthetic point of view. If any girl went out repeatedly in company that he found common or unsuitable for the Russian Ballet, without saying anything definite, he took steps to dismiss her from the company. He was no hypocrite, he did not preach a morality foreign to himself, but the whole tone of these servants of art must be maintained. Nothing could be allowed to interfere with the quality of their work.

Fortunately when the end came it was in Venice, a final wish fulfilled. His almost childish greed and love of sweet things certainly hastened the end. I have seen him eat almost a whole box of chocolates, chuckling at this defiance of the doctor's orders, strange contradiction in one so afraid. When it came, he was surrounded by those he loved, and who loved him. He, who was so terrified of suffering, went out quietly, all fears calmed by nature's soothing anæsthetic of unconsciousness.

" I feel fuddled, drunk," were his last words.

So passed this superman.

CHAPTER VII

FOUR CHOREGRAPHERS : NIJINSKY—
FOKINE—BALANCHINE—MASSINE

"Que ne pouvons nous joindre aux noms de ces grands hommes ceux des Maîtres de Ballet, les plus célèbres dans leur temps ! Mais à peine les connoit-on ; ce n'est pas néanmoins la faute de l'Art."

NOVERRE

M Y INTEREST in dancers had always been so strong that, apart from the direct lesson of *The Sleeping Princess*—that ballet to be good should show the dancer to the very greatest advantage—I had given little thought to ballet structure. Dancing is certainly the correct angle of approach, but it is only one of the many elements, perhaps the most important, and certainly, out of Russia, critically the most neglected. So perfectly did the Fokine ballets, my first, satisfy me that I took choregraphy very much for granted. It was only when, later, I felt that something was inharmonious, that I began to investigate the relationship between choregrapher, dancer, composer and decorative artist. The general public too takes choregraphy—clumsy word—very much for granted, scarcely distinguishing it from the putting together of some small dance or "routine." One old lady, with a delightfully antiquated hat, that only Bournemouth could still produce, was amazed at the fact that two performances were identical, and disappointed too. "I thought that those clever dancers made them up as they went along."

An extreme view, evidently, but not so far behind the accepted one, that takes it all for granted.

In the whole history of ballet, from Louis XIV to Fokine, there are fewer choregraphers of quality than men of value in any other branch of art; not surprisingly, perhaps, as choregraphy combines the elements of sculpture, painting, music and the drama. Any experienced dancer can arrange a small *solo* or a *pas de deux* for herself, that will be effective, by dipping into the large repertoire of ready-made movement; it is the *orchestration* of dancing that is the choregrapher's function. Like the sculptor, he is concerned with the organisation of the single figure and the group, and like the sculptor, too, he is limited by the particular medium in which he works ; like the painter, he is concerned with problems of foreground, background and space composition. There the parallel ceases, and his own particular problem commences. So far he is merely the producer of *tableaux vivants*. His particular problem is concerned with movement, and the transition from pose to pose. Many comparative amateurs can lift successful groups and poses from vases and sarcophagi; it is in the transition that the true talent is revealed.

Next comes his relationship to the drama. How to tell his story in pantomime in the simplest manner possible, without the need of extraneous literary explanation. Without resorting to paradox, there is a very definite ballet-realism. The whole of the theatre is a convention, and, once the particular convention that life is danced to music has been accepted, all that happens must be made consistent and plausible. There can be the fantastic ballet or the grotesque ballet, but each must be a harmonious whole. I remember Karsavina criticising *Le Fils Prodigue* on the score of realism. " It is a sign of decadence when

E

ballet no longer believes in its own conventions. A low barrier that is used as a gate and carefully opened and shut is ignored after a few minutes. That is a breach of realism."[1] The choregrapher is working in the medium of the human body so that the extreme distortion permissible in paint is not within his reach. Exaggeration of a particular pose may show a certain invention, but unless it is used for a definite purpose it is laughable, *unrealistic* and out of place.

There remains the relationship to music. Each ballet must be in close contact with both the form and the spirit of the musical score, so that this medium of the human body is still further restricted in its use. This implies in the choregrapher not merely a sound academic knowledge of music— a good ear is not sufficient substitute—but taste, discrimination and sensitivity. Stravinsky's *Oiseau de Feu* was actually worked out phrase by phrase with Fokine, who had heard the composer's *Fireworks* and had " seen flames in the music." " Stravinsky brought him a beautiful cantilena on the entrance of the Tsarevitch into the garden of the girls with the beautiful apples, but Fokine disapproved. ' No, no,' he said, ' you bring him in like a tenor. Break the phrase, where he merely shows his head, on his first intrusion. Then make the curious swish of the magic horse's return, and then, when he shows his head again, bring in the full swing of the melody.' "[2]

These questions bear pondering the next time you see " Choregraphy by Ivan " on a programme. They explain the paucity of fine choregraphers; they may also explain why you are pleased or irritated.

These three conversations with choregraphers will show

[1] In this particular case the weakness was recognised both by Diaghileff and Balanchine. A good work was spoiled by accessories.—A. L. H.

[2] L. Kirstein, *Study of Fokine.*

more thoroughly than I could, from just having seen them at work, their views and their individual methods. Fokine's " five points," first published in England in *The Times* of July 6th. 1914, contain the whole history of the birth of modern ballet. They are the Magna Charta of the chore-grapher, the whole basis of the art as we see it practised to-day. They may possibly seem obvious just because we are so used to seeing their results. They are however a very great discovery. Without them ballet would have been dead as an artistic force, and could never have become the medium for the finest works of Bakst, Stravinsky and others. The enduring quality of Fokine's own ballets shows the worth of his dicta.

It is interesting to see that both Massine and Balanchine, after long explorations in the over-sophisticated, are each returning to simplicity and a new-found classicism of their own, a complete triumph for the cause that I championed while it was still unpopular and ballet was out of the control of dancers.

It will be noticed that in each one of these dialogues the choregrapher definitely denies to Diaghileff creative gifts, while Larionov, the painter the longest associated with him, affirms them, but explains it as in the case of Nijinsky, of all artists certainly the most Diaghileff's creation, as a process of throwing people together and waiting for the explosion. It is obvious that those who are the chief ele-ments in such an explosion cannot be conscious of the fact. In the case of Fokine, his statements are obviously correct, however biased they may sound. Diaghileff unquestion-ably treated him with injustice, as I can vouch for from many conversations. Diaghileff's statement, for instance, about Duncan's extreme influence is absurd, and of the same quality as his remark on Anna Pavlova. From the very moment that Nijinsky began to show the creative urge, there could be no room for the master choregrapher, and his leaving, an instinctive act, had to be justified subsequently in Diaghileff's own mind.

"Of course he made many mistakes," says Larionov, "but they were the result of love and can be forgiven to-day." In any case, his changes of choregraphers greatly benefited the whole art, whatever the motives at the time.

I. VASLAV NIJINSKY

Of Nijinsky's methods of work I can only write by hearsay, but they show such a difference from the usual—a groping in the dark, followed by a sudden inspiration—that it is important to describe them, especially as they had a far greater influence on the future than their number—three, only one of which survives—or their intrinsic merit might suggest. Larionov, who was in the Diaghileff cabinet at the time, tells me :

"We would all be seated round the table with a very animated conversation in progress. Someone would perhaps make such a casual remark as, ' What an interesting idea if the classical positions were reversed and movements made *en dedans* instead of *en dehors*.' The idea would then be discussed and expanded, but all in theory. ' That is interesting, Vatza ; think about it,' said Diaghileff. Nijinsky took no active part in these discussions, and even gave the impression that his thoughts were far away. But all the time he was listening, assimilating things. Then he would go and lock himself up in a dark room for hours, and let all that he had heard take effect, perhaps in actual images.

" Then began the endless rehearsals, sometimes by the hundred, but not rehearsals in the ordinary sense of the word, to add in a touch here and there to a work already conceived, but actual laboratory experiments in movement, attempts at creation. Sometimes after an hour's work only a single movement would be fixed. Like a sculptor or a painter with a lay figure, he took hold of the dancer, moving his limbs in different directions, stepping back to judge the effect. ' No use, no use. Wait, hold it ; not bad like that. That's right now.' Sometimes nothing at all would please him, then suddenly came a pose that seemed interesting ; he would retain it and begin to build around it, always experimenting and groping for something that was not quite articulate. It was not a deliberate, highly conscious method at first, but in this way he enriched choregraphy, by adding to the repertoire a new variety of movement, naturally varying greatly in quality. That was one of the ways in which Diaghileff worked, throwing young and impressionable material into the company of the leading thinkers of the day, while remaining ever watchful in the background."

II. MICHAEL FOKINE : PARIS, FEBRUARY 1934

These conversations took place during the time that Fokine was hard at work, preparing four new ballets for Ida Rubinstein. I watched some of the early stages. Fokine entered armed with a large portfolio of musical scores and notes. First he sorted his dancers into groups, explaining carefully the setting of the scene, and what each one represented. He told them also the chief characteristics of the period. Then he went ahead of each group, dancing, letting them follow, dancing again. He made them try a few bars a number of times, rejecting and building up again, but always as if he were perfecting a work already in existence. There was nothing tense in the atmosphere, no trace of impatience. The company was good, and he had plenty of time to laugh and joke, while carefully indicating every shade of his intention, explaining by example, skilful parody and over-emphasis the meaning underlying every movement, splitting it up and analysing it in a manner I have never seen done before, but always allowing a certain individual latitude of expression. Also he related the movements of ballet to the natural movements of everyday life. He did not impose himself at all, but worked up a genuine mass enthusiasm. (The good choreographer always welcomes signs of individuality, realising that a strong personality will carry his work much further than a highly trained automaton. The Svengali attitude does not exist outside the imagination.) He is the easiest to follow of any *maître de ballet* I have ever seen at work.

To-day he is nearly bald, Napoleonic in appearance, more striking even than in the early days, and still dances with great fire and the most perfect control.

He greeted me with :

" You are just in time to see me setting a *gaillarde*. It is a beautiful dance. Do you know anything about it ? I myself knew little about it till just lately. I have been getting it up from old books. It is the first time I have ever worked like that. I usually ' feel ' the period from my artistic knowledge of it, and then justify myself afterwards. Sit down ; when the rehearsal is over we must have dinner and a long talk."

Fokine is easy to talk to and immediately finds the right word. He sounds dogmatic here, but he is not to the extent that this dialogue form, devoid of the frills, makes him appear. He is fully conscious of his worth and his achievement, and naturally eager that certain misunderstandings should be set right. He never takes disagreement with any of his opinions as an affront.

(During dinner.)

Fokine : Before I reply to your question as to how I actually create, I must tell you of the method that underlies all my work. Early in my career I was so disgusted with the stilted " unrealistic " side of ballet that I nearly left it altogether, when my memorandum was shelved by the authorities, to become a painter. I have always been deeply interested in painting, and I took to it again when I was forty-three. I dropped it when I was appointed a teacher in the theatrical school. At once I felt happier, and began to put into practice my new tendencies towards a ballet realism. From the first, people greeted me with, " Why do we need this young Fokine, when we have the glorious Petipa ? " Petipa himself was more generous, for after the production of my first ballet, *Acis and Galatea,* he sent me a card with the inscription, " Cher camarade. Enchanté de votre composition. Continuez et vous serez un très grand maître de ballet." I felt from the very first that no matter how obscure, fantastic and unrealistic the art form of dancing may seem, to be of any value it must have its truth in life. That was my first urge.

A. L. H. : How deep was the influence of Duncan on you ? There is a passage in a letter from Diaghileff, published in Propert's *The Russian Ballet, 1921–1929,* that reads, " I knew Isadora well at St. Petersburg and was present with Fokine at her first début. Fokine was mad about her dancing and the influences of Duncan on him lay at the base of all his creative work."

Fokine : That is absurd. Diaghileff could never have believed in such a statement nor made it with the slightest degree of sincerity. He watched my rehearsals and saw me compose. He knew perfectly well the differences between my new Russian Ballet and Duncan's dance. I remember going to see her with him. I had already been engaged as *maître de ballet*, and had by that time carried out considerable reforms on the Russian stage. The reason for my very great enthusiasm was just because I felt that here were so many of the elements that I was practising and preaching. I found naturalness, expressiveness and real simplicity. There was a similarity in our aims, but in method an enormous and obvious difference. My Russian and Oriental compositions and my romantic ballets, *Les Sylphides*, *Carnaval* and *Le Spectre de la Rose*, have nothing in common with her. The resemblance is only in *Daphnis et Chloé*, *Narcisse* and the bacchanals from *Tannhäuser* and *Cléopâtre*, and that is because our sources were the same, the same vases and sarcophagi in the same museums. The similarity there only lies in the static, the design of the poses ; the differences are far greater. Her dance is free, mine stylised, and my movements are mechanically highly complex. I was working on dancers with a fixed technique and an old tradition, she for an individual, herself. I am very happy, though, that in the treatment of ancient Greek themes, her speciality, I have something in common with her, just as I am delighted to differ from her in other moods and styles. She stood for the freedom of the body from clothes, while I believe in the obedience of the movement to costume, and its proper adaptation to period. She had only one plastic conception for all periods and nationalities, while I am essentially interested in the difference of the movements of each individual. She had, for instance, the same form of dance for Wagner, Gluck, Chopin, the Spanish dances of Moskovski and the waltzes of Strauss. The national character is absent; only Greece existed for her, as if it could be adapted to all periods. Diaghileff was far too keen an observer not to know all this, especially as his opportunities were better than anyone else's. His statement was made with some purpose or other.

As you know, early in my career I laid down five main principles for the production of ballet, which are, in brief:

To invent in each case a new form of movement corresponding to the subject and character of the music, instead of merely giving combinations of ready-made steps.

Dancing and gesture have no meaning in ballet unless they serve as an expression of dramatic action.

To admit the use of conventional gesture only when it is required by the style of the ballet, and in all other cases to replace the gestures of the hands by movements of the whole body. Man can and should be expressive from head to foot.

The group is not merely an ornament. The new ballet advances from the expressiveness of the face or the hands to that of the whole body, and from that of the individual body to groups of bodies and the expressiveness of the combined dancing of a crowd.[1]

The alliance of dancing on equal terms with the other arts. The new ballet does not demand " ballet music " from the composer, nor *tutus* and pink satin slippers from the artist; it gives complete liberty to their creative powers.

A. L. H. : These artistic principles are so much a part of

[1] What finer example than Fokine's own *Petrouchka*?—A. L. H.

your whole general outlook that they are no longer consciously to the fore each time. How in detail do you
compose ?

Fokine : There are no fixed rules there; in various ways,
as the mood occurs. Only yesterday, for instance, I sat up
in bed all night, surrounded by sheets of music. Once the
score has become a part of me images are formed, which
I occasionally fix in little drawings. That is the general
plan, but the fantasy comes during rehearsals. *Carnaval,* for
instance, was literally an improvisation during one rehearsal for a charity performance ; two further rehearsals,
with some thought in the interval, and it was complete.
To-day it takes many more rehearsals than that to put it
on again. *Igor,* which is to me my most perfect work—there
is nothing that I would want changed in it—also came very
easily in about eight rehearsals. It is the most complex of
all my ballets to revive without my direct supervision, just
as *Les Sylphides* is the easiest. Some of the groups in that as
it now stands were actually arranged on the stage a few
moments before the curtain rose. *The Dying Swan* too was
done hurriedly for Anna Pavlova at a charity performance,
the concert of the artists of the chorus of the Imperial
Opera in St. Petersburg, 1905. Small work as it is, and
known and applauded all over the world, it was " revolutionary " then, and illustrates admirably the transition
between the old and the new, for here I make use of the
technique of the old dance and the traditional costume,
and a highly developed technique is necessary, but the
purpose of the dance is not to display that technique, but
to create the symbol of the everlasting struggle in this life
of all that is mortal. It is a dance of the whole body and
not of the limbs only; it appeals not merely to the eye but
to the emotions and the imagination.

A. L. H. : How far do your dancers collaborate with you in a production ?

Fokine : Not at all. I never conceive works for particular artists, but the particular artist does lead me to make modifications. I did not create *Le Spectre de la Rose* for Nijinsky, but because of his particular style it became less masculine, and quite different from what I myself made of it. *Petrouchka* also I did not compose deliberately for Nijinsky. He left his mark on it, but there are various possible interpretations. That is why these works can be so constantly revived.

A. L. H. : What do you think of recent choregraphy, beginning with your immediate predecessor Nijinsky ? *L'Après-midi d'un Faune,* for instance ?

Fokine : L'Après midi d'un Faune was purely *un succès de scandale,* later becoming *un succès de snobisme.* It is fundamentally a work of no importance. Nijinsky's own rôle, with its oblique movement, is lifted straight out of the bacchanal from *Tannhäuser,* which I arranged for Karsavina and him.[1] The same archaic poses, only he substituted for the final embrace the act of onanism which I find most displeasing. Also the music, décor and choregraphy are definitely out of sympathy, even hostile to one another. There are moments when the public laughs instinctively, and they are perfectly right; they have felt the error. Notably when the nymphs run in flight, heel to toe. As you know, the correct walking movement is heel to toe, while with running it is precisely the opposite. He has therefore adopted a meaningless and unrealistic distortion, which the public has sensed.

Frankly I find that recent choregraphy has all the faults

[1] I have verified this from many dancers and *balletomanes,* who saw both works. It is beyond dispute.—A. L. H.

of the pre-Fokine ballet, only with added pretensions. Style has been completely forgotten, " points " and arms express different things. Such Greek themes as *Apollon* and *Mercure* should not be danced in ballet shoes, any more than a ballet on a purely Russian theme like *Les Noces*. Also, just as in the old days, there is far too great a reliance placed on programme notes. Most of the ballets I have seen are not expressive in themselves. They are far too closely involved with literature, and consequently appeal only to a small specialised *côterie*.

A. L. H. : In order then to purify choregraphy can you conceive of it as an entirely independent art, of dancing alone without music or costume ?

Fokine : No. Absence of music is only justified at some particular point, so as to emphasise and bring out a definite dramatic meaning. Dancing always implies noise, stamping, clapping, singing, drums or percussion of some kind from the very times of its origins. To-day it is no longer interesting to return to such primitive sounds. I prefer therefore to use the more highly developed forms of music. Yes, music is essential, while décor is of lesser importance, an embellishment that can add much, but that cannot disguise unsound work.

Yes, of course, museum study is an essential. I have just been spending several weeks in the Assyrian section of the Louvre for *Semiramis*. That does not mean a slavish imitation, but one must get soaked in the art of a period to render the correct style.

A. L. H. : How far was Diaghileff creative ?

Fokine : As far as I can see, not at all. I admire him immensely, and there is no one in a better position than I to judge the full extent of his achievement. Why lessen it by ridiculous claims ? He was a genius as a propagandist for art, and as a business man. He was something more besides. But many books have recently given an entirely false impression, and I hope that you will not perpetuate these mistakes. No one has ever claimed that he wrote the music or painted the décor. I cannot remember one single choregraphic idea of his. Cocteau, Vaudoyer, Benois, all gave ideas, but never Diaghileff. I had created before he ever came on the scene. The whole idea of the one-act ballet, and the other reforms that made the enterprise possible, were already accomplished. Before I joined him I had already composed *Carnaval*, *Les Sylphides*, *Cléopâtre* and *Le Pavillon d'Armide*, the ballets that established the first big triumphs. That is in itself a sufficient answer. It is Alexandre Benois who first wrote to me suggesting that Diaghileff should take my ballets to Western Europe, and I am deeply grateful to him for all the opportunities he gave me, but the early ballet was the Fokine Ballet. Diaghileff's creation, then, at any rate consisted in changing a few names. *Nuit d'Égypte* became *Cléopâtre*; *Chopiniana*, *Les Sylphides*. That is the clever business man. Then there is the story of *L'Oiseau de Feu*. Music had been commissioned from Liadov for a ballet to be composed by me around that old Russian legend. After very many months, when it was long overdue, Diaghileff met Liadov. " Well, is my ballet ready? " " It won't be long now; it is well on the way," was the reply; " I have just bought the ruled paper." As you know, Stravinsky subsequently wrote the music and had his first triumph, but meanwhile a new ballet of that name was awaited. Diaghileff found the solution simple. He took the old *Blue Bird*, not yet known in Paris, and it was temporarily renamed *The Firebird*.

I have in all created sixty-five ballets and the majority have been done either before or after my association with

Diaghileff. Without him my work would not have been universally known, but it exists just the same. *Orphée* of Gluck is one of the finest things I have ever done.

A. L. H. : Amongst all the dancers you have seen is there any one obviously outstanding ?

Fokine : No. It is never possible to say in an unqualified manner that a dancer is incomparable. Nijinsky was incomparable in *Le Spectre de la Rose*, and very bad indeed in *Prince Igor*. Pavlova, Kàrsavina, Fokina were each incomparable in certain rôles and types of dancing.

A. L. H. : Is the great dancer a thing of the past ?

Fokine : By no means. There are to-day so many admirable schools, those of the great *ballerinas* in Paris and others. There are many young dancers developing rapidly into something big. To-day I can assemble a troupe of dancers as fine in quality as at any period. There are some magnificent dancers in America to-day, waiting for the chance to do important work; there are also your young " loves " of the Monte Carlo Ballet. Have you seen my pupil Patricia Bowman ? There is an absolutely faultless technique.

A. L. H. : What would you save out of the old repertoire ?

Fokine : Giselle, *Lac des Cygnes*, *The Sleeping Princess*, *La Fille Mal Gardée* and *Coppélia*. What a delicious ballet, this last. I once put it on in Chicago in the old manner. The only time I have ever worked in that way.

A. L. H. : And now for your views on the new Central European dance of Wigman, Laban and their followers. It is a sore point with me.

Fokine : Must we talk about that, and spoil a good meal ? You know my views so well. I have often spoken and written to you about it, on the last occasion when poor Simeonov died. As it is important I will just go over some of the points. I was glad to hear from you that England has rejected it, for it is a development of dilettantism unparalleled in the history of the dance, a definite step backwards. This so-called innovation is built up on a total absence of a real knowledge of the grammar and syntax of dancing, and, in order to revolt against anything, it is essential to know it in close detail, perhaps even more thoroughly than its devotees. Musically it is wretched. I find this association with percussion and undeveloped music highly significant.

It is very typical of the Wigman school to substitute elbow for arm movements. For instance, in the gay happy mood of a gypsy dance, the elbows are moved; for a sad dance they are raised, letting the hands hang down helplessly. But most of all they are used to express energy, the strained energy of trying to force one's way into a crowded subway during the rush hours. I went once to an explanatory lecture by Mary Wigman. Nearly the whole time she gesticulated with clenched fists, and the clenched fist and the elbow seem to be the symbols of this movement. Then someone in the audience asked for the reason for the exaggerated turned-out position of her feet in dancing. She explained that it was for the elasticity of her jumps, to gain elevation. This is, of course, quite inaccurate. Immediately after I had denounced in the Maryinsky Ballet the old-fashioned superstition of turned-out feet (dancing *en dehors*) Nijinsky surprised the entire world by his tremendous elevation without ever turning out his legs *à la* Wigman or in the old Italian manner. Incidentally Wigman herself has no elevation.

A. L. H. : But is there anything new in it at all ?

Fokine : Absolutely nothing. I have seen each movement in ballet before, and can always tell you what they are attempting to reproduce. It is all hopelessly old-fashioned.

Ballet has already outlived such "modernism." The Diaghileff Ballet in its last stages, and the Swedish Ballet of Rolf de Maré, became so radical that no German dancers can ever catch up with them. I am in disagreement with much in modern choregraphy, but that is another matter. It is a disagreement in the same family, and fundamentally we think alike, and have the same groundwork.

The possibility of creating something really new is unlimited, as unlimited as the experiences of life itself, but only when the dancer has a strong technical foundation. The Germans, through lack of experience, invariably confuse the technical exercises with the real thing. One of them once said, " The ballet is horrible, look at this fifth position "—which she then made incorrectly. " How can you do a Greek dance like that ? " But there exist a number of ballets in which the points and the five positions are not used at all ; ballets which are based entirely on natural movement. I illustrated this by saying to her, " In order to lift their arms, your girls lift first their shoulders, then their elbows, and only after that the entire arm. That is not natural ; when I go to take my hat off the peg, I lift my entire arm to reach for it." " Perhaps ; but, just the same, your movement really comes from here," she explained, pointing to my solar plexus. "All movement does; you breathe." " Yes, that's true. I always breathe," I admitted, and we got no further.

The teaching of dancing consists to a large degree in the constant elimination of unnecessary strain.

With them everything is cut and dried, quite remote from reality. The chest caved inward expresses hate or envy, yet when we approach the bed of a sick friend the chest is caved inward to express, not our hate, but our sympathy.

The true and final answer is, of course, that we can do everything that they do, while they in their turn can do nothing of our work. I have noticed that as a teacher. In the classroom it is ten times more convincing than on paper. Pompous words such as " free impulses," and the whole phraseology that goes with it, cannot give them a mastery over their bodies, which are always tense and strained. Do you notice how their followers always call it " a sad art " and talk of " dark souls " ? People explain it as an after-war neurosis, the spirit of a defeated nation, but the reason is, doubtless, that the portrayal of sadness calls for very little movement. The more joyful we feel the more we desire to move about. The dance is primarily an expression of joy, though sadness of course may be a subject for the dance, as all the other emotions. Yet it is not for nothing that so many have copied Pavlova's *Dying Swan*, and no one her many fast and joyous dances.

This is not Duncan at all. The great Isadora Duncan has reproduced in her own dancing the entire range of human emotions, but when I think of dancers *à la* Duncan, I always picture a girl in draperies with her hand on her head in the manner of the funeral processions on a Greek urn.

. . . .

And so we take leave of the rebel composer of *The Dying Swan*, in a fighting mood that to-day he rarely shows. Perhaps I have spoiled his dinner. He is still an insurgent, fighting against all standardised formulæ, save the basic principles that first inspired him. Time cannot make his immortal dramas, *Petrouchka*, *Igor* and the like, appear old-fashioned. They have already survived the most rapidly changing of all periods. In New York, 1934, Paris and London, they are still the certain successes of a programme.

As he takes his coat from the *vestiaire* and goes out into the street, the gestures of the waiters and the passers-by will have taught him something new about movement that he will store up and translate into the dance, which he has bound so closely to life itself.

III. A CONVERSATION WITH LEONIDE MASSINE

On board M.S. *Lafayette*—New York bound, December, 1933

It is always difficult to catch Massine in a free moment. His work now is incessant, with young dancers to train, new ballets in mind, old ones in constant rehearsal, and the necessity of continual practice as a dancer. His last Italian *holiday* was spent in the creation of *Choreartium*. I had tried in vain to catch him in London, Bournemouth, Birmingham and Plymouth. My chance finally came on the *Lafayette*, with the boat too unsteady, and many of the company too ill, to make serious work possible. Even then he worked daily in his cabin with his wife, Delarova, and any survivors, and spent many hours a day listening to Antal Dorati, the Hungarian conductor, a veritable one-man orchestra, playing and singing scores that might provide an inspiration for ballet.

Massine to-day is at the very height of his powers, both as a creator and as a dancer. There are obviously greater technical performers, but no one who is even nearly his equal as an artist. It is in his case that I have felt the same concrete audience-contact as with Pavlova. I was watching

Le Beau Danube from the wings, the moment where Massine stands motionless, centre stage, remembering as he hears the strains of the famous waltz, and then very slowly raises his arm above his head as the crowd of idlers and midinettes passes him by in scorn. I looked into the auditorium by chance ; like some big wave the audience rose in their seats, craning forward, as if his hand had pulled some unseen string. There is no one else who could achieve such a result by standing almost motionless. It is quite another thing to whip an audience into excitement by a complicated technical feat. The mature Massine is the biggest personality I have seen in ballet, and certainly the most intelligent. Diaghileff once told me that Massine was the only dancer who was his intellectual equal. Coming from Diaghileff, at a time when Massine was no longer in the company, and was actually promoting a rival ballet, it was the highest praise possible. Massine's knowledge in every branch of art is encyclopædic. It is never used for conversational effect. Every reproduction or scrap of information that may be of use he pastes into a large volume, and several such books accompany him everywhere. He is exceptionally calm, with a quiet, dry humour, and is a very strong disciplinarian. I have seen him quell an unusually self-satisfied male dancer, leaving him in tears after a few short, quiet sentences. As he is to-day, his company loves him. There is never any unkind gossip; he is far above their jealousy. He is friendly, but there is always the barrier of his achievement, not brought forward by him, but which they feel and respect. He does not command, but asks for things to be done, and they are.

I have seen him compose and rehearse on many occasions, sometimes seated quietly on a chair, at others in the front row of the dress circle, armed with a megaphone,

shouting in three languages, and actually dancing in the
limited space, to illustrate some point.

There may be a strong connection between his present
dancing form and his fine burst of creation. Most choregraphers have created during their own dancing zenith;
all have been outstanding performers. In a discussion one
day, Marie Rambert advanced the theory that the stimulus
to create was the result of an unconscious reaction from the
daily grind at purely classical exercise.[1] I have put the
question to him, but the fact that it is an unconscious
reaction makes it impossible to answer. It would at any
rate account for Nijinsky, classical dancer *par excellence*,
creating in a manner diametrically opposed to his training.
Fokine and Massine are far more deliberate in their
manner of work.

I have watched Massine at work for a very long time
now, and it has taken me several years and an American
tour to get to know him, and to penetrate his natural
reserve. More and more his particular vision has coloured
my own views on dancers and has widened them considerably. I have seen him discover and develop talent that
was suspected by no one. He is in his right place in charge
of a young company that needs such expert guidance
between freedom and tradition.

A. L. H. : How do you create a new work ?

Massine : The first time I hear the music my mind is a
complete blank. I am then conscious of the volume, and the
pattern takes shape. I write down what I visualise to fix the

[1] It is certainly due to more than a coincidence that our English choregraphers miss
greatness in very much the same degree in their dancing. The two are very closely
linked together, actual physical experience and capacity with creative ability.—
A. L. H.

actual form, but at the first real contact between music and movement it may well alter.

A. L. H. : Are the interpreters of your rôles in any sense collaborators ?

Massine: No. They alter absolutely nothing in the general scheme of the composition, and the work is never composed with particular persons in view. They may of course alter a step or a detail, but that is unimportant. I first of all compose, and then look out for the ideal person to interpret. One must not adapt oneself to persons, but fit persons into one's scheme.

There is a very definite system of choregraphy that should enable anyone understanding it to create sound, if uninspired, works. English choregraphy fails because it is not based on any system. One day, when I have the time, and have ceased creating, I may perhaps teach it. There are definite laws of the sequence of movement. Why so many choregraphers imitate my works is because they see the finished thing without grasping the mechanics behind it.

A. L. H. : Is museum study a part of that system ?

Massine : Of course, intensive museum study. Any choregrapher is a fool if he doesn't understand that. Choregraphy cannot exist without it. Ballet is only three hundred years old, while in the museums of the world there are centuries of plastic genius to draw upon.

A. L. H. : And reading, literary inspiration ?

Massine : Literature is useful to us only in so far as it induces a plastic reaction, and so helps in a choregraphic structure.

A. L. H. : What are the most important works by which your artistic development can be measured ?

Massine : *Les Dames de Bonne Humeur, Le Chapeau Tricorne,* in which I enriched the repertoire of movement in ballet by translating the Spanish folk-dance, *Le Sacre du Printemps*, dealing with entirely fresh rhythmic problems, and *Les Présages*, my first symphony, the start of a new development, which should bring me back to pure choregraphy.

Choregraphy has too long followed in the footsteps of music and painting. Now once again it can take the lead and demand a new form of music and painting. I aim at something simple, healthy and purely plastic to take the place of the decadent, over-complex, highly sophisticated work of the late Diaghileff period. The ballet you like so much, *Le Beau Danube*, came as a reaction from the intense seriousness of *Parade* and *Le Sacre du Printemps*. It was an absolute necessity for me to create it. Curiously enough, that was in 1923, during the very strongest period of jazz, before there was any thought of a return to the Vienna waltz.

A. L. H. : And the new dancers ?

Massine : They are technically very advanced, but still lacking in finish and stagecraft. A dancer who can perform the most astonishing things will not know what to do with his hands in repose. But they overcome these difficulties very quickly, because they are all the time learning in practice on the stage.

A. L. H. : And that much debated point, the recent German school ?

Massine : Wigman has shown us some interesting new movements, but her dance is too personal and she fails with a group. The whole connection between dancing and music is weak, especially in the abuse of percussion. They also make use of a type of technique of dancing with absolutely no basic knowledge of movement, so that their discoveries are haphazard. It is not necessary nor possible to create an entirely new technique. With the old one as a basis there are endless ways of enriching choregraphy, a vast field of movement that has yet to be translated. It is not necessary to stick to the dance of Petipa. His was pure choregraphy, but created with a highly restricted vocabulary.

A. L. H. : How far was Diaghileff creative ?

Massine : As regards artistic expression, not at all. We were all of us caught up in the violence of the artistic creation in Paris of the period. No escape was possible, and the ballet expressed what the poets, painters and musicians had to say, ahead of its realisation by the public at large, but theirs were the ideas and Diaghileff followed.

Ballet, to survive, must be constantly freed from extraneous entanglements.

IV. A CONVERSATION WITH GEORGES BALANCHINE

New York, January 1934

I like Balanchine. He is so absolutely honest with himself that with him conversation is easy. He thinks aloud, and there is plenty of give and take. Also, he is one of those very rare people who can discuss their own work critically and dispassionately, and, what is more remarkable, will let his friends do the same without the slightest trace of injured pride. He is still experimenting, less positive of his direction than the more experienced Fokine or Massine. I am convinced that he is one of the few who will not feel slighted, whatever I write of him. In fact, on one occasion, when I wrote unfavourably of some of his work, the impresario considered himself an injured party, while Balanchine himself was in thorough and amused agreement with me.

I found him in a bare room, surrounded by pots, paint

and workmen, the headquarters of an important new
venture, the American Academy of the Dance, inspired
by the admiration my friend Lincoln Kirstein, a great
balletomane, feels for his work. Here he will train the wonderful raw material that exists in America, and will develop a company to show his new ideas. It is magnificent
pioneering work, in keeping with his story and generation.

Georges Balanchavadze was a pupil of the Imperial
School at St. Petersburg, which became the State school
before he had completed his education. He was the pupil
of Andreyanoff, Simeonov, Leontieff, Michael Obouhoff,
and also came under the influence of Fokine, whom he
admires unreservedly. His first choregraphic essay at the
age of fifteen was plastic, erotic in subject. " As I remember
it to-day it would be perfectly suitable for presentation in
a young ladies' seminary. I thought it very daring at the
time." His first mature theatrical work was as producer at
the Alexandrovsky and Michailovsky theatres, under State
control, but where some experimentation was allowed.
There he produced Shaw's *Cæsar and Cleopatra* and a play
by Toller. As dancer-choregrapher he appeared once at
the Maryinsky in a small work, *Enigma.* It was at the very
beginning of the revolution, but he was hissed off the stage
as being too revolutionary, and secured damning notices
from the powerful critic Volyinsky, who had always taken
a kindly interest in him. Next he organised a group of
young people and gave a series of recitals under the
uncompromising title of " The Young Ballet. Evolution
from Petipa–Fokine to Balanchavadze." The authorities
frowned and the young dancers were forbidden to appear
with him, so he was compelled to leave revolutionary
Russia for freedom to express ideas that were subversive
of the old order of the dance. He went to Germany with

a small group, the Russian State Dancers, consisting of Danilova, Gevergeva and N. Efimov ; and then to the Empire in London, where I first saw him. Diaghileff was attracted by *Enigma*, that had been hissed in Russia, and the group was absorbed into the Ballet. Balanchine, whose name was immediately truncated, created the new version of *Le Chant du Rossignol* for Markova, and so began his régime at the time of my first close association with the Ballet.

Balanchine : Yes, I collaborate with my dancers, create particular works for particular persons by drawing out what is in them, but they are quite unconscious of it and alter nothing deliberately.

I can always invent movement, and sometimes it can be fitted into the right place, but that is not choregraphy. It is the music that dictates the whole shape of the work.[1]

I do not believe in the permanence of anything in ballet save the purely classical. Classicism is enduring, because it is impersonal.

A. L. H. : And your own works, *La Chatte* or *Barabau* ?

Balanchine : I can assure you they are quite impossible now. They were made for another time. I have seen them both since their creation. They seemed very dull indeed. So many things have happened since.

Museum study ? Of course I believe in it, but not in the necessity for academic knowledge. It is a deep down love that is important, there must be a strong reaction to things seen. Even if they are ugly things, it doesn't matter. Apathy is the only enemy.

I have always been interested in the possibilities of the

---

[1] Balanchine is a magnificent pianist, who might easily have adopted that career. His whole musical education is far in advance of anyone else in ballet.—A. L. H.

film in rendering ballet. There is a wonderful unexplored field there. I worked out many ideas with Derain in Paris. Now I am in the land of films, and there may be practical opportunities

A. L. H. : But the loss of the third dimension always ruins all my pleasure in dancing.

Balanchine : Of course. I don't mean the mere photography of ballets we already know. That would give most unsatisfactory results. There is the exploration of pattern and new angles, with endless possibilities.

A. L. H. : But that sounds cold and dull. The greatest interest in ballet for me lies not so much in the pattern as in the exploitation of the personality both of a group and an individual. Mickey Mouse seems to provide the ballet need on the films ; a strong personality artificially created out of a pattern. Musically, too, it would be difficult to imagine a more perfect screen ballet.

Balanchine : I agree with all that, but you still miss my meaning. I can visualise ballet conceived for the screen that would possess everything, both pattern and personality. Imagine a great dancer in a specially prepared film version of *Les Sylphides* ; a close-up of the face, an arm, a wrist, the points, all so arranged that the full significance of the work could be revealed. Imagine the Sylphs flying through a wood, the Swans landing on the lake, Giselle's haunted tomb. There are countless devices that could be used. In actual ballet, after all, only those sitting close at hand catch any of the detail and expression, and that at the loss of some of the pattern. You have just been telling me of how you watch a work again and again, from the wings, the orchestra pit, the electrician's box and the front of the house, concentrating on some detail at each performance. Everyone cannot do that, and the very fact that you have shown the need is an ample justification of cine-ballet and its shifting viewpoint.

A. L. H. : I am still unconvinced, not about its justification—I can see many reasons for that—but of the pleasure that I personally would get from it, and that is my main concern. The whole charm of the thing for the *balletomane*, who goes nightly, lies in the difference in the performers on various days and their reactions to the ever varying audience. That is as much my reason as the shifting viewpoint for my many explorations back-stage. I do not want to see a Toumanova who is for ever fourteen years, ten months, one week, two days and so many hours old. The idea appals me. It is altogether too inhuman.

Balanchine : But I am not thinking in terms of the *balletomane* now. You are a part of our family. I am thinking of ballet in a much wider sense, of bringing it back to the masses as the ideal form of entertainment. The average ballet to-day is too complex, and is incomplete without programme notes.

A. L. H. : But does the story always matter so much ? And in any case they are usually simple enough. Anyone could understand your *Chatte* for instance.

Balanchine : The story does matter if ballet is to be popularised, also *La Chatte* is definitely too complicated. As a start, it embodies the idea of the transmigration of souls. I aim at a story so logical and so simple that all can understand it and follow its development.

A. L. H. : Then that implies a return to conventional mime, hand on heart, lovers' sighs.

Balanchine : Not at all. That is quite meaningless now and cannot express real things. It is so comical that it can only provoke the reaction of laughter. There are other ways of holding the interest, by vivid contrast, for instance.

Imagine the effect that would be produced by six negresses dancing on their points and six white girls doing a frenzied jazz !

A. L. H. : How big a rôle did Diaghileff play in the creation of ballets ?

Balanchine : Choregraphically none at all. *La Chatte* he only saw at its final rehearsals. He was very easy to work for and infinitely understanding. He left me a free hand always. Where he excelled was as a man of affairs. What a wonderful minister of finance he would have made !

. . . .

As we go out into the street Balanchine looks admiringly at the architecture of his new home, and tells me of his pupils and the qualities that young America can bring to the dance. With the paint not yet dry in his classrooms, he is already hard at work creating a repertoire, the first work of which is to be a homage to his beloved classicism. Lincoln Kirstein is proud and happy. Ballet to him is a necessity, so that he has taken practical steps to have it with him always, instead of wandering over Europe an exile. Would that there were more Kirsteins.

. . . .

HOMMAGE À FOKINE, MASSINE, BALANCHINE

At nearly every ballet performance I attend, the following scene is sure to take place. I am thoroughly weary of it, and must at all costs get it out of my system.

Elderly Russian Gentleman : Wonderful, the *Ballets Russes,* truly wonderful. What music, what art and what dancing. Beautiful women too. You love it, I know. You love our Russian art.

A. L. H. : Yes . . .

With my growing enthusiasm, he cools off visibly until he seems to become positively indignant. Now he is bristling all over.

E. R. G. : Yes, yes, of course. But what do you know of ballet? For that matter, what does anyone here know of ballet? . . . Nothing, absolutely nothing. You should have seen the Ballet as it was in Russia in the great days. What lavish décor, what music, what dancers. And the public too ; uniforms, jewellery and beauty. That was the real thing. This is not good, I assure you. It is bad even, very bad. What was the meaning of that last ballet? The programme said something about toys coming to life. Not at all my idea of toys. I don't know at all why I come, but I can't keep away. It makes me sad to see such decadence !

He then proceeds to revel gently in his sadness and I am sorry for him. I may so easily become that way myself some day, when new names will irritate instead of sending me off on long journeys of investigation. Besides, there are other grave reasons for his sorrow, associations which I must respect. He may or may not have been a *balletomane* in Russia. If he were, all things can now be forgiven him. If he dreams of Trefilova's *arabesque*, of Kchessinska's wondrous arms, we are brothers even. But he is entirely and utterly mistaken in everything he says. At the time I only nod sympathetically, any argument would spoil my pleasure for the evening and *Le Beau Danube* is still to come. There is no reason however why I should act the coward and hypocrite here; besides, it has been simmering for too long.

A. L. H. : My dear sir, we in Western Europe have seen everything that is finest in Russian Ballet, everything that is art in a universal sense, and not something that is purely local on however grand a scale. And what we have seen has been more truly Russian than what you can

remember, with its strong Italian influences. There were
magnificent exceptions, but many of your favoured dancers
might remind us too closely of acrobats. We too have our
series of *fouettés*, you have seen some to-night, but they are
used as the indispensable part of a choregraphic and
dramatic structure.

How do I know all this ? It is not merely hearsay, but
from circumstantial evidence as well as from innumerable
conversations with former dancers, many of whom agree
with me; from actually seeing ballets in the old style that
some of them have arranged or approved ; from listening
to the " music " of the ballets of the grand epoch, Minkus,
pah ! From studying photographs and *maquettes* of the
scenery, which was of a truly incredible magnificence,
closely approaching the dreams of Roxy. Your own Alexandre Benois, artist whom you venerate for his work and
his learning, deals the bitterest blow. " We were only
interested," he says, " in those ballets produced on the
Continent after 1909."

It is Fokine and his successors who have freed us and have
given me right in my argument—at this respectful distance—with you. They have honoured your country, that
is a consolation surely. In any case, how dare you complain. To-night, you have seen Baronova, Riabouchinska
and Toumanova. Your country is still unchallenged. You
should be happy.

But I fear this will begin all over again to-morrow.

CHAPTER VIII

TAMARA KARSAVINA

"Soulève ta paupière close
Qu'effleure un Songe Virginal ;
Je suis le spectre de la rose
Que tu portais hier au bal."

GAUTIER

"Une vapeur avec deux pieds."

Gil Blas, 1909

"Vous êtes une grande virtuose mais le prestige de votre métier s'efface sous le charme de votre art."

R. BRUSSEL: *L'Heure Dansante au Jardin du Roi*

IT IS A logical transition from the choreographers who freed ballet, to the dancer, of whom Robert Brussel wrote, "Vous avez compris, vous la fille la plus exquise du *classique chorégraphique*, que l'union était possible entre une tradition et une révolution artistique."

The great dancer is a rare and valuable possession, a national treasure. She is, in fact, potentially a living and progressive museum of plastic art, and an entire academy of music ; but, where the museum is lifeless, the dancer is an active and powerful propagandist, and on the many occasions when I am accused of making too much account of some young dancer, that is my justification. She may lack the great intelligence of a Karsavina, and, without appreciating her true value to art, concentrate exclusively on personal success. If she has the necessary gifts, in spite of her empty little head, she will carry the work of musicians and painters around the globe.

When, on the death of Serge Diaghileff, I organised an exhibition of works connected with his ballet, I was struck by the vast number of them that were intimately associated with Karsavina. It was clear that she had brought to us the glories of Russian music, the wealth of Russian legend and the bright colour of Leon Bakst. She revealed to Paris, too, a new aspect of its own artists. Where Trefilova represents pure classicism, Karsavina stands for romanticism and the drama in ballet, and with Fokine she brings it closer to life. Where Pavlova is an example of the outstanding individual, the solitary star, Karsavina is the very brilliant part of a very brilliant whole. It is impossible to compare them, so rarely did they stand on common ground. Karsavina has assuredly left the whole art of ballet richer than any other dancer, for, when I say that she brought these gifts to Western Europe, I mean it literally. There is no exaggeration or attempt to turn a phrase. The Diaghileff contract of the first few years depended on La Karsavina being in the company, the first and last time that such a thing ever occurred. His whole conception was opposed to stars, but Karsavina and Nijinsky were definitely stars, and they represent from a dancing point of view the finest period of the Ballet, the first, the Russian period, that had carried it the furthest from its Italian origins ; a rich, young, very national manifestation. Fokine, Nijinsky, Karsavina and Diaghileff were Russian, Stravinsky their favoured composer, and Bakst, perhaps more than anyone responsible for the popularity of the movement, were Russians too, and, if they did dance to the music of a Chopin, Schumann or Weber, the dreams they created could not be mistaken for anything but Russian, and the park of the sylphs was the park of a Russian palace.

Parallel with this, Karsavina was enjoying a career as *ballerina* of the Maryinsky, practically taking off her make-up on the train as she journeyed from St. Petersburg to the west and lived her double life ; enormous effort of mind and body, only possible in one extremely adaptable. When the change came, as logically it had to, she was ready to help the ballet in its transition from the rule of Fokine, her fellow pupil, with whom she had danced *The Fisherman and the Pearl* at her Maryinsky début, to that of Leonide Massine, the brilliant new discovery from Moscow. *Les Dames de Bonne Humeur, La Boutique Fantasque, Le Chapeau Tricorne*, a change of direction, but gradual at first, and then *Parade*, the cubist manifesto, led by a Maryinsky *ballerina*, who was dancing at home in *Raymonda* and *Paquita* !

Throughout her career Karsavina has shown a versatility unsurpassed by any dramatic actress ; from *Le Spectre de la Rose*, the personification of girlish innocence, " la grace ingénue et tendre," which has no significance without her, to *Thamar*, proud, sadistic Georgian Queen, feverishly awaiting still a fresh victim. The curtain rises with Thamar on her couch, waving to entice the passing stranger, and descends with her waving once again. What has gone on in between—the death of a young warrior prince—has been but an episode that could not quench her passion. Thamar is more than a vicious woman, she is a Queen in search of amusement ; pride as well as cruelty plays its part. The dancing is of secondary importance, all lies in the acting of this one rôle, and never did a poem translated into action retain its original spirit more intensely. Here is Lermontov's Thamar, realised in paint by

F

Serov, in human form by Karsavina, yet but a moment ago, the time to put on fresh make-up, she was Gautier's fragile dreamer. In *Petrouchka* she lays bare the simple pattern of all tragedy, the tragedy of the puppet, a *Coppélia* of deeper significance, mysticism instead of childish fun, far nearer to Hoffman than his own balletised story ; Karsavina as the eternal flirt without a heart, she who had been all heart in *Giselle*. Then *L'Oiseau de Feu*, requiring all the elevation and virtuosity of the *ballerina*, but so much more. To be the legendary bird of Russian folklore, lightness is not enough ; one must feel the passion of the imprisoned woman. To be all bird or all woman is to make the Fokine-Stravinsky dream into a Christmas pantomime, as it has appeared during so many revivals.

" Une légende," said Vaudoyer, " veut que l'oiseau de Paradis, qui passe, devant les yeux aveuglés, comme une gerbe de rubis et de perles, soit privé de pattes, qu'il ne se pose jamais. Légende dont il est impossible de douter lorsque Mademoiselle Karsavina, *Oiseau de Feu*, devant les fantasmagories du décor, obéit aux vols obliques ou circulaires de ses ailes cachées."

Karsavina made one believe, and all the works of this romantic period are fatally easy to spoil. They were created for the finest talent, without which they are barren ; *Le Spectre de la Rose* becomes sentimentality plus cheap virtuosity ; *Scheherazade*, the Oriental scene from a revue ; *Petrouchka*, a small item from Balieff's *Chauve Souris*. The ballet of the emotional subject is always dangerous. Karsavina made it possible.

Then the Massine ballets in a new key : *Le Chapeau Tricorne*, a peasant theme from Alarçon, the Spanish dance balletised and incredibly difficult of execution, devoid of all the cheap allure that makes Spanish dancing so easily effective, *Les Dames de Bonne Humeur*, Goldoni with its lighter note of mischief, a living picture by Longhi, and the fun mixed with sadness of *La Boutique Fantasque* with, as in *Giselle*, a difficult change of emotions between the boisterous *can-can* of the first scene, and the romantic reverie of the second.

Each one of these rôles can be repeated, but not all again by one interpreter.

During the little season of *divertissement* that I arranged for her at the Arts Theatre, I gained an insight into her method of working up a dramatic rôle, from its early plastic suggestion to its complete intellectual justification. I have always been interested in the genesis of any particular dramatic interpretation. In ballet-mime, the very basis of all acting, it is easier to seize upon ; neither the choregrapher nor the composer impose themselves on the performer in the manner of the author and producer of a play. The rôle when it comes to her is more fluid. She may feel it or reason it out. With Karsavina it is a combination of both. During that season there was a small *divertissement* that stands out as a little masterpiece, *Mademoiselle de Maupin*, to the romantic music of Liesberg, an unknown pupil of Chopin's, the discovery of Edwin Evans. I watched the evolution of the whole idea. It came vaguely at first through the memory of a black velvet *travesti* riding-habit *à la* 1830, curls, a black hat with feathers, then the desire to do a dance in that spirit, and a few mimed poses, with the playing over of countless melodies till the one that could extend those poses was found. This was followed by a reading of books and poems of the period till finally dance, story, music and costume met in this exquisite study. And so it was in the bigger rôles. The choregrapher found the movement, but he could only indicate the mime, and the problem was hers. *Thamar* was at first the most difficult; neither music nor poetry would reveal it fully, and right up to the time of the dress rehearsal it remained a complete mystery. Then, with the first make-up in front of the mirror, and a suggestion from Diaghileff that the eyebrows should meet in a line, the character stood revealed. What she had read could now be fitted in with what she felt.

It is this sensitiveness to plastic form and period, afterwards justified by knowledge and extensive research, that has made Karsavina an actress without equal, who worked parallel with her choregrapher. If we can think of her dancing for the moment as a thing apart, which in fact it is not, she would have made an equal success, through her fine approach to the problems of acting, when the parting of the ways came early in her life, if she had chosen the legitimate stage. Fortunately, in choosing the ballet she could speak the language of the whole world.

Karsavina I know perhaps better than any other dancer, but not in Diaghileff days. Then I was content to worship her from afar. We first met over a scheme to organise a world congress of the dance in London. The scheme itself came to nothing, but it provided me with a delightful friendship. It was through listening to her stories of other days, stories that were not mere gossip, but a vivid re-creation of the ballet as it had been, that I first hit upon the idea that she should record it in a book, and then by my wild enthusiasm I rushed her headlong into the adventure of writing, by phone calls, letters and visits, until finally I had persuaded her, conditionally. She would try, and, if it did not please her, would destroy the manuscript and nothing more was to be said. I had blind confidence in her ability to write from the very moment she consented. And so Karsavina became what she described to me as " a literary bloke." From time to time she called me over for " readings," her handwriting making it too laborious to take the work home. Whenever I have had a letter from her I have always been in some doubt as to its contents, until I rang up for confirmation. I heard the whole of that dance classic read by her in exactly the form that it appeared. Every line of it was written by her alone, with the aid of one of the biggest dictionaries I have ever seen. She, who, but a short time ago, had started with a boast about her " beautiful pork [pigskin] bag," now speaks faultless, almost pedantically correct English, with the very strongest of Russian accents.

When the great work was finished we had a long session to assemble the mass of material and to view the final results, her husband and I suggesting the cutting of a few of those passages " where she had let herself go." One in particular I remember; she was so proud of it, it contained the word " kaleidoscope," and its suppression, on her husband's advice, seemed to rankle for quite a time. Wisely I remained silent; marriage might stand such conduct, friendship never. In my own edition she has added it in longhand, and I also possess the original manuscript.

No one was more relieved when the work was finished than Joey, the Sealyham, who tried his best on so many occasions to chew the manuscript to pieces. He had sharp teeth, and, as if by instinct, on the very first day, when I entered full of the book, had chewed up my hat and a pair of gloves.

I find it difficult to write of Karsavina as a person, because it is not possible to gossip about her. " She was quite different from anyone in the company, aloof but never stand-offish. She seemed herself to be part of the dreams she was enacting," said Sokolova to me. She herself in *Theatre Street* has only revealed the woman by inference. " I will write of myself as a child, then when I join the theatre; and it is *the* important thing in my life, I become entirely the artist, and my private affairs can interest no one," she says in a letter to me, discussing the plan of her book, and so in the middle we have a bare statement, " I was married then."

She can discuss literature, ballet, painting and music, but always in a large objective manner. She is full of the give and take of discussion, with a sense of humour in the true English manner; she is a great lover of Dickens as well as the Continental type of wit ; she relished an incident that I had overheard at the Coliseum. On the entry of her partner in a Cossack solo, " Is that Tamara Karsavina, dear ? " " I dunno; thought Karsavina was a woman, but you never do know with these Russians."

There is nothing in her attitude to remind one that here is one of the most applauded artists of the day. But she has an aloofness that many find frightening. She is certainly difficult to know. It is her guard against a too great sensitiveness, the fear of being disappointed in people. She is dignified, a " blue stocking beauty " and always an artist. The type of work that she created called for the analytical mind. Every triumph was as fully and consciously calculated as her faultless period house. I remember her amused annoyance at a long florid description of herself in which the words " exotic," " lotus " and " orchid " appeared many times. The exciting, remarkable thing about the real Karsavina is the very fact that she has never once imagined herself an exotic, a Thamar in real life. The " artistic temperament," she once insisted, should be kept for the stage.

It is a very great loss to me that she is no longer in London, and it is a great blow to English dancing. She was our only Maryinsky *ballerina*.

CHAPTER IX

THE TWO LYDIAS

LYDIA SOKOLOVA

" Hilda Munnings alone [among the English dancers] possessed that indefinable spirit that made her one of us. Like the Russians, she possessed that humility of heart, and a fervour almost religious, that gave her the same attitude towards her work as we had."

LYDIA LOPOKOVA'S PARIS DÉBUT

"She won a place of her own in the hearts of the public, and there was a touch of tenderness in the eulogies of which the papers were full."

HER RETURN TO THE BALLET

" When she came back there was a mastery in her technique which fully qualified her as a star; in some marvellous way her spontaneity, and the unique blend of eagerness and naïveté, had remained unimpaired."

TAMARA KARSAVINA in *Theatre Street*

TWO OF THE EARLIEST CHARACTERS in this book, Markova and Dolin, happen to be English, both of them closely identified with the last years of the Diaghileff Ballet, and with dancing in England since. They have made and deserved international reputations, but it is admittedly Lydia Sokolova who stands out amongst English dancers in a position all by herself.

Hilda Munnings, famous as Sokolova, a name first honoured in the annals of the Imperial Russian Ballet, made her career in the very greatest days of Diaghileff, at a time when competition was feverish and the supply of dancers from Russia still unlimited. It is from such a background, the richest in the history of the dance, the period of Karsavina, Fokine and Nijinsky, that she must be judged. Her work has a depth, intensity and versatility that places her next to Karsavina alone. She is at once the complete actress-dancer-personality that I have always set up as an ideal. She arrived at her summit through a bitter struggle, and a rich and early experience of life, added to the ordinary daily grind of the dancer, and she arrived " consciously," rationalising the experience, and storing up every detail, so that to-day it is a commonplace to be told, " Ask Sokolova," for any special information about the ballet. It is these adventures that the small Hilda Munnings had, so very rare for an English girl before the war, but now shared by the war-revolution generation of Russians, that have brought out these extraordinary qualities of a kind that one does not expect in the English dancer at all, and only rarely in anyone. She is not frightened of showing her emotions; all natural reserve has been banished, so that she can express the beautiful, sad, grotesque or terrible with complete freedom. I have " asked Sokolova," and bit by bit I have pieced together the story of how it all came about.

The start is the same as with everyone in this book, and most children—a keen love of dancing, and improvisation at home; unlike so many, it did not remain there long. The little Hilda Munnings, Sokolova-to-be, was given a very thorough musical education, and by the age of twelve had already passed many advanced piano examinations. As her passion for dancing grew, she was sent to Stedman's Academy, where Hilda Butsova[1] and Vera Savina[2] were her

---

[1] Hilda Boot, afterwards chief dancer in the Pavlova Company.
[2] Vera Clarke, a *soliste* in the Diaghileff Company and Massine's first wife.

fellow pupils, and her first rôle was that of a lobster in *Alice in Wonderland*, with Butsova as chief lobster.

After she had been learning for six months, Pavlova and Mordkin came to the Palace Theatre, and Pavlova, as always, was the big creative inspiration that made childish dreams into something positive. Little Hilda spent her lunch money in going to the matinées, and her parents stinted themselves to give her a course of private lessons with Mordkin, for which they paid the enormous fee of £5 a lesson ! Whether she learnt in proportion to that sum or not, it gave her a first footing in a serious ballet atmosphere, and made the great ones conscious of her existence.

Then Pavlova slapped Mordkin in full view of the public ! He had lifted her in some manner not to her complete satisfaction ; an historic event, that affected at least a hundred careers. The results of that smack can still be felt in England to-day. It was on account of that that Anna Pavlova filled her company with English girls, whose loyalty she could always count upon in any civil war. Then, it meant an immediate declaration of war. Factions were formed, and the strong Polish contingent, with a few Russians, went over in a body to Mordkin, who immediately formed a company to tour the United States in *Le Lac des Cygnes*, *Giselle*, *Coppélia* and the *Russian Wedding*, taking with him Gheltzer, the great Moscow *ballerina* of to-day, then already over thirty, Sedova, Gluck, Kuhn, Morosoff and Volinine, cream of the Pavlova Ballet, together with thirteen-year-old Hilda Munnings, and nine other English girls.

The trip on the *President Lincoln* started ominously, Mordkin having to be operated upon suddenly for appendicitis in mid-ocean, which left him weak, and depressed the company. Hilda, doubtless feeling a little frightened and homesick, celebrated her fourteenth birthday on board. The tour started at the Metropolitan Opera House, but almost at once Mordkin and Sedova quarrelled with Gheltzer, and fresh factions were formed.

In the whole of the first part of her career Sokolova was destined to rise and gain knowledge through the disputes of famous artists. She and her English companions, pawns in his game of foreign quarrels, went on with Volinine and some Polish girls for a long tour of one-night stands. For three months they slept on a train, two in a bunk, dancing nightly. Their salaries were meagre, and Volinine generously supplemented them by five dollars a week from his own pocket. Then one night in New Orleans they played *Coppélia* to a house empty save for three negroes in the gallery. They did not get beyond the first act. The Poles struck, and the manager wisely disappeared for a time. They were stranded.

The Consul could do nothing but write to New York and hope for the best. Then they decided on their own to send a threatening wire to the impresario. This had an immediate effect. A cart was sent to take their luggage to the docks, and the girls perched themselves on top of the pile. I have seen a snapshot of this. They looked more like schoolgirls from a junior form coming home for the holidays than a hungry and stranded theatrical company. They returned to New York in extreme misery, eight days in a smelly cargo boat. On arrival they decided that they had had more than their share of discomfort, and put up at one of the best hotels, informing the manager, who must have been both sympathetic and an optimist, that they were staying indefinitely. They found the impresario, and took it in turns to camp on his doorstep. He arranged, suspiciously quickly, for them to sail back on the *Lapland*, but still managed to give them one final shock by not turning up on the quay, until the girls, in absolute despair and looking like nothing on earth, had seen the gang-plank taken up and heard the final siren. Mordkin's own impressario, Mr. Mitchell, who was travelling on the boat, gave them every penny he had, and as, surprisingly enough, they were travelling first class this time, they had a thoroughly enjoyable trip. They could not guess the reasons for this luxury, and they were ready to accept it without much thought. This time they were pawns in a game between a business man, his wife and H.M. Customs officials. This man's wife was an actress, who was bringing over with her several baskets of very expensive costumes. The task of the English girls was to pass these safely through as their personal property. They were useful, and could therefore be allowed the resulting comfort. Had the fellow been a bachelor they might still have been in New York —as far as he was concerned !

All this was the prelude to a career : unique haphazard training. It had naturally made a deep impression that could be used later ; meanwhile Hilda was ready to receive a more systematic tuition. The sympathetic Mitchell, exceptional in his profession, had immediately put himself in touch with Pavlova, and had arranged an audition. " Madame " was impressed, and agreed to have them trained at Ivy House by her own *maître de ballet*, Cheraieff, an expert in character dancing. It was then that Pavlova " discovered " Hilda as a coming dancer, a fact that she reminded her about in their very last meeting. All through her long career Pavlova sowed these seeds of ambition. When her jealousies and tantrums are brought up against her they are more than balanced.

After Sokolova had been learning for a few months,

Theodore Kosloff arrived in England to produce *Schehera-zade* at the Coliseum ; with Baldina, his wife, Alexis Kosloff, Becheharoff, who had been in the Diaghileff company, Morosoff, Zvereff, and others. Again chance helped her, and she was ready to profit by it. Baldina had to be absent for two or three performances, and Kosloff was not over-eager to draw attention to the fact. Physically there was some resemblance between the two ; both were plump and blonde. Hilda was carefully made up in Baldina's wig and costume, and at the age of fifteen danced this exacting rôle with Kosloff. This lasted sufficiently long to reveal her full merits, so that, when they went on tour to Vienna and Buda-Pesth, she was given Brahms' Czardas to dance with Alexis Kosloff. It was the success of the programme, and in a country where every movement of that dance was known and understood. After the tour they returned to the Coliseum.

Diaghileff meanwhile had come to Covent Garden with Nijinsky for the historic season of 1912, with the production of *Le Sacre du Printemps* in mind. Hilda, two of the English girls and Zvereff went up for an audition before Diaghileff, Fokine, Nijinsky and Cecchetti—a nightmare audience, and at a time when there were only Russians in the company. All were accepted, but later the other two dropped out, and only Hilda remained. She left the Kosloff company at Cheltenham (curious contrast, New Orleans to Cheltenham, as first stages in an artistic education!), and joined Diaghileff at Monte Carlo, where so many careers have started. Her first contract allowed her the magnificent sum of 720 francs a month, which was increased yearly, until it stood with the very highest.

Chance immediately helped her. One of the small *solistes* was expecting a child, and Hilda stepped straight into all her rôles. The first act of *Sacre du Printemps* was already known to the company, but she learned it in a few rehearsals, her musical training making the difficult rhythms easy. All the time she was busy with Cecchetti, adding pure dancing technique to her knowledge of music and life.

This is the sum of her achievement in one month, her first : *L'Oiseau de Feu*, in which she was one of the Princesses, was learned in a dress rehearsal and a general rehearsal, *Thamar* in two rehearsals, while *Prince Igor* had to be learned while the overture was being played, and *Giselle* second act, danced as an impromptu, following as best she could ; in *Carnaval* she danced in the " Valse Noble." That was not the end. Nijinsky selected her as one of the nymphs for his creation, *L'Après-midi d'un Faune*, with its difficult rhythm, its entirely new technique and record number of rehearsals.

Naturally she collapsed, and lay for days in a fever, dancing all the time in her dreams, memorising and counting beats. There was work to be done, her chance had really come, and she could not allow herself the luxury of a breakdown.

Fokine selected her and a Polish girl, out of the company of sixty, to perform the dance of the veils in *Daphnis et Chloé*. It was the first time that a subsidiary rôle was entrusted to two dancers, a system that has since increased the interest for the audience, led to the discovery of new talent, and saved the Ballet in many emergencies. It can be imagined how much jealousy was added to her already great difficulties.

At the *répétition générale* in Paris before a smart audience, the Polish girl, who was given the first turn, became entangled in the veils, and, on a reprimand from Fokine, promptly answered him back ; an unheard-of occurrence.

Diaghileff was furious. " Give the veils to the English girl"; and so through these words she made history, and had her first small creation in the Russian Ballet of the glorious days of Michael Fokine.

But Sokolova always helped her luck. That year, for the first and last time, *Maestro* offered two prizes for the greatest technical progress. Hilda won the first—his photo in a silver frame, inscribed to " Ida," his name for her, and one of the many she was known by until " Sokolova " was truly created, through character, hard work and experience born of amazing chance.

All that had happened so far was but the prelude to further adventure, and but a mild acclimatisation, as it proved.

She left on the famous American tour under Nijinsky's artistic direction, and witnessed the beginnings of his appalling tragedy. The breach with Diaghileff and the sudden assumption of unaccustomed responsibility undoubtedly hastened the end. It was and is an impossibility for even the most balanced of men to dance, create, manage, and to be lionised at the same time. Serge Grigorieff, who could have taken so much of the burden from his shoulders, was left behind at Nijinsky's own request ; a bad initial blunder. Then the two fanatics began to exert their harmful influence on him, hastening the destruction of a weakened mind, upsetting both his newly married life and his career as an artist. The public wished to see him in his great rôles, and him alone, but often he refused to dance at all, or assigned himself some subsidiary part such as the eunuch in *Scheherazade*, and a distracted Kremneff had to come to his hotel, to suffer many difficult scenes and to implore him to dance, where Diaghileff could have ordered.

From the first he took an interest in Hilda, whom he had previously selected as one of his nymphs, and chose her to dance with him in *Le Spectre de la Rose*. "It was terrifying; he seemed to have altered so completely; he would throw me high into the air, and became increasingly difficult to follow as performance succeeded performance."

With the production of *Tyl Eulenspiegel* came the complete fiasco. Extravagant ideas entered into his mind, he selected a group of walkers-on, gathered from hobos and down-and-outs, and suddenly expected them to dance a complicated *pas de six*. Then, when the last day arrived, only the first portion of the ballet was set, and Kremneff, in complete despair, had to arrange with the company to improvise the rest, during the actual performance. Highly trained dancers, they just got through with it. But the work had to be abandoned. Without Diaghileff and his careful tutoring the once creative mind had ceased to work.

On their return to Europe they found *La Boutique Fantasque* in active preparation. The brilliant reign of Leonide Massine had begun. Hilda was assigned a Venetian dance with Gavriloff, which later was given up in favour of a tarantella with castanets to be danced with Felix, who became too insane for it ever to be carried out. Finally she created with Woizikovski the tarantella we know so well.

This same Gavriloff shortly afterwards suffered from one of the most curious dancing accidents on record. Dancing in *Les Sylphides*, in an antiquated theatre in Saragossa, just before the final leap his leg crashed through a rotten board. He pulled it out, and was able to continue. The next week, in another Spanish town, at the very same moment in the dance, there was a loud crack, and he fell in agony to the boards, and crawled into the wings. His leg had been wrenched above the ankle, had seen him through the week, but now it was completely broken. He was on crutches for a year.

The next tour of the Ballet was in South America. It was war-time, travelling was difficult and the company was to assemble by groups in Spain. Hilda travelled alone, and struck up a casual friendship with a sympathetic woman on the boat. They travelled together as far as the frontier at Hendaye, when she saw this woman in apparent difficulties at the customs, surrounded by important-looking officials, the contents of her trunk spilled all over the floor. Immediately she went up to offer a helping hand. " So you know her ? " said a gendarme. " That is interesting " ; and she was promptly arrested and locked in a room under a military guard. The woman was a spy, and none of Hilda's protests was believed. Fortunately, by sheer good luck Grigorieff was still in the town and able to vouch for her, but she had had a very narrow escape from spending the rest of the war in a concentration camp.

The South American tour was a fiasco, almost a repetition of the North American venture, but it held many thrills for Hilda. In the meantime she had been married and was expecting a child. One day, in a tunnel on the line between Santos and São Paulo, a truck-load of scenery caught fire. The men fought valiantly to save it, with only three buckets and their bare hands. They were badly burned but succeeded in salving the greater part.[1] The shock, however, upset Hilda, and on September 1st, 1917, her little girl, Natasha, was born, a month before her time.

[1] *Contes d'Enfants* was burned and the doors in *Scheherazade*. Zvereff painted a new set that was used for many years.—A. L. H.

It turned out to be a fortunate event, in spite of the serious operation required, for she had planned to sail to Buenos Aires in a boat that proved so derelict and suffered so many delays that, with no doctor present, mother and child might well have been lost. The very day before Natasha's birth, Hilda was teaching the Bacchanal in *Narcisse* to Klementovitch !

On their return to Madrid, Spanish 'flu was raging, and the entire company went down with it, Sokolova the last. She was forced to remain behind with Kremneff, her nurse and baby. Then, still weak, she travelled to Lisbon to rejoin the troupe. When they arrived at the station, all was dark, and they could clearly hear the rattle of machine guns. They had landed in the midst of a revolution ; from frying-pan to fire, Spanish 'flu to Portuguese revolution. A porter conducted them through heavy machine-gun fire to a *pension* off the Avenida, the nurse dropping the baby in her panic. No sooner had they arrived in their bedroom, and placed the baby safely on the bed, than the mirror on the wall opposite was smashed to fragments, and bullets ricocheted round the room. They spent a miserable foodless night in a cellar, and moved the next day to a quieter place, where they were besieged for five days. It was then that she learned her first Spanish dancing from Felix, Diaghileff's new discovery.

The revolution over, they danced for a three weeks' season, but were stranded for the rest of the spring. Diaghileff went to Barcelona to try to fix a season, but an impostor had forestalled him and was trying to present a ballet with some of the original dancers. Both the bogus and the genuine engagements fell through. They were able, however, to make a tour through Spain on very bad terms, and returned to Madrid penniless. The company disbanded and lived on their own as best they could. Diaghileff, ever sympathetic, was able to scrape together enough money for Sokolova to take a third-class ticket to Lisbon to fetch her baby, who had been left there, and to return. But Diaghileff was starving, and only the kindness or apathy of the hotel proprietor kept a roof above his head. This is a picture that few who knew him in opulence in London, Paris or Venice can visualise.

Hilda's baby was ill through lack of nourishment and proper medical attention. She was in despair. One day Diaghileff called her; he was unpacking an old trunk and had come across a collection of coins of various nations. He gave them to her to sell for what she could get, and the baby was saved. Diaghileff went without meals for many days then. Nightly they met, and Sokolova helped him as translator in his negotiations with Sir Oswald Stoll, but, though both were eager for a contract, war-time regulations proved a hindrance. Once she was wakened at four in the morning by Diaghileff standing at her bedside— how he got into her *pension* she never knew—feverishly waving a telegram that he could not understand. It read, "Try from your end, impossible from ours," and he went wearily home again. When finally negotiations were complete and an advance had been sent, weakened by hunger he fell across his bed in a faint, sobbing with relief.

London received them with joy and the period of suffering was over, but the memory of those events created a deep and lasting friendship between Diaghileff and Sokolova. She had seen a Diaghileff very different from the unapproachable autocrat whose presence frightened so many of his company. These actions of his must be balanced against all the rest, if we are ever to know the complete Diaghileff : rich and poor, weak and strong, petty and jealous, generous and sympathetic, dangerous enemy and staunch friend. There was a man!

The rest of Sokolova's career in the Ballet had its difficulties, and more than its fair share of illness, but adventure proper was ended, only artistic adventure remained, and those creations that have built up her name.

During the last two months of the Ballet's lifetime, as if by a presentiment, she was given a new lease of life in the middle of a serious illness, and her performances as the Chosen Virgin in *Le Sacre du Printemps* will be remembered as a magnificent climax to the Russian Ballet, bringing back memories of its greatest days. When the curtain went down at Covent Garden, and a doctor and anxious friends rushed to her aid, a chapter of ballet history ended.

To-day she is teaching, giving her fine experience to her pupils, in an attempt to repeat in another that marvel of another great English dancer-artist-personality. Here then is the opportunity to learn at first hand.

Lydia Sokolova has made the journey from England to Russia; to-day Lydia Lopokova is making the journey from Russia to England, and from ballet to the legitimate stage. Her story has been less varied, but no less full; it is marked from the very first by a success which she has done her very best on many occasions to destroy, but without avail. Her luck, or more accurately her charm, has fortunately always prevented her in time. The artistic pattern of her career is especially rich : as a dancer, she was a pupil of Fokine ; as a conscious artist, the pupil of Massine, at a time when he was still learning, beginning to discover, and developing rapidly.

She was sent to the Imperial School following a brother and sister, at the age of eight, and went through easily,

uneventfully, but with the beginnings of a reputation[1];
pink dress, grey dress, the coveted white dress, and gradu-
ation with her first important solo, Columbine in *Casse
Noisette* ; and Columbine is the *leitmotif* of her career. She
was only on the Imperial stage a few months before she
was invited to join the Diaghileff Ballet in Paris, then
in their second year and at the very height of their
popularity. Karsavina in *Theatre Street*, has given us a
delicious description of her first bewildered arrival in
Paris.

" Young Lopokova danced this season ; it was altogether her first journey abroad. As she was stepping out
of the railway carriage, emotion overcame her. She
fainted right away on the piles of luggage. It had been
her dream to be in Paris, she told the alarmed Bakst, who
had rendered her first aid ; the lovely sight (of the Gare
du Nord) was too much for her. A mere child, she
reminded me again of the tiny earnest pupil when, in
the demure costume of *Sylphides*, she ecstatically and
swiftly ran on her toes."

As a pupil of Fokine's she was immediately given small
rôles, and immediately she attracted attention, amidst all
the brilliant stars of that period. She was different. J. L.
Vaudoyer wrote of her with his sure instinct for divining
that difference :

" Sa virtuosité est ingénue, et l'imperceptible gaucherie
de l'âge la tempère. Mademoiselle Lopokova ressuscite les

[1] " Out of the group of small pupils given now into my care was littleLopokova
The extreme emphasis she put into her movements was comic to watch in the tiny
child with the face of an earnest cherub. Whether she danced or talked, her whole
frame quivered with excitement ; she bubbled all over. Her personality was manifest
from the first, and very lovable."—Karsavina in *Theatre Street*.

poupées de Hoffman et de Schwind ; et sans doute
mordait-elle encore, l'an dernier, dans les tartines que
distribue Charlotte."

Luck soon came her way, for after a few months Karsavina was unable to dance for a time, and Lydia was
given Columbine in *Carnaval* and L'Oiseau Bleu with
Nijinsky in *Festin* (she was just eighteen). Only the
young dancers of to-day have met with such rapid advance-
ment; then she was alone. Then, when Karsavina returned,
they shared the rôles, which definitely established her, not
as an understudy, but as a star in her own right. During a
further absence of Karsavina she was given *L'Oiseau de Feu*,
and all the time with an increase of salary. She should have
been content with this, but success always seemed to bore
her, and she went off to seek the customary fortune in
America. She was there five years before she rejoined them
again, and her path was made easy, for it was the ballet
that came to America at the time of Nijinsky's famous
tour. She danced as *ballerina* during those difficult days
when it was almost impossible not to take sides. Then from
1917 to 1919 she remained *ballerina* of the company, and
one of the most popular dancers who ever appeared in
London. It was the period of *La Boutique Fantasque* and *Les
Dames de Bonne Humeur*.

Once more success seemed monotonous, and she ran
away suddenly, again to America. But " I was a flop," she
says, " and thoroughly deserved it." In 1921 she returned
for *The Sleeping Princess*, to dance the Lilac Fairy, and
sometimes Princess Aurora herself. Truly Diaghileff must
have been long-suffering ; it was a rare compliment that he
never paid to any other dancer. She had deserted him
twice, and yet he let her return as if nothing had happened,

and after the first reconciliation he never mentioned it or let her feel it.

After *The Sleeping Princess* things were difficult. No salaries were forthcoming, and she joined Massine in a new venture. With the exception of *Le Beau Danube*, in which she created the rôle of the Street Dancer, the work was singularly uninspired. While Diaghileff was alive, away from him, the most brilliant minds seemed dulled, as if he possessed a hypnotic power that could travel over space. She met him during this engagement, and he gave her a half-hearted peck instead of the hearty kiss reserved for a favourite artist. " Sergei Pavlovitch, why are you so angry with me ? Haven't other people the right to produce ballets ? " " No," he replied, " I am a bar-tender, and have invented certain cocktails. Now other people come and steal my recipes ; certainly they have not the right." When, unabashed, she asked for the third time to be taken back once again, he replied rather ungraciously that he did not want grandmothers in the company. But his actions belied his words, and she appeared for him again many times, but only as a guest-artist during the London seasons.

Lydia Lopokova has given to ballet a quality all her own, the quality of inspired mischief. To call her a *soubrette*, as is so often done, is an understatement. It may cover her rôle in *Les Dames de Bonne Humeur*, but not the memorable *Sylphides*, or the deliciously sentimental doll in the second scene of *La Boutique Fantasque*. So shrewd a critic as André Levinson failed to understand the real Lopokova, and never did her justice.

It was during her reign in the Diaghileff company that I began the habit of going nightly to the ballet. I still have the photograph, the first one in my collection, for which I waited so anxiously outside the stage door. It shows a red-cheeked doll, heartless coquette, who played with poor Petrouchka, and if in her performance the mischievous girl was more in evidence than the puppet, and some of the feeling of witchery was absent, it was all the same memorable for its beauty of movement.

In private life Mrs. J. M. Keynes is the Lydia Lopokova of the stage, in a series of her most enchanting rôles ; quick, provocative, intelligent, a trifle sentimental. She has an earnest, at times almost pathetic, manner that can allow her to say the rudest or most argumentative things in such a way that the truth of them only dawns upon one some considerable time after, and then leaves no hurt. She is also that rarity, the dancer who cares so little about criticism, that she will read adverse notices with obvious relish and even sympathise with their author. There is never any coldness in meeting her after a non-adulatory article. In many things she can be highly intolerant, but never about anyone's opinion of herself. She shares with Georges Balanchine almost complete objectivity of outlook, and it is this gift that makes her experiment so recklessly, and then step aside and coldly judge the result.

Finally, there is a quality that she possesses that it might be damaging to relate about anyone less obviously enchanting (a subtle mode of attack that would leave no possible grounds for a libel action), simply that she is essentially good and right-thinking. Many times I have discussed the latest ballet scandal with her, only to find her taking both sides in turn, and in a perfectly logical manner. She has always an infinite sympathy and understanding of other people. I have seen outbursts during our Camargo venture and even suffered from them. They always arose through the tolerant desire to be reckless in giving other people a chance to create; a temporary victory of heart over reason.

Yes, I love the real Lopokova, though at times she has driven me mad. I have come to the theatre to admire the artist I know, only not to find her there at all. She has carefully hidden her humanity under a mechanical-doll buffoonery. I hear people laugh and applaud, and I am furious. I hear them say, " What a clown ! " and I am still more furious for the Lydia Lopokova whom I know to be an artist.

To me Lopokova failed the moment she stepped out of her own particular field to undertake a classical *ballerina* rôle. *L'Oiseau de Feu* was not for her ; its whole tempo, its mood of mystery and legend, left on the stage a little girl who had wandered into the magic garden by accident. That was not her fault ; it was a case of miscasting. The failure was an honourable one. But for me, jealous of my memories, it is in English ballet that she has failed con- spicuously, and for a very understandable reason : the choregraphy assigned to her was insufficient in complexity to extend a dancer of such wide experience. She forced her effect and earned applause through over-acting, where before she had been subtle and restrained. However naïve she may appear, she is in reality, both by training and temperament, highly sophisticated in her reactions, cer- tainly more sophisticated than those who have recently created rôles for her. This mixture of an old tradition with a new development can never succeed. It shows neither in a flattering light. Fokine and Massine put so much wit into their dances, and wedded it so carefully to the movement, wit of a quality that she could understand, that there was never any need to come to the rescue by violent methods. The *can-can* in *La Boutique Fantasque* was as high-spirited as any of the dances in *Façade*, but so much more complicated in its presentation. Andrée Howard succeeded admirably in *Façade* where Lopokova failed, because she was part of the thought that produced it. Outside that ballet no one would yet compare her to Lopokova, highly promising artist though she is.

Lately Lydia Lopokova has taken to acting. I managed a brief season for her at the Arts Theatre. The *clou* of the performance was Shakespeare's *Lover's Complaint*, acted with members of the Cambridge University Dramatic Society. She looked right, and moved with a rare distinction. She understood the poetry too, but a strong Russian accent, amid the faultless but lifeless declamation of the University men, resulted in a poor unbalanced performance. Later, at the Old Vic as Olivia in *Twelfth Night*, she earned many critical rebukes. One of them said that it was as daring as if Henry Ainley had taken to *pirouettes*—a far-fetched statement, for Lopokova by her whole training has the basic material of dramatic acting at her command. Again it was the accident of her foreign birth, and not that she was a dancer, that made the performance an incongruous one, a fact that she fully realised afterwards when she decided to leave Shakespeare alone for the future. She was reckless enough to try it, critical enough to let it be for the last time. Later she fully proved her dramatic ability by a fine performance of Nora in Ibsen's *Doll's House*. It was only natural that someone who could understand the intensity of the drama in *Giselle* should give an unforgettable performance of the tarantella in the second act of the *Doll's House*, but it was not just a dancer's performance and a dancer's climax ; the true climax came, as it should, with the quiet seated scene of revolt at the end, where with a beautifully modulated voice she proved conclusively that the highly trained dancer could gauge the tempo of spoken drama. And there, after the first few moments, the accent did not matter.

Lopokova, through her restless nature and her love of experiment, will try many things yet; she will fail and succeed in many things, but it is by her many magnificent performances with Diaghileff that she occupies a big position in the history of ballet.

CHAPTER X

ENGLISH INTERLUDE

" The hypnotised audience, crowded tier above tier of the dark theatre, held itself strained and intent in its anxiety not to miss one gyration, one least movement, of the great dancer—that dancer who had enslaved not only New York and St. Petersburg but Paris itself . . . she revealed to them new and more dazzling visions of beauty in the union of colour and motion. She hid herself in a labyrinth of curves . . . a mist of iridescent light. Gradually her form emerged from the riddle, triumphant, provocative, and for an instant she rested like an incredible living jewel in the deep gloom of the stage."

Adeline Genée—THE JOURNAL OF ARNOLD BENNETT

" Vrai Dieu ! Ne suis-je plus La Camargo ? "

Les Marrons du Feu: ALFRED DE MUSSET

INTEREST IN DANCING IN ENGLAND, after the great days of the *pas de quatre*, revived with the success of the Empire Ballets, but essentially through the art of one really great personality, Adeline Genée.

I imagine that the Empire Ballet was choreographically, musically and artistically negligible, just a form of light entertainment, where the tired business man could drop in late after a good dinner, instead of going to the cinema as he would to-day. I have seen a revival of one of these ballets, *The Débutante*, at the Coliseum. Its presentation was a disaster, especially as it was shown in a burst of patriotic fervour, always a silly mistake in matters of art, as English work for English dancers. The subject was identical with Massine's *Scuola di Ballo* and Ashton's little

Foyer de la Danse, but where they had, by careful study and a genuine feeling for their respective periods, produced something living, that will not easily date, *The Débutante* visualised the Paris opera as being somewhere in the English suburbs. Massine's dancing master, interpreted by Woizikovski, was a true figure of the *commedia dell' arte*, Ashton's definitely more realistic, French, true to type and period, while here we had the monstrous incongruity of a Svengali doing classical ballet exercises. This ballet, which may possibly have suffered something in revival, was in any case devoid of all choregraphic interest, save for a scarf dance, that no parodist, no Nervo and Knox at their most inspired, could have equalled. An audience that might have applauded some thirty years ago, just yawned and consulted their programmes anxiously for the next item. It was a certain indication of the development of taste. The coming of the Russians had banished that type of thing once and for all ; even without the Russians it would have perished of an old age that the far more ancient *Giselle* has never known. The Empire public was certainly never Diaghileff's. From the first he created a fresh public of his own from the people who understood painting, followed concerts and loved the theatre. The word *ballet* may even have been something of a handicap, for apart from the Empire it was associated with the light relief of an evening at the opera, the jam in the powder, that made so many swallow " the art " without undue complaint. There is still, as a survival of those days, the fixed superstition that opera is something educational that should be subsidised by the self-respecting State, and that it is a crying scandal to have no permanent opera. Why opera should be a necessity and ballet a luxury it is difficult to understand.

Theoretically in their composition the two arts are very closely related, in opera the voice taking the place of the dance, but opera needs both movement and mime, so that what in theory is logical, in actual practice becomes an impossibility. How can one ever find a Melba-Pavlova, when each one is such a rarity? The very intensity of the training required would make it impossible. Pavlova was the complete artist in what she undertook; Melba a voice. When we have acknowledged Chaliapine as a magnificent exception, we are left with the undoubted fact that on the stage there is little true opera-realism. One of the most comical and crudest theatrical sights I can remember was Melba as Mimi, slowly dying of consumption, her muff piled on top of her, with a wildly gesticulating Caruso, in appearance the perfect *maître d'hôtel*, lamenting by her bedside. When I closed my eyes it was truly glorious, but they had undertaken to *show* me something, as well as to let me *hear* it, and my complaint was fully justified.

This is not a quarrel on a petty point. *Madame Butterfly* is definitely unrealistic from the Japanese point of view; the whole musical idiom is different, the costumes, décor and make-up far from the actual truth, but, when it is well acted and produced, it has a truth of its own, outside of Japan, and is complete. Before the spectacle begins one concedes two things: the general one, that everything in life is sung; the particular one, that this is a Western interpretation of Japan; just as one concedes in *La Bohème* or *La Traviata* that the many unpleasant medical details of phthisis are hidden and that stage consumption is something really poetical. One can easily believe all that, but one cannot credit a fat and ungainly stage consumptive, even though in life the hospitals must be full of them.

The ballet available immediately before 1909 was not sufficiently complete in itself to make this truth self-evident. The opera at any rate was one up on it, in having good music. When Diaghileff came, that truth was made clear, and the word *ballet* assumed a new significance that the composer and the painter realised even sooner than the public at large. They transferred their allegiance, and have since produced their most significant work for ballet. Diaghileff himself experimented in the reform of opera in his famous production of *Le Coq d'Or*, where he found the only possible solution, the leading dancers of the day to act and mime, the leading singers as voices, and the programme was divided logically into a *partie chorégraphique* and a *partie vocale*, with a double cast ; La Reine de Chemâkha, Karsavina in body, Dobrovolska in voice. To take an extreme case, this is the only manner in which Strauss's *Salome* can ever be performed.

This failure of ballet to point out such a self-evident truth was the case in Russia too, to a much lesser degree, and in our own experience with Anna Pavlova's company. It kills completely the dancer of small talent, leaving the true *ballerina* to shine alone. One may talk of wasted talent, but the *ballerina* will transform the work of the inferior choreographer into something intensely personal, and at any rate so reveal herself.

Adeline Genée, judged by any standards, is a very great artist, as well as a great dancer, which we can take for granted. Without both attributes she could scarcely have survived. Her training and environment in Denmark were much the same as in Russia, and the traditions of that country are parallel to Russia ; the tradition of the Bour-nonvilles that gave Johannsen and Legat to the Maryinsky. Genée is the sister of the great Russian *ballerinas*, a fact that

Diaghileff instantly recognised when he told Karsavina how much he coveted her for the company.

The Genée that I can remember so well belongs to the Coliseum and not to the Empire ; the Coliseum—it is significant for English dancing, the Mecca of school-children home from the holidays, future audiences, future dancers. I can remember her every movement, but nothing of her *corps de ballet*, décor or choregraphy. People have called her cold ; she was nothing of the kind. She added to that aristocracy of movement that makes her as regal in private life as on the stage a rare and sparkling quality of wit, very fine and subtle. She was not only commanding on the stage,[1] her movement appealed to one's reason as well as to the emotions. It was the revelation of a very brilliant personality. She retired while this was still a precious, exciting memory, while she could go on dancing in our imagination for ever. The public clamoured for her, but she possessed a strong enough sense of proportion to halt in time.

Then in 1932 she made a reappearance at the Coliseum in the same programme as the unfortunate *Débutante*. One feared a tragedy, it was a triumph. She was the true *débutante*, the Genée of old with something different, a new tenderness added to the sparkle. With amazing skill she had chosen a suite of the old French dances, conventional but skilfully arranged.

She danced with the young Dolin, but their styles blended admirably. The uninitiated might have said that it was all so easy, well within the reach of anyone, but it appeared easy only because a great artist made it so.

[1] " What dominion in that face, what assurance of supreme power."—*The Journal of Arnold Bennett*.

IRINA BARONOVA
in *Les Sylphides*, 1934

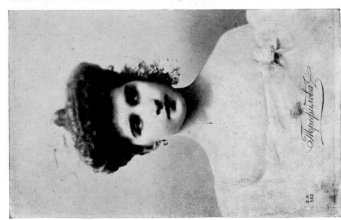

Three Maryinsky Ballerinas

MATHILDE KCHESSINSKA

OLGA PREOBRAJENSKA

Преображенская.

Трефилова.

(Goldberg)

LUBOV ROSTOVA
in *Jeux d'Enfants*, 1934

(Iris)

HELEN KIRSOVA
in *Les Sylphides*, 1933

ALEXANDRA DANILOVA and ANTON DOLIN
in *Le Bal*, London, 1929

ANNA PAVLOVA—Maryinsky period

VERA TREFILOVA
Paris, 1925

ALEXANDRA DANILOVA
The Can-Can from *La Boutique Fantasque*

(*Iris*)

ALEXANDRA DANILOVA
in *Choreartium*, 1934

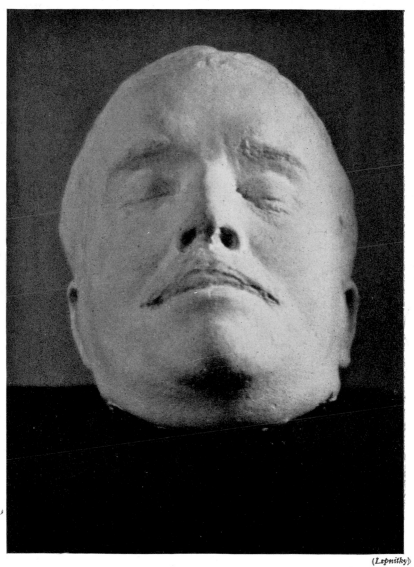

(*Lipnitky*)

SERGE DIAGHILEFF
Death Mask

MICHAEL FOKINE
from a self portrait

VASLAV NIJINSKY—Maryinsky period

(*Iris*)

ANNA PAVLOVA
on her last visit to Paris, 1931

ALICIA MARKOVA in *Le Lac des Cygnes*, 1925
(Inset : with the AUTHOR at Monte Carlo, 1925)

(Lipnitzk)

OLGA SPESSIVA in *Le Lac des Cygnes*

LUBOV TCHERNICHEVA
in *Apollon Musagètes*

TAMARA TOUMANOVA in *Le Lac des Cygnes*, 1934

(Iris

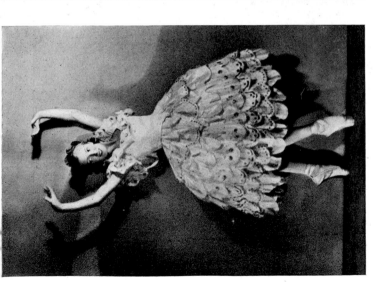

TATIANA RIABOUCHINSKA
in *Carnaval*, 1934

(Iris)

TATIANA RIABOUCHINSKA, 1933

(Iris)

LEONIDE MASSINE
in *L'Oiseau de Feu*, Paris, 1934

TAMARA TOUMANOVA in *Prince Igor*, 1934

(*Iris*)

TAMARA TOUMANOVA in *Mozartiana*, 1933
(inset : aged 7)

(Brewster)

IRINA BARONOVA and DAVID LICHINE in *Les Présage*. 1933

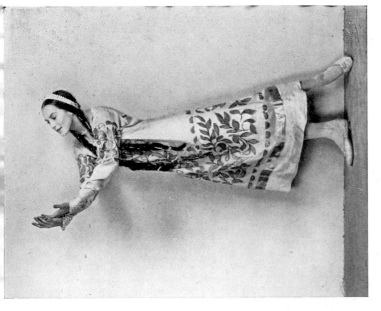

TAMARA SIDORENKO
as the **Princess** in *L'Oiseau de Feu* 1934

TATIANA SIMEONOVA
in *Scuola di Ballo*, 1934

(*Brewster*)

ALICIA MARKOVA in *Le Lac des Cygnes*, London, 1933

(Gothe)

LEONIDE MASSINE and COLONEL DE BASIL in conference
The Alhambra, 1933

(Goldberg)

IRINA BARONOVA and YUREK SHABELEVSKY
in *Le Beau Danube* 1934

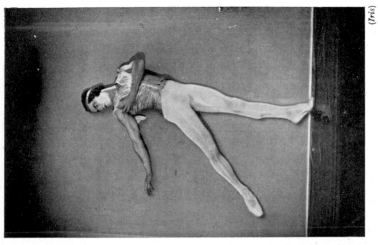

SERGE LIFAR
in *L'Oiseau Bleu*

(*Iris*)

FELIA DOUBROVSKA and SERGE LIFAR
in *L'Oiseau Bleu*

(*Iris*)

(Goldberg)

TAMARA TOUMANOVA
in *Les Sylphides*, 1934

TAMARA KARSAVINA
as Echo in *Narcisse*

LYDIA SOKOLOVA as the Chosen Virgin in *Le Sacre du Printemps*,
London, 1920

LYDIA LOPOKOVA
in *Les Dames de Bonne Humeur*

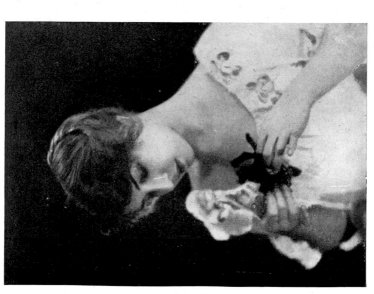

LYDIA LOPOKOVA

(*Iris*)

TATIANA RIABOUCHINSKA and LEON WOIZIKOVSKI
in *Cotillon,* 1933

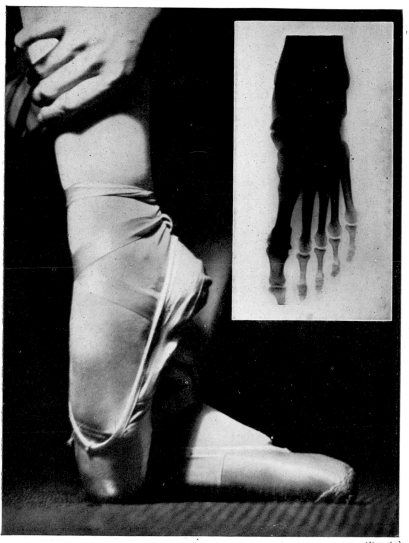

(*Brewster*)

TAMARA TOUMANOVA's feet
(inset : X-ray photograph, showing supplementary bone)

(Iris

TATIANA RIABOUCHINSKA
in *Les Présages*, 1933

(Iris)

LEONIDE MASSINE
in *Union Pacific*, 1934

(Glarner)

Conversation-Piece, Paris, 1934

RIABOUCHINSKA, BARONOVA, RAZOUMOVA, the AUTHOR, and SERGE GRIGORIEFF

IRINA BARONOVA in *Choreartium,* 1934
(inset : aged 7)

(Goldberg)

IRINA BARONOVA
as the Top in *Jeux d'Enfants*, 1934

Les Présages

First movement—NINA VERCHININA

(*Iris*)

NINA VERCHININA in *Choreartium*

(*Iris*)

on Monte Carlo beach, 1933

DAVID LICHINE

in *Choreartium*, 1934

(*Iris*)

(Glazner)

IRINA BARONOVA
in *Le Beau Danube*, 1934

(Glazner)

TATIANA RIABOUCHINSKA and
LEONIDE MASSINE
in *Le Beau Danube*, 1934

(Goldberg)

ALEXANDRA DANILOVA, J. HOYER, E. BOROVANSKY
in *Le Beau Danube*, 1933

(Iris)

LEON WOIZIKOVSKI in *Concurrence*, 1933

KCHESSINSKA in *Esmeralda*
at the Maryinsky Theatre, Saint Petersburg

(Goldber

IRINA BARONOVA
in *Les Sylphides*, 1934

VERA NEMCHINOVA in *Les Biches*
(inset : Nemchinova's bare foot)

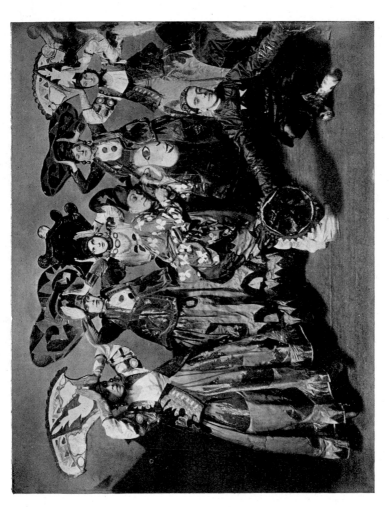

Le Soleil de Nuit, MASSINE's first production, 1915
(NEMCHINOVA third from left. MASSINE seated)

Only three of us actually watched the true world-farewell performance of this very great dancer. That is not quite correct, because I am told that there were many thousand, but they were invisible, and there were only three of us in the room.

An execution must be very like this ; cables and wires everywhere, the constant hum of electric motors, a warning signal, and silence. Beams of light leap out of a little box, and then a flickery signboard appears, gradually getting steadier—FAREWELL OF MADAME ADELINE GENÉE. A black-out, and another blaze of light, gradually dimming down, until a small speck takes shape. That is Adeline Genée, first like a passport photo that has been left overnight in the rain, then, as the details of her costume can be distinguished, like some old and faded family portrait. As she dances, the image takes on some meaning, perhaps because we know and love what it represents. We think we can see the fine carriage, the grace and precision of movement, and we realise that she is in the B.B.C. building with us.

I dash down a long flight of steps, along a corridor and into the studio, just in time to see the real Genée, and the finishing movements of her dance, cut up by the beams of light, black and white flickers—no, still not the real Genée. Then the flickering ceases, and there is applause, but the greatest part of the ovation cannot be heard. Genée approaches, and a close friend exclaims : " Genée, but with the face of Grock." For it is not yet the real Genée ; there is a heavy black make-up still between us.

It is imperfect, but it has been a beautiful, impressive farewell. The great artist, who paved the way for the vogue of ballet, once again a pioneer, paving the way for this new invention, that must in a very few years find perfection, and play a big part in spreading the knowledge and cult

G

of dancing. The wireless and gramophone have brought nothing to the dancer; television can; and Captain Robb, its enthusiastic director, has followed the dance with keen interest. He has already shown us Lydia Sokolova, Dolin and Brigitta, Alicia Markova, Penelope Spencer and others. Very soon every home will have its evening of ballet.

Later, I saw the principals of the Monte Carlo Ballet in the same studio. Still the imperfection, the irritating suggestion of something beautiful not quite within reach, but the compensation of the thoughts—that Hélène Kirsova's mother in Denmark was watching her daughter, and of the difference that a few years must bring.

A wonderful ending to a great record; and a wonderful beginning to new careers.

There are now many semi-official organisations in the dancing profession in England that have played an important part in recent local history. I wonder how many *balletomanes* realise the extent of the profession at all, or even the fact that there is this flourishing industry, something almost apart from the art they love? It came as a revelation to me, knowing only those few, who have been directly associated with the practice of the art, to realise the machinery they had set into motion; a first layer of their pupils, a second layer of the pupils of their pupils, and so on, until the last outer covering holds no knowledge of the stage, and only a very diluted knowledge of the great tradition. There must obviously be a demand for these teachers, if only to teach others to teach, for the results of their work are rarely seen on the stage. It is a little difficult to see why the stage-struck should go to some Madame Quel'conque, when for the same money they could learn from the very fountain heads or from the first layer.

So deep is the love of dancing in England that, formerly, it meant an assured income to set up an academy of the dance even with only the most slender qualifications. Adeline Genée has altered all that. The association of Operatic Dancing—horrible title, relic of an old superstition—of which she is the president, and P. J. S. Richardson the secretary, has laid down a full syllabus of education, and holds certain demonstration classes and examinations. To hold its certificate is at any rate a guarantee of a certain technical foundation. The statistics of those who are members and have entered the examinations are staggering.[1]

There is another equally valuable body, the Cecchetti branch of the Imperial Society formed to keep the *Maestro's* methods alive. Cyril Beaumont, a keen *balletomane*, writer, historian and publisher, has codified these lessons—a heroic task, since they were a living part of one man, rather than a standard method, and the personality of that man was so closely bound up with them. Beaumont knew the man, understood and loved him, and, together with Stanislas Idzikovski, dragged the knowledge out of him, and put it into a book, *A Manual of Classical Dancing*, which, if it has not been my Bible, has at any rate been my Bradshaw. Beaumont himself is one of the most interesting figures in the ballet world, a storehouse of knowledge, who under a very precise manner conceals a real passion, and is as gloriously mad as I am. To him, Taglioni, Elssler and the whole *pas de quatre* are still alive and dancing, always in their prime. When we meet it is with pleasure, but each of us is always a little on the defensive, having possessions that the other covets, and one can never quite trust an

---

[1] For 1933, the total membership was 2,075 *active* members, not including 178 in South Africa. Elementary and advanced examinations were taken by 1,207 students, with entries of 5,000 for the children's examinations.

enthusiast alone with one's treasures. There is a book that I have been trying to get out of Beaumont for a long time, a glorious album with photographs of Kchessinska. Still I do not despair, and, like all of us, I am in his debt for so many things. It is the members of this Cecchetti Society who have been the backbone of English dancing, Marie Rambert and Ninette de Valois, both *Maestro's* pupils.[1]

While these examinations ensure a standard, they do not pretend to turn out artists ; they have no control over that. The great artists of the present day have passed no such artificial tests ; they have received something invaluable from a Preobrajenska or a Kchessinska, have added of their own, and have danced. It sounds easy.

What happens to the thousands who enter for these examinations ? With few exceptions, little, unfortunately, that is the concern of this book ; the chorus, musical comedy, marriage, with, let us hope, a happy ending, and several daughters to continue " mummy's tradition " and go one better. They become a shade more graceful than they would have been, help a worthy profession and a few charities, while their number accounts for the really fine audiences we enjoy.

Let us take the path of one girl, who knows what she wants, and estimate her chances of success. Every week, nearly, I receive some letter asking for advice about the future career of some "Glasgow Pavlova" ("see local Press, attached "). I have a fixed formula for reply, polite but not encouraging :

---

[1] This is not the place to go into those small details of the differences between methods that shake the dancing world, as they do the worlds of economics and science. The fine teacher with good material will succeed with any nameless method, but Cecchetti's method seems to me to produce dancers from a definitely theatrical point of view, giving them confidence, strength and stage-craft. The classes that seem to me the finest of all are those of the Russian *ballerinas*, great individual artists, and no label will apply to their work.—A. L. H.

" First select a really good school; there are many to-day.
If your daughter is under eight, let her begin with two or
three lessons a week, after that she must go daily. Bear in
mind that she is too old at fifteen. If all you say about her is
true, the cost need not terrify you. The proper teacher will
always take a pupil she believes in at a greatly reduced
fee, or even for nothing. The advertisement of a fine pupil
will fill her school, even if her motives are idealistic. Give
her good music lessons, encourage her to draw and visit
museums ; but above all you must take care that she visits
every ballet performance of note. Continue like that for
four years, refusing every offer for lucrative engagements,
film and otherwise, that may come your way. Then, if she is
quite exceptionally brilliant, and has worked very hard,
there is just an outside chance that you may get her into the
corps de ballet of a good company, at about 1,000 francs a
month ; of course, she will have to buy her own shoes and
tights, and live, while on tour. Again, once there, if she
is brilliant, hard-working and *lucky*, she may make a small
reputation, in which case she can hope for 2,000 francs a
month. Do not be discouraged ; a few people have actually
got there, and, at any rate, the work will keep her out of
mischief."

Usually they reply that they have sent the girl to some
" barefoot school " that guarantees really speedy results,
and I never hear the end of the story. The difficulties are
not exaggerated, and explain at any rate some of the
reasons for the praise I lavish on those who have had the
will to get through.

The whole development of dancing depends, not upon
the teachers alone, but on the choreographers, who will use
the material that is given them. When Diaghileff died, followed so shortly by Anna Pavlova, we realised that this

mass of well-trained machinery would be wasted if some-thing were not done quickly. Both troupes had found use for English dancers, and the vague hope of being received there some day was their only inspiration and incentive. We ourselves had never attempted to make use of them. With Diaghileff alive, such competition as we might offer would have been comical. Indeed, the fact that there ever could be such a thing as English Ballet had never occurred to me, not through any snobbery, but because I was well satisfied with things as they were. The most important thing seemed to be that there was a large permanent audience ready to welcome the best, and among the best were many English dancers, though their nationality was of minor importance. To-day, with Russian dancing so firmly re-established, that is once again my feeling. It is impossible to think of such matters in terms of nationality ; Diaghileff himself never did, as the list of his collaborators proves.

Then, the need was urgent. There was a gap that the Russians themselves seemed too stunned to fill, and the reaction of their English admirers, too, was that ballet itself had died with Diaghileff, a belief that I never at any time shared. Immediately the dancers split into small fac-tions, and were swallowed up by their own jealousies or the commercial theatre. Two or three abortive attempts were made, and contracts drawn up by optimists, crooks or lunatics. One in particular, a self-styled Dutch millionaire, raised great hopes, gathered the whole company together, made a few speeches, and then waited. The dancers waited too, but no engagements or money were forthcoming. The gentleman vanished, and the company melted away. We did not know that de Basil, surrounded by a few children, was soon to prepare to fill that gap—fortunately perhaps, for our efforts saw the birth of English choregraphy, and gave our dancers a self-confidence that has had lasting results that will only be fully revealed in the future.

I was discussing this situation one day with the editor of the *Dancing Times*, P. J. S. Richardson, in a restaurant appropriately enough called Taglioni. Richardson and I invariably disagree on almost every point in our assessment of dancers, choregraphers and artists, but, as we agree whole-heartedly on the importance of ballet in general, we have always got on surprisingly well. He has done invaluable pioneer work both through the *Dancing Times* and the Operatic Association, a whole-hearted enthusiast, and a remarkably fine organiser, the rare practical man in this crazy world of charming but difficult people. An academic discussion immediately took a practical form. " Why not form a society for the production of ballet, and use our own talent ? " said Richardson. Why not, indeed ? It seemed easy, and, even if it came to nothing, it was always a consolation to have tried something. We jotted down a score of names on the back of an envelope, and the Camargo Society was conceived. We invited a chosen few to a preliminary meeting in a Soho restaurant, and the response was promising.

Gathered there together, everyone talked at once in a variety of languages, but the general impression was that such a society could and should be formed. I talked with one guest in particular, who was more quiet and practical than the rest. We had in common an intense admiration for Trefilova. He seemed unusually well informed, and I could not quite place him. Whenever I tried to nail him down to a definite branch of art, he always escaped. Afterwards I found it was J. M. Keynes, who practises, of course, the most fantastic of them all.

At a second meeting, when the noisier ones had talked themselves out, we proceeded to elect a committee under the chairmanship of Edwin Evans, who had hit upon La Camargo of the shapely legs as our patron saint. The name has since been misspelt in a quantity of different manners, from the usual Carmargo to the deliberate " Ca Margot," sign of our success. There were many eager candidates for the committee, but Lydia Lopokova, whom we wanted in particular, took a great deal of persuading ; she had never belonged to a committee before; one could not do such a thing at once; perhaps she had better be a kindly spectator; after all it was a serious step, "like parting with one's virginity." She finally capitulated, and we now had enough of the " old gang " with us to give our venture a sporting chance. All that remained was to find the neces-sary money, and to agree upon a programme. Both were difficulties throughout our existence, both were linked together. After a few committee meetings we could usually agree as to the ideal programme, but when came the treasurer's turn to speak, it would be whittled down, the number of dancers employed cut in half, cloth substituted for silk, and a hundred and one small things.

Lydia Lopokova (always very correct, once the great decision of joining a committee had been made) : I propose, Mr. Chairman, that we put on *Casse Noisette* on a grand scale, as it was done in Russia.

Constant Lambert : Yes, and with a really fine orchestra . . .

A. L. H. : We must get Benois or Doboujinsky to do the costumes.

The Treasurer : I can allow you exactly £57 3s. 4d. Will that be enough ?

We would go on discussing the scheme with all its tempting possibilities, relying on the intervention of some mythical millionaire, till the calendar reminded us that we had to be practical. The whole system of occasional production was extremely wasteful. Each performance cost somewhere around £500, the majority of the expenses being the same as for a long run. The dancers, as usual, gave their services, and I believe that ultimately they benefited. It is a miracle how Alfred Tysser, and later J. M. Keynes, steered us clear of debt. Theirs was the task of curbing us, without throwing too much cold water on our efforts. Keynes was unfailingly optimistic. When things were at their very worst he found a good reason why people should subscribe; when things improved, a still better reason, and thanks to his own efforts he was usually right. An hour on the telephone, and a few tea-parties, always produced the necessary guarantee. He was at times dictatorial in his methods. A very quick thinker, he could not suffer elaborate discussion, and acted at times while things were still being debated. That he acted wisely one cannot now deny, but, at the time, some of us were a little irritated at being kept in the dark about so many things.

Our secretary was M. Montagu-Nathan, author of several volumes of Russian musical history and criticism, and a man of exceptionally wide general culture, who could turn his mind from musical scores to box-office arrangements, and, at his most inspired, to the resurrection of a dish in honour of our patron—*La Bombe Camargo* at the Savoy. The whole time Montagu-Nathan practically was the society, the one tangible person with a definite telephone number. He strongly believed in a Utopia, where artists in different media would find a common enthusiasm in ballet and our Society. To-day he still believes in it, but he truly knows it to be Utopia. He received the complaints, while the praise was given to the large and elastic committee. Montagu-Nathan can organise anything. He is meticulously exact, and his schedules, agendas and minutes terrified some of our dancers, and were a highly comical contrast to the actual conduct of most of the meetings, where separate conversations were carried on across the table that often wandered very far from the point. His record of telephone conversations was a constant source of amusement : 12.51, Miss Jones rang up to say that her shoes had been dyed purple instead of blue ; what should be done ? 1.28, Baroness Y complained that her seats were not good enough, also she wished particularly to be near Lady X. 1.30, Lady X wished on no account to be anywhere near Baroness Y. 1.40, Mrs. J would resign unless the society revived *Scheherazade* at once. 1.45, So-and-so read a long scenario based on an old Indian legend, and thought it would be a good ballet for Lifar to produce. 1.55, Miss Jones-Smith considered that Madame Lopokova had treated her with insufficient respect. She must protest energetically. (She did for ten minutes that day, and for very many days after.) These are actual examples, and so it went on the entire day.

The inaugural event was a large banquet presided over by Adeline Genée, during which Lopokova made an admirable and impassioned appeal in English, and a characteristic letter from Bernard Shaw was read, which naturally monopolised the Press reports. The dinner brought us good results that more than offset the many complaints from offended people who had not been sufficiently well placed. Montagu-Nathan was already then a master of the soft answer.

In summing up the results of all our work I will not plead a lack of money. It is a grave handicap, with which nearly every organiser of ballet, from Diaghileff himself, has had to contend.

The inherent weaknesses lay in having a committee—perhaps the very best that could be obtained, but nevertheless a committee—instead of a dictator with advisers. No one had the time or the inclination to take the post, so that money finally dictated and our policy was one of compromise. It was impossible to run on any one clear path.

The other weakness was the lack of a permanent company, and without it the difficulty of rehearsals is always too great. Artists who are giving their services cannot be disciplined, and choregraphers have no ready material at their beck and call. During the summer season, when the company was paid and stable, this difficulty was less in evidence. We suffered too from a lack of harsh criticism, perhaps because all those who could have spoken with authority were members of committee. We met with kindness and indulgence everywhere. The Press talked of ballets worthy of Diaghileff ; we knew quite well that they were nothing of the kind, but this may have made us take matters a little too easily.

The society wound up magnificently with two gala performances at Covent Garden for the edification of the members of the Economic Conference. It solved our own immediate economic problems by turning a large deficit into a small balance, now the nucleus of a fund for the Vic-Wells. After this effort I shall aways be a firm believer in any move that J. M. Keynes advocates. He was our inspired chancellor.

On the positive side we accomplished much. We

overcame a national inferiority complex, and also paved the way for the triumphs of the Monte Carlo Ballet the following year. Many of the works presented were economy scraps, and are best forgotten; a few find their way into ballet history, if only local, and are fortunately preserved in the Vic-Wells repertoire.

Obviously our choregraphy to-day is still immature, as is most of our dancing, and it is quite impossible to judge it from the same critical standards as we adopt for the Russians. We have no choregraphers sufficiently inspired themselves to inspire a company, or with sufficient authority to discipline them perfectly. Most important of all, they have not yet a full knowledge of the actual possibilities of movement, either physical or academic, so that the vocabulary in use is an extremely limited one, and the performance of any work is apt to depend on one brilliant dancer alone. Markova and Dolin have enhanced the face value of English choregraphy a hundredfold, but English choregraphy could never have given them either the initial experience or a name, and is therefore greatly in their debt. It has not yet reached the formative stage. At present, aided by dancers of experience, it can provide adequate theatrical entertainment—a very great stride, bringing it rapidly towards this second stage. Its ultimate development should now become the concern of painters and musicians, who must realise its vast propaganda value, as the Russians and the French have done. No Exhibition of British Art in Burlington House can have the same effect as one world tour of a really fine national ballet, that is not praised on patriotic grounds, but on account of its intrinsic merit.

The pioneers of this " new art " in England are Ninette de Valois and Frederick Ashton.

Ninette de Valois was a valuable *soliste* of the Diaghileff Ballet and a favourite pupil of Cecchetti's. When she left the Ballet, she took charge of the dancing at the Abbey Theatre, Dublin, and the Festival, Cambridge. This entailed work with amateurs and novices, with a consequent concentration on group effect rather than movement. Her big chance came with the Camargo Society, and in Vaughan-Williams' *Job*, an outstanding example of collaboration in the arts, she created the most important English ballet, a work that can be appraised by any standards. It is big in conception, simple in the grand manner, and the story is told with astonishing style and economy of means. Here is the true dance drama towards which Wigman and Laban have been so vainly striving. There is one virtuoso rôle that stands apart from the pattern, dominates it and makes the masque into a ballet proper—that of Satan. Dolin was Satan, superb in the powerful conception of the rôle, a Miltonic interpretation of the fallen angel, replacing the customary demon king of pantomime ; and Dolin could forget completely that he was a *premier danseur classique* in his surrender to that conception.

I remember well the many meetings we had to decide the delicate point of how to name the Deity in the programme. A bald Mr. X as God would have been out of place and the censor of *Green Pastures* would certainly have intervened. Finally we compromised on Job's Spiritual Self. When the ballet was performed in Denmark, P. J. S. Richardson showed his height and editorial authority to full advantage in this, his first part, and has never appeared since. Any lesser rôle would be an anticlimax.

De Valois' choregraphy to Milhaud's *Création du Monde*, with Edward Wolfe's beautiful scenery and costumes, was also an outstanding success. In her treatment she made the extremely wise choice of retaining a negro conception of Genesis, the only manner in which she could make it anthropomorphic and moving. Again she excelled in pattern, starting with an intricate group, unravelling it bit by bit as the trees and animals found life, and winding up with a dance in celebration of the birth of Man and Woman. A really superb piece of craftsmanship.

In these heroic canvases, where details of dancing are not paramount, de Valois has found herself, and has given a valuable contribution to our ballet, but in her smaller work, where the individual dances are the main point, she seems to me to be musically sound, but finicky, boring and uninspired. She is not even saved theatrically by any display of elegance. Such a ballet as *Douanes* (Geoffrey Toye) reveals a lack of originality and some poverty of movement. Round just such a simple frolic Massine created his *Matelots*, valuable only because it reveals dancers, and finds new uses for their limbs. Most classical of dancers herself, she must leave classical sources far behind and seek inspiration in themes that are in themselves of value. The *ballet bouffe* is not yet for England. More than anything it needs a great directing mind in the background to solder its elements together. I value her work very highly, because, when she does succeed, she owes nothing to prevailing fashion, and can strike out a line of her own. In this way schools are made and traditions founded.

Our other choreographer is Frederick Ashton, most prolific and versatile, who may influence the whole of English dancing. His story is an interesting one. A public school boy,[1] he started late by taking weekly lessons with Massine, who has greatly influenced him. Then he went to Marie Rambert, who made him into a competent and

[1] The term is always used when anyone takes to crime or dancing.—A. L. H.

interesting dancer, discovered and encouraged his gifts, and turned him from a love of the *chic* to more serious things. For a time he danced with Ida Rubinstein, and came under the powerful personality of Nijinska, a valuable way of making up for lost time.

He has usually excellent taste, a good sense of atmosphere and of the stage. His limitation is the general one of an insufficient experience in movement, and the personal one of an enormous facility for producing temporarily effective work that has hampered the creative struggle. Ashton's work as a whole is not yet truly personal and inventive ; it has still to bear a definite unmistakable signature. If he can avoid commercial work, and handle one group of dancers for any length of time, I have faith in his future. Pavlova believed in him ; inspired by her, and cut off for the moment from the prevailing fashions, that he so readily assimilates, he would have found himself, and international importance. Now who knows?

Constant Lambert's *Pomona*, in our very first programme, was of a very high standard, and in it he showed his gift of being able to produce his dancers to full theatrical advantage. Anna Ludmila had appeared in London under a grave handicap. As Dolin's partner she had stepped straight into Nemchinova's classical shoes, and the contrast of types was so striking that Ludmila was found wanting. Beautiful American blonde, she should have been a Follies girl, but, unfortunately for her pocket, she happened to be born an artist, who might have fitted into certain of the rôles made famous by Lopokova, but who was lost without careful treatment. Ludmila translated sex-appeal into terms of ballet. In *Pomona*, Ashton made full use of this, and showed an adorable and very human little goddess, who could move with immense charm and softness.

Ashton's other important contribution was Constant Lambert's *Rio Grande*, in which he chose for his interpretation an *étude de mœurs* of the ladies of the port. Logically enough this displeased many, as it clashed with the original poem and the words that were being sung during the action, but the composer himself was satisfied, and Edward Burra's scenery and costumes echoed Ashton's intentions. Choregraphically it was weak, but theatrically admirable. His best liked work for the Camargo was a suite of dances to William Walton's witty *Façade*, a blend of vulgarity, satire and humour, in which he made excellent use of popular dance idioms. Again, if he did not enrich choregraphy, it was first-class entertainment that amused one, cabaret fashion ; the incongruity of a classically flawless Markova in a cheeky straw hat, removing her short skirt to dance a skittish rag polka, was in itself almost a discovery. *My Lord of Burleigh*, to music by Mendelssohn, skilfully sewn together and wedded to Tennyson by Edwin Evans, was an attempt to do one of those difficult feats of harmony between a living choregrapher and a dead composer, that a Fokine, Massine or Balanchine alone can do. Only the finest dancing could have saved it from tedium. Ashton's other work in a more restricted field belongs to the Ballet Club.[1]

A producer of one work, *Adam and Eve*, was Anthony Tudor, whose most interesting activities belong to the smaller stage of the Ballet Club. He has yet to arrive, but his method of tackling material, his struggles, and even his failures, point to him as a potential leader in English Ballet.

One small *divertissement, A Willow grows aslant a Brook*

[1] Since this was written Ashton has had success in Hartford and New York with his production of the Gertrude Stein–Vergil Thompson opera, *Four Saints in Three Acts*.—A. L. H.

(Frank Bridge), was infinitely fresh and charming. Wendy Toye, its arranger and principal dancer, unspoiled heroine of a hundred charity matinées, and everyone's pupil in turn, has yet to find a home. Hers is one of the real talents that we have. She is infinitely musical, with a personality far beyond her years. Her versatility of interest is too great. She dabbles, where she should concentrate. She must make a name, but probably it will be outside ballet. A year or so with a big company, and plenty of rivalry, and we should see the real Wendy, that I know exists.

All this activity, and the talent of de Valois, made the Vic-Wells into a permanent home of ballet. There, at cinema prices, an audience can enjoy a whole evening of dancing. It is always full, always appreciated by indulgent audiences. It has yet to prove itself by creating its own *ballerina*. So far it is an encouraging local phenomenon, a plucky prelude to bigger things. Its much-stressed financial difficulties should not be an insurmountable hindrance. The Monte Carlo Ballet, with no permanent home, has had to go through far worse times before its final success, and the need for funds can sometimes be made to cover too much. The revival of *Carnaval* in brand-new costumes, when the work was devised as a whole—Schumann—Fokine—Bakst—is a disquieting mistake, that indicates a whole wrong manner of thinking. Before building up, it is necessary to have an infinite respect for traditions, that are in this case the result of the careful collaboration of the finest creative minds of their day. In reviving *Casse Noisette* there was also a mistake of taste, more debatable this time. Unlike *Giselle*, which depends on one fine dancer who was to hand in Markova, Ivanoff's ballet is a spectacle, that needs a lavish Maryinsky presentation, and a whole body of flawless classical dancers, as well as a fine mime, in Lopokova's old rôle of the little girl, Clara. Without such a company the Snowflake interlude becomes cheap provincial pantomime, unbearable at the present day. Hedley Briggs' pleasing costumes cannot turn a small and comparatively inexperienced company into a Russian *corps de ballet* at its most inspired. The Vic-Wells has vast opportunities, and it would be an unfriendly act to damn it with faint praise, or even just to be grateful for what it gives. It can do so much better, and I like to believe that it will.

The formation of the Ballet Club was altogether an easier venture. It had no committee, but was the child of Marie Rambert and Ashley Dukes, child of her artistry and his theatrical sense, organisation and industry. Ashley possesses a passion for building theatres, his wife a passion for building dancers. Their union had to result in the Ballet Club.

Marie Rambert was first engaged by Diaghileff to analyse for his dancers, especially Nijinsky, the principles of Dalcroze Eurhythmics. The whole trend of Nijinsky's development, and the use of new and complicated music, made this important. Whether she taught them anything or not I do not know, but she herself learned their secrets from Cecchetti. We first met at the exhibition I had organised in memory of Diaghileff, and squatting on the floor discussed the whole situation. We both agreed that the only solution was a return to the classics. She told me that her girls could dance Petipa variations. I listened, the talk was good, but did not for a moment believe her, though now I always believe in what she says. She is at times honest almost to the point of rudeness. Then I assisted at a lecture she gave on Petipa that was absorbing for the future that it promised. The hall was disgustingly draughty and uncomfortable, and her pupils performed in practice costumes to a tinkling piano on a dangerously rickety platform.

The effect was admirable. They " came across " with no bluff, as promising dancers and real personalities. They showed that luxury presentation was no longer necessary. They even had that vague glamour previously so lacking in our dancers.

There was a gloriously beautiful and serene Pearl Argyle, an outstanding dancer anywhere, who still awaits the choregrapher who will reveal her to herself and to us; Prudence Hyman, vital and mischievous, with a lovely long line; the stately Diana Gould, perfect in poise and balance, to-day a really fine artist, who awaits "discovery," and Andrée Howard, a real stylist, who reminded one of a hundred old prints; also the boy, Harold Turner, a fine athletic young animal. One in particular, Maude Lloyd, was quite in a class of her own. She lent distinction to everything that she did, and promised something really good.[1] They still had a long way to go, but they were magnificent material on which to build. I went to the class almost daily. I had found a new headquarters. Marie Rambert treated each one as an individual problem, moulding character as well as body. She had to master the reserve of Pearl, harness the vitality of Prue, give Andrée self-confidence. She praised and cursed them all, but each in a different manner. She tried to give them theatre consciousness, as well as efficient machinery. She devoted herself to them the entire day. In Ashton she fostered the creative urge, in William Chappell his fine natural gifts as a designer. There were children also, who were being

---

[1] She is teaching in South Africa when she should be dancing the whole time.

nursed and developed. It is a tragedy for our many fine dancers that English choregraphy has not kept pace with them. It is always a story of " not yet discovered." She took me in hand too, and polished up my rusty technical knowledge. To-day, she is one of my dearest friends, whose frank opinion I can always trust and value, whose standards are high and invariably disinterested. Her vitality is a tonic. After a busy day at the theatre, when others were irritable and depressed, I have seen her turn cartwheels in the street, to the amazement of the police, and then stop for a careful analysis of their mechanics.

The first matinées at the Lyric, Hammersmith, followed by seasons at which Karsavina danced, showed not pupils, but a young and inexperienced company, that knew how to behave in front of an audience and that continued to improve. It seemed a shame to scatter this little band, and so the Ballet Club was formed as a permanent home and a workshop, where chamber ballet could be presented.

They invited me to become a founding director, and I gladly accepted. I have yet to discover my duties ; so far it has been a one-sided arrangement, with no risks, no hard work, only continual pleasure in the society of these fine friends and artists. I have criticised, offered advice, and my applause may have counted for something on the sad occasion when I was one-fourteenth of the audience, that is all. I intend to hang on to that directorship, to have at any rate a nominal responsibility for the Pearls and Dianas, and the rest of " Marie Rambert's jewels."

The first season was only survived through the invincible optimism of Ashley. " How many in front to-night ? "— (Fifteen and no paper !) " Not at all bad, a decided improvement." I called him " the mad King of Bavaria," as he sat in his almost empty theatre, enjoying the performance with no apparent thought of the box-office. Meanwhile the church next door, a tabernacle of the Four Square Gospel, was playing, as we should say, to crowded houses, the " House Full " boards up nightly. They could afford a poster campaign and dramatic flood-lighting effects denied to us. They looked like the prosperous opera-house, we like the small chapel.

We persisted, till all of a sudden it became fashionable, and people began to be turned away nightly. A few faithful friends came throughout the season. Then we suffered from our success. Various managers took our girls from us, and offered them important engagements. They danced some absurdly simple steps for five minutes at anything up to fifteen times the salary they received for the complicated work they gave us. Not one manager has yet known how to use them, but the engagements showed at any rate that the work had been thorough and effective. But it meant closing down on week-days. Now on Sunday the whole company is united again, save the fortunate ones who have joined the Russian Ballet. Serious dancers never rest.

It is necessary to keep a sense of proportion, and the achievements must be judged on the same small scale on which they are presented. At times, on that scale, they have reached real perfection. The Ballet Club has been the main recruiting ground for English dancers. None of them can be called great as yet, but they are *solistes* who must be treated seriously by any standards, and even among the Russians they are at home both in class and on the stage. Pearl Argyle, Prudence Hyman, Betty Cuff and Diana Gould were valuable aids in the difficult season of *Les Ballets, 1933*, taking their places at short notice, and later, when three of them joined de Basil on tour, they went straight from the station on to the stage, a striking tribute to their training. They have danced in miniature revivals of important works before hypercritical audiences, who in the tiny theatre could see every mistake ; they have produced their own choreographers and decorative artists.

The revivals have been *Le Lac des Cygnes* and dances from *Le Mariage d'Aurore*, *Carnaval* and *Le Spectre de la Rose*, with a delightful Prudence Hyman in Karsavina's rôles, *Les Sylphides* and *L'Après-midi d'un Faune*; daring ventures all of them, but fully justified by the results. The company has been assisted by Alicia Markova, not as a solo star, but as one of its members, naturally the most brilliant dancer, but each one has given a positive contribution to the result.

The most interesting creations are Frederick Ashton's *Foyer de la Danse* (Berners) and *Péri* (Dukas), the truly Pre-Raphaelite *Lady of Shalott* (Sibelius), a genuine English ballet, and, the finest of his works, the early *Capriol Suite* (Warlock), a perfect translation of country dances.

Anthony Tudor, the other choreographer, has a great deal to say, and sometimes a little difficulty in saying it ; he strikes dull patches, where he cannot get himself out of musical difficulties, but those very mistakes, and the manner in which they are made, show the essential honesty of his purpose. He will not bluff his way out just to satisfy the non-critical in the audience. His first work, *Cross-Gartered* (Frescobaldi), earned praise from Massine, his second and best, *Lysistrata*, from the composer, Prokofieff, both of whom felt the working of an original mind. His last work, *Atalanta of the East*, is a striking example of research into entirely new material, not yet fully assimilated and translated into ballet. Poses are there, the style is fine, but it is heavy and lacking in movement. For all that, I find these three works amongst the most interesting yet produced by an Englishman.

Susan Salaman, one of the most ingenious people I have ever met in the theatre, who can create scenery out of nothing, carpenter, electrician, designer and artist, has produced three small sporting sketches, *Rugby*, *Boxing* and *Cricket*, excellent examples of English humour in dancing, that are based on sound, elementary movement. She has been working with *La Compagnie des Quinze*, and it is in applying movement to drama that her real future lies.

Andrée Howard is the latest choreographer, with *The Mermaid*, a small work, full of feeling and real style. She has used Pearl, too, as no one else, and penetrated her reserve.

This entry of ballet into the little theatre movement, which has already been imitated in Rome, would be valuable in every country, and especially in America, home of the little theatre. It is the one manner in which choreographers can be trained, and, even if it is only regarded as a means to an end, our results have proved that it is a hundred times justified.

Fortunately these organisations are working in perfect harmony, each realising that the other is working at a different aspect of the same thing. There is an interchange of artists that helps to broaden the outlook and prevent parochialism.

If, in this survey of ballet in England, I have been cautious in my praise, it is because I am viewing these achievements from the absolute standards of the main tradition. The progress made, which is remarkable in three years, has placed these activities far beyond the need of any charity. There is still only one Lydia Sokolova, a glorious bewildering phenomenon, one Markova, one

Dolin, but, in these three years, our machinery has been given personality, and the old catch phrases, to the effect that English dancers have no temperament or charm, now belong to the past, just as leadership in the art may possibly belong to the future.

Meanwhile the cause of the ballet in England is safe in the hands of such fine connoisseurs as Mrs. Edward Grenfell and Captain Bruce Ottley, to name but the leading spirits among our ever growing, active audiences. We owe to them at least one season of unforgettable memories, and the opportunity of learning from the finest, and doubtless keeping something for ourselves.

CHAPTER XI

BALLETOMANE IN WAITING

IN THESE LONG YEARS of waiting we saw many manifestations of dancing, some of them called ballet, others frankly dance concerts.

The most ambitious was the season of Madame Ida Rubinstein at Covent Garden. She had spared no expense. She recognised the finest creative minds of the day, and promptly bought them. Unfortunately she always insisted on dancing herself, in a manner that even in her youth was unfamiliar to her. She had been famous as a mime, but here she was showing us an extensive repertoire that only a Karsavina could have carried, from the cold classicism of *Princesse Cygne* to the thrills of Spanish dancing in Ravel's *Bolero*. There were near-masterpieces presented that season, that made one lament the fact that their inspirer was not content to play the rôle of super-impresario. Nijinska's *Valse* will long remain in the memory, with its impressions of a whirling mass of couples in an enfilade of brightly lit and mirrored rooms; Massine's *David* had a simplicity and grandeur that gave one a taste of his new development. This magnificent failure was valuable as a nursery for the new and the real thing. There, under Nijinska, Lichine was first disciplined. Frederick Ashton learned his earliest lessons in chore-graphy, and Nina Verchinina danced in the perfectly trained *corps de ballet* ; also, sad reversal of things, there was a St. Petersburg star, Ludmila Schollar, who had delighted us in *The Sleeping Princess*. Even so much in the background, she was a menace to the star, a reminder of the value of a sense of proportion, and of the value of money too. This was so nearly the real thing that, *faute de mieux*, we were grateful and went nightly to applaud.

The dance recital, so much an institution in Paris and New York, has never become popular in this country, where dancing is best loved and understood. Argentina alone has enjoyed a real success, and then for brief visits. I would not place her at the top of all the Spanish dancers I have seen, as representing the Spanish dance at its purest and most national. In that respect Argentinita, best loved dancer in Spain, reigns supreme. Argentina as a concert *soliste* has refined the Spanish dance too much, without having translated it completely into ballet. She has made us forget its origins in the people. In that form it is corseted and unhappy on the concert platform, a respectable compromise. In her use of the castanets she is, of course, unique. Whatever she does, her ear is never for an instant at fault. Argentina, with Escudero and her full company, is complete, and that is how she must be seen. Then all criticism is out of place. Argentina is too big an artist for the restraints of the concert hall, too magnificently theatrical. No one has shown the essential vulgarity of the Spanish gypsy dancer better than Tina Meller, who can transform the most respectable theatre into a cabaret, and her smart audiences into quayside loungers and tourists. She is certainly less consciously an artist, much more limited in expression, but the results she gives are exciting, and excitement is the chief reaction that Spanish dancing should provoke.

In truth, the dance concert is usually a piece of monstrous

impudence on the part of its giver ; the sole motive being to follow the lines of least resistance. When we consider that Anna Pavlova, for all her art and personality, never appeared unsupported, and that her famous solos, *The Dying Swan*, *The Dragonfly* or *The Californian Poppy*, lasted but two minutes each, what can we think of those who ask us to watch them for an entire evening in the triple rôle of artists, dancers and choreographers ? The usual pretext is ample opportunity to display personality, and full freedom for self-expression. Actually the true reason is, that the performer is not sufficiently good to appear with any company, and is aching to be seen, if only by her family and friends—a form of exhibitionism—so that we have a whole class of " inspiration " dancers, expressionist dancers and exotics, whom Nijinsky so happily labelled " mushroom " dancers. Isadora Duncan is their goddess, but they have not understood her, for Isadora alone was the great exception. Even in her case one cannot help feeling that, had she possessed a background of orthodox technical training, we should never have seen the pathetic spectacle of a prematurely aged woman, unable to control her body, forcing an inspiration that she could no longer completely command. In her prime, her art and her message shone through all these self-imposed handicaps.

The Sakharoffs, most uncharacteristic of Russian dancers, belong to an opposite school, the costume school, the triumph of *la haute couture*. With them everything has become so stylised, so mannequin-like, that nothing human is left. When they enter, one asks oneself, Which of the two is Clotilde ? There is no male dancer, so complete is the illusion of those Parisian carnival dolls. A Botticellesque costume and a few poses are not enough to make a dance. For such dancers a knowledge of art is a positive danger, because it is apparently so nice and easy to translate art into the artistic. I have the illusion that one morning at breakfast Alexandre says to Clotilde, "My dear, I saw the most *divine* material at Schiaparelli's this morning, Madonna blue, and an enchanting picture in the Louvre, with just the same colour; let's make a dance round them." And that Clotilde replies : " That *will* be jolly. Let's."

Alanova, too, with all her training and experience, has succumbed to the temptations of easy success, and become the complete *Elizabeth Arden* dancer. Her true place is with a company, where she can shine, as she has done in the past.

Pretty, devilish pretty, all this. No one could ever have accused Isadora of that. She was a statue carved by a master, and not a finicky Parisian doll, or even a Pompeian fresco. When the end came, she was still a statue, magnificent if weathered and broken.

There is another type of concert performer, whose aim is, through the medium of gesture and movement, to convey a series of character sketches and impressions, ranging from the beautiful to the grotesque. This type of dancer does not lay claim to any pretensions of regenerating the dance, but of entertaining her public. As with all dancers, the measure of her success depends on the technical means at her disposal, and what she actually has to express. Her task is less difficult than that of the classical dancer, because she is aided by the literary idea, and is not expected to show us pure dancing.

While in New York, I had an interesting conversation with Maurice Goldberg, amazing photographer of dancers and keen *balletomane*, on the technique of the solo dancer. He has advanced the theory, after many photographic investigations, that the success of the solo dancer depends on kino-æsthetic memory, the ability in an executant to feel exactly the last position she was in, and to take up the new one in complete harmony with it. The audience, he claims, can sense this without being able to express it. The solo dancer must compensate for the deficiency of standing alone by making out of herself a complete harmonious company. I have seen his photographic results. He takes the first pose; then, still with the same plate, tells the dancer to move, and to touch with the tips of her fingers, where her outstretched arms have been, and so on till a complete frieze has been made by one woman. The results of this memory test are amazing. In some cases it is so accurate that it is difficult to imagine that one person has made the intricate pattern, just by dancing with herself. I have no doubt at all that it is the possession of this gift that explains so many questions of failure or success, that makes one performance seem thin, while the other fills the entire stage.

By far the finest dancer-*diseuse* I have seen is the American, Agnes de Mille, niece of Cecil B. I believe that she has been greatly handicapped by her relationship to that illustrious man. Agnes is not a wealthy *dilettante*, who felt that she had to practise some art or other, but a very thorough and hard-working professional, whose inspiration and technique are of a very high order. She could step straight into a ballet company to-day, and find herself fully competent. In that respect she is unique. De Mille has understood her medium, and expresses herself completely in movement, so that all programme notes are unnecessary ; and all the time she dances. Her range is wide, from the brutal realism of *The Ouled Naïl*, the satire of *The Audition*, to the white ecstasy of *Hymn*. Her two Degas sketches, fatally easy pitfalls for the merely artistic, show an extraordinary assimilation of material. The one is the painter, the other the sculptor, and they are not just period pieces with a snatched pose or so; they are pure Degas throughout. Gifted with a mobile and expressive face, she usually resists the temptation to gain easy applause by clowning. *The Burghermaster's Bransle* is genuine mime of a very high order. De Mille is really important, not just another wordless Ruth Draper.

Angna Enters, another American, an exceedingly sensitive artist, sketches lightly in sanguine, where Agnes paints and sculpts. She has ideas and taste, but her limitations as a dancer are soon revealed and make for monotony, so that one misses the medium of speech. She has one little masterpiece of pantomime, a flirtatious woman in the park during church parade, and that I could willingly see many times.

We have one such dancer in England, Penelope Spencer, who has also failed to reach the summits, only through a lack of technique. She is definitely an artist, but her inspiration is more developed than her muscles. She is beautifully built, and it is a pleasure to watch her in that little masterpiece *Laideronette* (from Ravel's *Ma Mère L'Oie*), where she portrays a timid Javanese taking a bathe by moonlight. This is far more effective than her famous *Funeral March on the Death of a Rich Aunt*, that depends so much on a joke and a mask, excellent though they are.

Then there is the long list of " exotics," whose work it is so difficult for us to judge, through lack of standards : Uday Shankar, a Hindu Nijinsky in one rôle, beautiful but limited ; Nyota Inyoka, who has borrowed so much from the West that one can judge her by our ideals, and still find her exquisite, again within limits; and, finest of all, Raden Mas Jodjana, Javanese with a tradition and a religion of movement that were old and formalised when ballet was still undreamed of. All these are justified, through necessity, in adopting a form that is definitely untheatrical and destructive to all illusion—curtains, piano interludes and long waits.

These things could not long console us for ballet, that contains the possibility of everything. The finest theatrical Spanish dancers I have seen are Karsavina and Massine ; the finest light comedy jazz, Irina Baronova in *Plage*; the finest character mime, Cecchetti in *La Boutique Fantasque* ; dramatic mime in recent times, Toumanova in *Cotillon*, and Baronova in *Presages* ; the finest tragedy of all, Nijinsky in *Petrouchka*; and there is all the rest they have to give so lavishly. It was hard to have to wait, snatch feverishly at substitutes, and to praise them exaggeratedly at times, because one wanted so hard to believe.

We heard with pleasure that Vera Nemchinova was established with Obouhoff, Zvereff and a large company in Kovno, Lithuania. Happy country where a large proportion of the small budget is devoted to a first-class theatre, opera and ballet. There she dances *Lac des Cygnes*, *Raimonda* and *Giselle*. Since, I have only seen her work in Paris, away from the ideal surroundings, but I have seen a new Nemchinova. Before, she had been cold and remote, a hardworking, almost flawless machine, who dazzled us in such a carefully created rôle as in *Les Biches*. Now she is a deeply moving Sylphide, a personality as well as a dancer, and yet her dancing has still further improved ; she has gained an elevation that allows her to do thirty-six consecutive *entrechats six* ! Disgusting feat in a machine, glorious in an artist. It would be ungracious to call Kovno a backwater, but so is London to the artist who remains there. People remembered and discussed the old Nemchinova ; they must see the new one. At that time the news of her triumphs, and of what Kovno could accomplish, was no consolation to us, who were anxiously waiting for something to happen a little nearer home.

The English experiment had been definitely worth while. It was honest. It had kept together the nucleus of an enthusiastic public, had given opportunities to young dancers to perform serious work, and so provided a stimulus to the dancing schools and organisations, from whom come the expert section of the public, the old guard, who cheer enthusiastically from pit and gallery. It had done more than that, it had shown works that could really be classed as choregraphy, instead of the usual depressing " dances arranged by Miss X," or the exceptionally daring and exotic " Madame X." But, in spite of all our enthusiasm, we realised that so far all this was of local importance, a pleasant, colourful backwater, apart from the main stream of ballet tradition. Ballet had settled in France, Italy and Russia. In England it was welcome, understood, but not yet indigenous. There could be no question of an English school, with characteristics that become distinguishing virtues.

Strangely enough, while London was a hum of ballet activity, so much so that the late André Levinson, writing in the Paris *Comœdia*, could acclaim it as the ballet centre of the world, his own Paris, of late always completely indifferent to the finer points of dancing or anything that was not a startling novelty, was preparing dancers, inspiring choregraphers, painters and musicians, to take up the great tradition, where Diaghileff had left off. Whether Paris is vitally interested or not, France has again and again reaped the reward of her hospitality to foreign emigrations, by keeping unchallenged her supremacy in the plastic arts. Jongkind, Van Gogh, Picasso, Larionov, and the many

Russians assimilated into Parisian life, have given to French art, without swamping it, a fresh point of view, and a new vitality. Ballet is a true synthesis of the arts, and the French, above all nations, have never kept their arts in watertight compartments.[1] Their poets have been in the vanguard of plastic development, sympathetic to, and often practising, another art, as in the case of Victor Hugo and Baudelaire; their authors of repute are critics and fervent collectors of pictures; both collaborate with the musicians in opera, ballet and now the films. Chaplin inaugurates a style, René Clair makes it into a school. So that it would not be surprising to see France, within very few years, gain complete fiim superiority, if the financiers will forget their superstitions about the box-office, and give the artists a free hand. Already Jean Cocteau, poet, artist, inspirer of ballet, has made one important experiment. It is not French originality that counts, but this whole conception of parallelism in the arts. Every period of French art underlines this. In the great romantic movement, Delacroix, Berlioz and Hugo are making the same discoveries at the same time, and, up to a certain point, from English sources: Constable, Bonnington, Walter Scott, the rediscovery of Shakespeare. It is only with such a parallel outlook that ballet can achieve its full expression. France has never in modern times provided dancers of genius; England has done so once, and can do so again, but in England the dancers are not a part of the general artistic activity. They remain in the atmosphere of the classroom, and are thought of mainly in terms of the light musical show. In France perhaps this interchange of ideas between artists in different media takes place in the café.

[1] Thank God for the Sitwell family and Lord Berners ! They are the great exception to everything I have written about the narrow views of English artists. Their rôle has already been a great one.—A. L. H.

H

Impressionism, the *fauve*, cubist and *surréaliste* movements in literature, painting and music, are born round a table, laden with bock, liqueurs and wine. No club can ever replace the informal, free and easy interchange of ideas that takes place in the café. Certainly no committee of artists, solemnly convened to meet, complete with secretary and minutes, can ever fuse the various artistic elements. In England, while this is so, we shall continue to provide the raw material for fine artists; occasionally one, such as Sokolova, will escape into the main stream; but it is always others who will provide the ideas. The very essence of ballet, that is of more than local importance, is a permanent touring company with its roots in Paris.

The *balletomane* began to come to life in the season of 1933 with the announcement of four visiting companies : Ballets Jooss, Ballets 1933, Serge Lifar and Ballets Russes de Monte Carlo, each one with its different æsthetic. Discussion and rivalry would take place once again, and that, both between companies and within a company, means life and creation. There was only the fear that, with such box-office competition, they would all fail, and failure meant another long wait, the gradual fading away of the small public, and the rise of " mushroom dancers " and exotics, with hundreds of English girls waiting desolately at the *barre* with no potential artistic home. It was a question of an immediate decision as to which company was in the true line of succession. When the choice came, the public had no difficulty at all in deciding.

The first arrivals, and fortunately for them, were the Ballets Jooss, fresh from a victory in a choregraphic competition organised in Paris by the Archives Internationales de la Danse. They made an undoubted success of the kind where nearly everyone spoke well of them, very well, and then stayed away. I find it difficult to write of them, or even to think of them yet, as a fully established ballet company. They have still to prove themselves. They are the creators of one successful work, *The Green Table*, a political satire, that is effective, up to a point, the first time that it is seen, and that varies from an original angle of thought, more literary than plastic, to a complete banality, that is not saved by richness and beauty of movement or execution. In the first tableau, where the performers are hampered by dress clothes and masks, they succeed admirably. These artificial limitations suit their style by concealing short-comings, and the effect is marvellous theatre. Later in the action one has the vivid impression that an extra medium, that of poetry, is missing. *Le Théâtre des Quinze* had expressed the same thing so completely and powerfully in André Obey's *Bataille de la Marne*. They have created an entirely new medium, a successful marriage between ballet and the theatre, by resorting to the old method of writing the play for the actors actually in the theatre, under the guidance of a producer-choreographer of genius. In *Noë*, *Lucrèce*, *Don Juan*, and especially *La Loire*, they have made admirable use of this near-ballet technique, that calls for the added element of declamation. Saint Denis, Marie-Hélène Dasté, inspired designer of costumes and magnificent actress, and André Obey have found the perfect Diaghileff method of collaboration, without a gap between the media. There are moments of *La Loire*, where the river is shown in flood, that are pure ballet at its finest, but, because of the limitations of the movement, they never make the mistake of believing that it is enough in itself. By resorting to art and artifice, they have produced the most realistic drama of war that I have seen.

In their mechanics, the Ballets Jooss are a compromise

between ballet and the German school, but nearer to ballet. This compromise leaves them weak to express vital ideas, and they so clearly have ideas. Also it places an immense onus on the choregrapher never to be able to allow an interval between ideas, since the dance itself cannot hold the audience. This well-disciplined troupe is like a picture that contains a vast expanse of admirably painted background with no clear focal point of interest. There is none of the glamour of outstanding personality. Usually, after nightly visits to the ballet, I recognise each member of the *corps de ballet* as an individual artist with something of her own to express. Here names meant nothing. It is not a question of stars, that are created film fashion with an eye on the box-office, but of individuals that are picked out by the public because of their work. In ballet, with the exception of Anna Pavlova, the public has never been attracted or kept away by a name, but by names, and the choregrapher has been the main attraction. The true ballet company solves the whole " star system " controversy in an admirably logical fashion. It is led by dancers who, because of their attributes, are better qualified to be in the foreground, but it contains a *corps de ballet*, any member of which is able technically to assume a leading rôle at a moment's notice. With Jooss all are good, but none outstanding. The preliminary ballets are but a prelude to the main attraction, *The Green Table*, so far their whole *raison d'être*. *The Vienna Waltzes* can be dismissed as " charming." Massine, with the same material in *Le Beau Danube*, has created a work that has already survived for ten years, and that is a fine vehicle for his own genius as a dancer and for such artists as Danilova, Riabouchinska, Baronova and Lichine, whom it helped to create. In this lies the true difference between the ballet proper, and the group of dancers. In an interview, Jooss outlined certain principles for his method of working, but all of them principles that had been discovered and worked upon by Fokine and his successors, who were using material that enabled them to be exploited to the full. His main point was that mime did not exist apart from dancing and that every portion of the body should be expressive. To-day that is a truism.

I believe that Jooss has the makings of an important choregrapher, but only after additional study in the classroom with some Maryinsky teacher, who has a rich repertoire of *enchaînements*. At present he is like a pianist deliberately limiting himself to one hand, but playing without doubt brilliantly, in spite of his self-imposed handicap.

TILLY LOSCH AND LES BALLETS 1933

This first taste of ballet left us more eager than ever to welcome the next arrivals. Here, there would be less of a surprise. Balanchine, Derain and Milhaud had proved themselves, in the great days.

In its origin *Les Ballets 1933* was a fragment of the Monte Carlo Ballet, the result of one of those quarrels unfortunately possible at any moment in the dancing world.

Diaghileff had always foreseen this, and, rather than risk the wreck of his enterprise, had kept such a hold on his company that it was an impossibility. Anyone whom he suspected of such ambitions would be speedily thrust into the background. He was as expert at unmaking reputations as at making them. On one occasion a secession on a very large scale nearly occurred, when the majority of his company tried to fix up an engagement without him. He waited till their plans were well advanced, then let them know that all the music copyrights were in his possession. The revolt promptly ended. There is never room for more than one such company at a time, and the individual shines only as one of its members. The best proof is the tragic case of Nijinsky, inside the ballet a popular hero, but afterwards alone, pathetic and homeless. I imagine that dancers will never learn this, and it is a constant threat to any organisation, when things are going too well. If the head of a company is called a slave-driver and plays one element against the other, he has all my sympathy. He is protecting the interests of everyone, as well as his own.

This quarrel between de Basil and Balanchine must have been a bitter one, for there was a constant drifting of dancers from one company to the other, and for a time it was difficult, without the very latest news, to know where anyone belonged. At mid-day one of the artists could not tell me where she was going to dance that night ! What an opportunity too for the mothers to play one manager against the other, for rôles and money.[1] To increase the bitterness, Balanchine played in Paris at the same time as de Basil, and reached London first, with a clear field and a hungry public.

Les Ballets 1933! A name that did not imply any permanence or stability, the first presage of misfortune ; and if it had only been 1933 ! A real title to attract the snob, the amateur of the *dernier cri*, with the brightest, newest and *funniest* artists. This venture was doomed from the first, without any competition even, by the nature of its composition. Born of a quarrel, it was called into being by Edward James, a young Englishman of taste, culture and wealth, but with absolutely no experience, and most

---

[1] The order is significant ; the dancer always places the rôle before the money ; it is always, " What am I going to dance ? " first.—A. L. H.

certainly not born to command, as an offering to his wife, a Viennese dancer, who had never worked with Russians. There was a remarkable but still inexperienced child prodigy, and a thin *corps de ballet*, the whole to be set into motion by a highly sophisticated choreographer, who, more than anyone, needed ideal conditions under which to work.

Tilly Losch, the reason for the whole venture, is an artist of taste, talent, beauty and positive personality, whom I have always greatly admired in her own sphere. I was perhaps the first, in our little world, to acclaim her, and have always had a strong belief in her future. An early success in a small Gothic *divertissement* in a Cochran revue, an admirable number within its limitations, led her to forsake ballet half-heartedly for a Gothic-plastic form of the dance, of her own imagining, whose possibilities of expression are exhausted after a few moments. Her Nun in *The Miracle* was a success, and served to confirm her in that direction. She was beautifully, deeply moving, aided by a physique perfect for the rôle, but there was no question of great miming there. The whole surroundings were a colossal " bluff," that was sufficient to bring her to the fore, and obscure the real talent of such a proved artist as Leonide Massine. In fact, given the requisite physique, it was well within the reach of many, as the understudy, Phyllis Stanley, a gifted and inexperienced pupil of Karsavina's, so rapidly proved. In truth this rôle, like that of the Madonna, is practically fool-proof. The whole subject of Roman Catholic ritual, treated in the direct manner, is quite out of reach of the choreographer, for the reason that it is already so dramatic and moving as a spectacle, traditionally so much older than ballet, that there remains nothing for him to say. The wedding in *Les Noces* was a genuine creation, as Nijinska and Gontcharova,

wiser than Reinhardt, transferred it from the religious
ritual to find the deeper significance that underlay it.
Saint Denis with his *Companie des Quinze* could have made
a masterpiece of this simple legend. It is quite impossible
with such treatment as in *The Miracle* not to achieve something superficially effective, that will not bear close investigation, and I saw it several times with lessening effect.
By this, I do not wish to imply that Tilly Losch is one of
many. At any rate there is no reason at all why she should
be. I remember well, when she first arrived in England,
ravishingly fresh and beautiful, like some young girl just
out of a finishing school, and very full of interesting ideas.
One in particular, that she elaborated for me—the composition of a baroque ballet—still remains an exciting
possibility for a Sitwell to devise. Since this first success, so
rapid and complete, she has taken the line of least resistance, till a technique, grown thin through disuse, has had
to be replaced by dresses, lighting and literary conceits ;
a losing struggle for a choregrapher with something to
express.

The results : *Anna-Anna*, the main attraction and the very
latest novelty. German masquerading as American, just as
Berlin sometimes plays at being New York, with Kurt
Weill, composer of talent, trying to do " Frankie and
Johnnie " all over again in a Louisiana setting, that could
have meant very little to him. The novelty lay in the fact
that Lottie Lenja sang Anna, and Tilly Losch danced
Anna, an expression of dual personality by no means
novel, being the subject of the original *Lac des Cygnes*,
where Odette and Odilia, two aspects of the same person,
were danced by different *ballerinas*. No ballet, no trace of
Balanchine anywhere. The fact that the rôle gave no
opportunity for real dancing, does not mean that it gave

any opportunity for mime, which must have been its whole object. Those would-be erotic movements from the hip, so abused by the plastic dancer and so cheaply effective, become monotonous and meaningless through constant repetition.

And then *Errante*, the story of the wanderings of a lost soul in search of something or other—I have mislaid my programme—with Losch manipulating a gigantic train, show-girl fashion, amidst scenery reminiscent of a " big white sale." She certainly manipulated it very well, never once got caught up in anything or anyone, but then Loie Fuller had done precisely the same thing, twenty, thirty, forty years before; Losch has real talent, and it is 1933 on programme, poster and in fact ! Then, the worst of all, *Waltzes from Beethoven*, with the crudest décor I have ever seen in ballet, the pathetic showing up of a neglected technique by a thin and uninspired *corps de ballet*. Still no trace of Balanchine, who had succeeded with the finest artists of all, who had succeeded for Cochran and Sir Oswald Stoll with a troupe of girls. Twice only he appeared that season, working with congenial material, and two real memories he has left, with *Mozartiana* and *Songes*.

For me the whole point of the season was the first appearance in London of one of the major artists of modern ballet, Tamara Toumanova, a first appearance that was nearly a disaster, for her childish weight hid the true extent of her artistry from the uninitiated. She saved the season from complete artistic collapse, and from the very first performance had a following of applauding, bravoing people, the good old guard.

For years I had read of this Russian child with as much scepticism as when I had been told of little Alice Marks, heightened in the interval through having seen one much boomed and thoroughly mediocre Russian girl. The minute that Toumanova stood on the stage I knew that a great artist had appeared once again, and already I felt a strong personal interest, I feared for her future career. Those few moments of Toumanova were painful. I knew that she did not belong there. I recognised in her the beginnings of a new chapter in the history of the dance. This fourteen-year-old could play with her audiences, make them infinitely sad, and then banish that sadness with a smile, that was all the more effective through being used so sparingly. She could soothe them with a dream, and then whip them into excitement by the thrill of some technical feat.

Two minutes in particular gave a thrill of such pain-pleasure, the real aim of fine ballet ; in *Songes*, the fantastic toy ballet of Derain-Milhaud-Balanchine, where the child, Tamara, already on her points in the dance has to indicate that she is tiptoeing gently, quietly out of the nursery. A subtle effect that is a *tour de force* of balletic acting, and that compelled one from the first to take her seriously.

Mozartiana and *Songes* may survive, in spite of what Balanchine said to me in the wings after the *première*; " I am no longer interested in these works, they already belong to yesterday. Only the classical lives."

The whole season was a repetition in miniature of the Rubinstein adventures, the certain proof that the money that makes possible the grouping together of the leading painters, composers and choreographers, around one person, who is anything less than a Pavlova, cannot create either an artistic or a box-office success. The public is always wiser than managers or critics imagine.

So far the *balletomane* could with the best will in the world— and since the deaths of Diaghileff and Pavlova he had the

best will in the world, and was no longer hypercritical—
return night after night, looking for something worth-while,
and finding it only in those few minutes of Toumanova,
the fine presence of Jasinsky, or in some odd movements of
Losch.

After Toumanova's very first performance, I went to see
her, tumbling headlong up a flight of stairs in my excitement. I told her what I had seen in her dancing. She cried.
I now know that Tamara usually cries when she is happy
(and sometimes when she is sad). She asked eagerly for a
list of her mistakes, and, when I hesitated, herself provided
the answers, promising better next time. At last I had
found someone to whom I could safely entrust a series of
letters I had from Elssler and the great dancers of the
past. She was of their breed and would understand. Of
course she cried again. At that time she was just three
months over fourteen.

Sandwiched in the middle of this unhappy season was
not a ballet, but a concert ensemble centred around the
virtuosity and personality of Serge Lifar : Jooss had been
all background, this was the very opposite. Lifar must
not be judged by these performances, of which an American
critic wrote with some bitterness, " Serge Lifar has done
nothing since the death of Diaghileff than to appear as
best man at the Mdvani-Hutton wedding." This *bon mot*
is less than just, as Lifar's main work has been at the Paris
Opéra, which in spite of its traditions has been of purely
local importance. Lifar is bringing it once again into the
great tradition, a curious position for a young Russian,
follower of the rebel Diaghileff. There his work has earned
the highest approval of André Levinson, greatest of all
ballet critics. In London he showed us a dance so very
near greatness that the failure was all the more evident.

It was his first visit as a great classical dancer, and he revelled in his virtuosity sometimes at the expense of the art, that he had so often proved. He danced like a god, yet shattered the delicate romantic dream of *Le Spectre de la Rose*. Since, I have seen him dance it at the Paris Opéra, where he is sure of his audience, as near perfection as we deserve to see. This time in London it was not the nymphless Faun, strange unsatisfactory experiment, that showed us something new, but *L'Oiseau Bleu* danced with an effortless brilliance that would have delighted Diaghileff, and that crowned Cecchetti's tireless work. Serge Lifar to-day has found himself completely, technically ; only the accident of imagining that that is the end will prevent us from seeing male dancing at its finest. But Diaghileff is dead, Cecchetti is dead, and there is danger.

Unfortunately I have not had an opportunity to study his work as choregrapher. Recently he has outlined to me, in movement, design and description, a new ballet that showed an interesting point of view. I believe in Lifar's ultimate triumph, because of his supple intelligence that has made him a collector and connoisseur of pictures, and has led him to the best in poetry and music. He is a fine product of Diaghileff's training, but he has had to fend for himself before his education was complete.

1933. A sharpened appetite ; the meal is yet to come.

CHAPTER XII

HOME AGAIN—LES BALLETS RUSSES
DE MONTE CARLO

TAMARA TOUMANOVA AND IRINA BARONOVA

" Ah, Tamara, que vous êtes brillante,
Mais qu'Irène, grands dieux, est ravissante,
Que vos pas sont légers, et que les siens sont doux.
Elle est inimitable, et vous toujours nouvelle.
Les nymphes sautent comme vous
Et les graces dansent comme elle."

VOLTAIRE on Camargo and Sallé, up to date

ON JULY 4TH came the long awaited *première* of
the Ballets Russes de Monte Carlo at the Alhambra, home of the greatest memory of all, *The
Sleeping Princess*.[1] They were the last of the four invaders,
and our final chance. Already well known on the Continent,
they were called the *Babies' Ballet*, the principals being anywhere between thirteen and seventeen years in age. Little
Tamara Toumanova, one of the original members, and
now in the rival show at the Savoy, had already taught us
how little extreme youth meant as a handicap, and how
much as a help, but we could take nothing for granted.
They had to convince us here in London, and, since Diaghileff, we had given our allegiance to no company, even if
we had admired and applauded individuals.

Les Sylphides, first ballet and greatest test, challenging
comparisons, awaking memories. It had been murdered for
so many years now, that one despaired of ever seeing it

[1] Thank you, Sir Oswald Stoll, for two such first nights.—A. L. H.

again. I was only conscious of two things, through the jarring new orchestration that cut into the dream, like pain through morphia ; Danilova at the very top of her form, a new young dancer, and the incredible lightness, charm and racehorse aristocracy of Tatiana Riabouchinska, whom I had seen as a child two years before in *La Chauve Souris*, with no impression at all. Dolin, too, was back in his right place, the *danseur noble*. Nothing had altered ; Fokine's masterpiece still hurt with its beauty. Already I was sad at the thought that the season must come to an end, and was making vague plans to follow them, anywhere, everywhere.

Then *Présages*, and the revelation that was Irina Baronova.

So God in His wisdom, through Olga Preobrajenska, had made two of them ; Irina and Tamara, each of whom would dance the better, for the rest of her life, through the very knowledge that the other existed, rivals who met at some points and in some rôles, yet each dissimilar and incomparable. I could foresee the fierce partisanship ; Taglioni and Elssler, Pavlova and Karsavina, all over again. Perhaps I too had already taken sides ; but, now that I know the minute details that go to the making of each of their rôles, I can see that preference becomes a matter of temperament. Tamara has a dramatic fire and a dominating personality that at its worst turns into over-acting, and a too keen awareness of the public; Irina a serenity and reserve that may mean a loss of contact. Tamara is grave, tragic and dark, Irina gay and fair ; between them they divide the emotions, with each one supple enough to challenge the other on her own *terrain*. Theirs are the big names in ballet to-day.

Something of all this flashed through my mind a few

moments after Baronova's unforgettable entrance with Lichine, so beautifully, poetically tender, the finest interpretation of young love that I have seen on the stage.

Finally *Le Beau Danube* ; Leonide Massine with his contrasting partners, Riabouchinska light, delicate, a true maiden, whom the spectre of the rose might visit, and Danilova, the beautiful shrew, balletically coarse ; and Baronova again, a subtle mime this time, in the light, almost insignificant rôle of the midinette, which she has made memorable. In it she was the very synthesis of the *soubrette*, a vast jump from the destiny-haunted maiden of *Présages*. No contrast could have shown her to greater advantage. She was a part of the music, expressing every shade in face and body.

There was enough that night to set one's head in a whirl ; Massine choregrapher, Massine dancer, the glorious reappearance of Danilova, Woizikovski and Dolin, Nina Verchinina, by herself the complete answer to the Central European school, the bounding fiery Lichine, triumphant Hero of *Présages*, and the others, but to me, as to so many, this night was Baronova's, the second great revelation in one month of the fact that the Maryinsky principle was alive and situate in Paris. Great dancers, who were artists too, could still be formed. Both girls had their faults. I was never blind to them, but they were superficial and could be remedied.

This was a greater surprise than the first Diaghileff visit, and because of that a greater triumph too, for it was Diaghileff who had formed our tastes, taught us all the finer points, and the great fact that he himself so clearly realised : memory magnifies impressions of the past.[1]

[1] When the question of a revival of *Scheherazade* was mentioned to him, he said, " It would have to be with brighter colours. Memory has made it all seem very vivid ; to-day those same colours would seem drab."—A. L. H.

People arrived at the Alhambra on the defensive—" We shall never see another X again," " I wish, dear, that you could have seen Y in *Les Sylphides*; nothing can ever be the same." In spite of the fact that X and Y would have been the first to disagree with these opinions, the new company had to struggle against an exaggerated sentimental memory. X and Y were young then, and so were their beholders; income tax was a shilling in the pound, and life was worth living—for the few. When the curtain went down that night no one said anything of the sort. It was all forgotten. They applauded without reserve—not the smart, frightened-to-split-new-kid-gloves sort of thing, but the wholehearted enthusiasm of people who are supposed to take their pleasures quietly and sadly. The ground was unprepared, most of the names quite unknown, and the material difficulties had been enormous. Yet it was no feat of divination on the part of the audience, so obvious and abundant were the merits. At last the growing superstition that the dancer was only in her prime after thirty had gone for ever. Already that night they were no longer *de Monte Carlo*, but *Les Ballets Russes tout court*. They now had the full allegiance of the faithful old public, so constantly disappointed, and of a larger new public of their own.

" Bravo—bravo—*bis*—*bis*—hurrah ! " Stamp—stamp—stamp. " Speech ! Speech ! " . . .

De Basil came towards me smiling, and slapped me on the back.

" Well, have I learned now ? You wouldn't say rotten any more ? But I shall go on learning. This will be better soon, much better. There are still many mistakes."

He resumed an argument of years ago. I had only met him once before in an interval at the Lyceum after his first night of ballet, during the Russian Opera season.

" Well, and what do you think of it ? "

" Rotten," I told him, " we can do much better than that in England."

" Perhaps," he beamed at me. " Perhaps. I have only just begun. But I will learn, certainly I will learn. We shall see—you will see. Good-bye."

I was as impressed by his long memory as by the definite manner in which he had got the better of me in this long-delayed discussion.

Colonel de Basil is a remarkable man, as his achievement after the failure of so many others clearly proves, but I very much doubt whether anyone will ever give him full credit. (The memory of Diaghileff will prevent that.) He will not mind in the slightest, but just go on smiling, learning and showing concrete results.

He has in no sense modelled himself on Diaghileff or attempted the comparison. He has taste, but none of the vast erudition of his predecessor. How then does this many times war-wounded Cossack come to be involved in ballet at all, and what is his particular contribution ? De Basil is a man of action, and a keen business man, whose great interest lies in the handling of people, difficult people. Where Diaghileff maintained discipline through aloofness and fear, de Basil seems to court trouble through an intimacy with his company, and then to avoid it at the very last moment. He smiles, never raises his voice and generally gets his own way. He is popular or unpopular in the company at any given moment as he himself wills. I have seen a dancer come in to him furious, only to come out again and tell me how wrong she was in judging him, and how sympathetically he spoke to her—an opinion she kept, until she had had a little conversation with her mother. His problems are endless in a company whose leading dancers are school-children, and spoiled ones at times, backed up by their querulous mothers, ever on the look-out for trouble. He is expert at gaining results from these jealousies, by opposing one to the other. No one could have kept the company alive by any other method. For a year before the London triumph there was a terrible struggle for existence ; one night stands in Holland and Belgium, where only the generosity of a friend, in lending motor coaches for the journeys, made the venture possible. It speaks a great deal for the dancers that under such financial conditions they did not desert him for better-paid engagements, but it is essentially a tribute to his manner of handling them. I can well imagine him at work, betraying no excitement at all : " All right, of course you must go if you are dissatisfied. In any case X dances your rôles more brilliantly, so that everyone will be satisfied. You, with five times the salary, X with the rôles, and myself and the public with her success." And then a phrase that I have heard him repeat so often; " But come and see us. I like you personally very much, and such a business disagreement cannot be allowed to interfere in personal matters."

No one of any consequence left, and now they can be grateful to him. One story that I heard in the company may or may not be true ; I hope that it is. One of the male dancers flatly refused to take on a rôle as being too unimportant and so beneath his dignity. De Basil left him alone, but summoned his wife, whom he had recently married. " It is a great pity that you should put such exaggerated ideas into his head. Now on account of that I shall have to lose a very excellent dancer. His career will be ruined, and it will all be your fault."

That same evening the young man performed, and nothing more was said about it.

Undoubtedly de Basil is a master psychologist, but such moves take time, and this is only one phase of his work ; there is all the business to be done, and also the reactions of the public to be gauged.

De Basil has had many important decisions to make, and each time any hesitation or compromise would have wrecked the affair. He is a clear thinker of immense courage. The first was when he turned his activities from opera and occasional ballet, to ballet alone. From that very day the fortunes of the opera declined. Next came the question of the composition of that ballet. He immediately decided on a new young company under the guidance of experts. During the *pourparlers* with Monte Carlo they naturally wished for well-known names and established favourites. He temporised, and started the season, saying that the well-known dancers would join them later. By that time, as he foresaw, his unknowns had established themselves, and the question of the others was not even raised. With certain exceptions, from the very first he was opposed to mixing the old and the new, which would have involved so many cruel comparisons in both directions. Then during the difficult year came a brilliant offer from London, better financially than the one that he later accepted. He refused it, fortunately for our Camargo season, realising that his company was not yet fit for our critical audiences, and remembering, perhaps, " We can do better in England," and his reply.

At last, when success was really his, after nearly four months at the Alhambra, he decided to risk all on a large expenditure in the final week—a new ballet, *Choreartium*. " I must end," he told me, " on a new note that will prepare next year, and leave people with a memory. Already I have stayed the whole hot summer against all advice and

have succeeded. Now people will remember the ballet
that came for three weeks and stayed four months."

Those were big decisions, and they reveal a big man. So
far he has concentrated on dancing rather than the embellishments. Soon he will learn still more, and, with a rapidly
improving company, we shall have the annual treat of
ballet, perfect in all its details, music and décor, together
with dancing. Unlike Diaghileff, he may not directly inspire
the artists, but he can use them so that they give of their
very best. His work may be carried on quietly, but, as the
"non-dancing" member of his company, I know that his
influence is to be felt everywhere.

I. THE CHOREGRAPHY

The company first started around the work and personality of Balanchine, always ready to search for new talent,
and with him lies the credit of discovering Baronova and
Toumanova in Preobrajenska's studio.

Balanchine in all his work has a dual outlook that produces remarkable results, so long as he is interested. More
than anyone he requires the inspiration of fine material.
He is enamoured of classicism, and at the same time pas-
sionately interested in contemporary life and thought, so
that he gives to his work a twist that attempts to reconcile
the two. He is a poet, and it is fantasy that appeals to him,
the curious results that modern thought can give, when
dressed in the garb of what has gone before. His *Concurrence* is a dream, and not a fairy-tale ; it is a commentary
on life, in which the incongruous happens in the most
logical sequence, all bound together by the dreamlike
presence of the young girl, who, Alice-like, fits so very
logically into the life of the ballet, if not into the printed
synopsis of the humorous little story. The same is the case in

Cotillon, the first creation of the Ballets Russes, and Balanchine's masterpiece.

In the conventional setting of a ball, amidst dance and
gaiety, there is the ominous feeling that something is hap-
pening involving the fate of all the revellers, and that they
are powerless to understand or to intervene. Like a dream,
when transcribed on paper it is vague, while during the
dreaming all seems so straightforward, and afterwards in
the memory it leaves a vague disturbing impression. When
the curtain goes down on the light-hearted fun of the
Cotillon, one asks oneself, Has it all happened? What
exactly has happened?

These ballets show the true Balanchine. In them he has
created something permanent, instead of giving rein to the
facile and witty diversion of one season, his great self-
confessed temptation, and so often his fault.

From the dancing point of view, Balanchine's distortions,
typified in such a work as *Mozartiana*, bear the same relationship to classicism as new wine does to old ; an analogy
that can even be followed up quite closely. The new wine
is made of the same grape, is exhilarating, rapidly intoxicat-
ing, but does not produce the full satisfying effect. Balanchine has been greatly copied by young choreographers,
and it is a mistake. He is not essentially the *chef d'école*. His
vision is too intensely personal for that, and his movements
are an interpretation of that vision and not part of some
system that can be learned. Balanchine without doubt
possesses a brilliant mind together with a rare choregraphic
talent, but of the hit-or-miss variety. If, and when, he fails,
he does not produce a sound and uninspired school-piece,
but something that is complex to dance in, and tortuous
to follow, but that has a strong justification in his own
mind, and almost certainly musical truth. In the past I

imagined that he was insincere; now I know that that has
never been the case. When he is complex and appears to
exaggerate, it is on the contrary his sincerity in following
through a conviction. His whole method of creation
depends on a spontaneous inspiration at the very start,
without which it is no good continuing. With all his experience he has remained unsettled, still the revolutionary,
not always quite sure what cause he is supporting.

With Balanchine's departure Massine was the ideal man
to lead and mould the young company. It is for them that
he has done much of his finest work, and they bear un-
mistakably the imprint of his personality. Were I writing
of Massine a little time ago I would have referred to his
past achievements, and then have mentioned a decided
falling off in inspiration, a feverish hunting after sensa-
tionalism. His exaggerated movement, that, as in the later
Raphael, so often destroyed the unity of a composition,
gave to his work a lack of that repose that every great work
must show. It developed into that *tic* that his imitators
have seized upon. All the praise would have belonged to
the past, his early years. After his Roxy interlude I regarded
him as finished, a brilliant man trying to make up for his
brilliance by earning a comfortable pittance before retiring.
In fact; even in dealing with his ballet achievements, in
a past work I have done him less than justice. I would not
now acclaim *Les Matelots* as a masterpiece; to do that would
be to lose sight of the essential Massine who created *Le
Chapeau Tricorne*. It is an agreeable novelty that has worn
remarkably well, but it is worth far more than I originally
found, when to my shame I accused him of *épatisme*. I could
not know how much he was wishing to escape from the
current artistic formulæ, waiting patiently for time and
opportunity. My criticism at times must have echoed his

thoughts. Then, thinking of his best, I called him a fine choreographer of unusual intelligence; to-day I know him to be an inspired leader.

There are three well-defined Massines : the satiric, the period and the symphonic. *Le Beau Danube* is pure period. Here the creator of the highly sophisticated *Jeux d'Enfants* is not afraid of sentimentality, and succeeds admirably on that account. He underlines it and treats it quite frankly as something artificial. By his own dancing in it he sets the whole tone. It is a period piece, as is *Scuola di Ballo*, which is in such perfect harmony with the music and thought of the time. Neither is *pastiche*. They are original creations in the correct atmosphere, a gift that the translator of Goldoni and Calderon possesses to an unusual degree. He never makes the common mistake of taking his poses direct from pictures, but conceives the action as a whole in the first place. These two ballets are immense favourites with the company, so natural are they to dance, and to dance with the maximum of effect. *Jeux d'Enfants* is the first truly *surréaliste* ballet, the expression of a former theme, *La Boutique Fantasque*, which was treated in a more direct and conventional manner. Once again, for the hundredth time, toys come to life, not as they actually appear, but as they seem to the subconscious in the little girl.

In all these different works, with their varying moods and intentions, there is invention and richness, but no forcing of effects and not the slightest taint of eccentricity. Moreover, the dancer is left with a latitude of interpretation that is rare in contemporary ballet, so that when the rôles are taken by different dancers the work as a whole does not suffer. That is a sign of their essential classical foundation and their permanence.

The true greatness of Massine lies in his very latest phase, the choregraphic translation of symphonic works. *Les Présages* to Tchaikovsky's Fifth Symphony is the first step. The music is still close to conventional ballet music, and suggests a definite programme, so that it is possible to conceive of a theme—destiny and the final triumph of the individual—and to co-ordinate the development of that theme logically with the development of the music. Choregraphically the weakest portion, the third, coincides with the weakest in the music, but throughout, the two are so close together that it seems possible to see the music and to hear the dancers. The Central Europeans have aimed at just such expressive mass movement drama. Massine has utilised the classical training to arrive at a result that is technically complex, theatrically effective and yet that is simple in the grand manner. The German school goes after mass movement, for the simple reason that it cannot develop the *soliste*, or that, when it does, she is merely a concert dancer, incapable of being inserted into a complicated *ensemble*. Here is a work with some of the most effective mass movement I have ever seen on the stage, because that mass is composed of individuals, who are treated as such at the same time, and, in addition, the ballet is enriched by five solo dancers of the front rank. Stamping, gesticulating machine-emulating groups grow wearisome in a very short time however impressive on the rise of the curtain. In conception the rôle of Fate is as banal as Death in *The Green Table*, with the difference that the movements are varied and enjoyable in themselves apart from the conception. For into this classicism has been imported and skilfully woven a whole fresh field of dancing ; the alliance between Duncan and classicism in the first movement, and the tribal dance of natives, at the

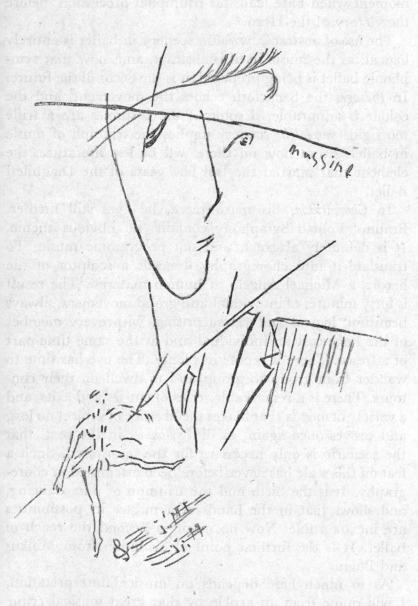

moment when Fate leads his triumphal procession, before
the victory of the Hero.

The use of abstract, *surréaliste* scenery in ballet is entirely
logical, as the music itself is abstract, and, now that symphonic ballet is being prepared, it is the décor of the future.
In *Présages* the backcloth echoes the movement, and the
colour is admirable, if some of the costumes are a trifle
too rigid. *Surréaliste* scenery implies the triumph of music
in ballet. From now on there will be less literature, the
element that marred the last few years of the Diaghileff
Ballet.

In *Choreartium*, his masterpiece, he goes still further.
Brahms' Fourth Symphony contains no obvious theme.
It is definitely abstract, and not programme music. To
translate it into choregraphy it needs a sculptor of the
heroic, a Michael Angelo in human material. The result
is forty minutes of individual and group movement, always
beautiful, logical and yet surprising, with every member
of the huge cast an individual and at the same time part
of a fresco. There is repose in plenty. The eye has time to
wander from group to group and to dwell on their con-
tours. There is a remarkable series of entries and exits, and
a variety of moods that makes the absence of subject no loss,
and proves once again, as did *Sylphides* in the past, that
the scenario is only necessary for the uninspired. Such a
feat on this scale has never before been attempted in choregraphy. It is the birth and the triumph of pure dancing,
and shows that in the hands of a master its possibilities
are inexhaustible. Now no music is beyond the reach of
ballet. It is the furthest point of evolution from Minkus
and Pugni.

As so much here depends on musical interpretation,
I will quote from an article by that great musical critic

Ernest Newman.[1] He is in no sense a *balletomane*, and was not present, as I was, to see the latest Massine, but to hold a watching brief for Brahms :

"Massine showed the common sense we might have expected of him when he put aside all thought of reading a story into Brahms' symphony and decided to approach it as music pure and simple. . . . If music is to be ruled out from ballet when it is ' pure ' music, what justification is there for *Les Sylphides*, for example? There is no more programme in Chopin's music than there is in Brahms' ; yet the enduring success of *Les Sylphides* proves that choregraphic figures can be devised that are felt to be not in the least alien to the spirit and the build of this music. We are bound to grant, I think, that there is nothing *a priori* incongruous in the mating of ' pure ' music, whether that of Brahms or of any other composer, with the lines and masses and movements of the ballet. . . . The only question is to what extent the choregrapher has succeeded."

After an interesting discussion on nationality, in which he justifies Massine for a non-German interpretation, he goes on to say :

"What has Massine done with the remainder of the symphony ? Here I can only wonder at the lack of imagination that prevents some people from seeing the points of genius with which Massine's choregraphic score, so to call it, positively bristles. There can, of course, be no question of a translation of the ' meaning ' of this music as a whole into terms of another art : this kind

[1] *Sunday Times*, October 29th, 1933.

of music is just itself, the expression of something to which there is no real equivalent in any other art. But if there is no equivalent, surely there can be parallelisms ; surely certain elements in the musical design, certain gestures of the music, certain softenings and hardenings of the colours, can be suggested quite well in the more objective medium. I found myself profoundly interested in watching these correspondences, many of which gave me a fresh respect for Massine's genius. Unfortunately, as I have remarked before in a similar connection, there is no way of making these correspondences clear to the reader without quoting the musical passages in question side by side with photographs of the particular moments of the ballet with which they are associated. But how any musical listener in the audience who knows the Brahms score and has any imagination at all could fail to perceive these extraordinary parallelisms I confess myself unable to understand.

" The opening entry of these two figures for instance, with their curious gliding, undulating motion, seemed to me as perfect a translation into visible motion of the well-known dip and rise of the first phrase in the violins as could possibly be conceived. I could cite similar felicities of parallelism by the hundred ; the sense of the musical design conveyed for instance by the entry of the same two figures each time the first subject of the symphony assumed a leading part in the structure, the subtle distinctions invariably made in choregraphy between the basic elements in the music and the transitional passages —between the bones as it were and the cartilages—the curious correspondence between harshness in the harmonies and musical colours and angularities or violences in the gestures, and so on. In the finale, which, as the reader no doubt knows, is in *passacaglia* form—a series of variations upon a ground fugue—Massine seems to me to have done wonders. He typifies the commanding *theme* by six black figures that persist through the whole movement, as the ground bass itself persists in the music ; and he intensifies or thins out the action and the groupings in accordance with the changing texture of the variations."

II. THE COMPANY

To have achieved these things, more especially *Choreartium*, in so short a time, calls for a company of extraordinary training and versatility, and, from that point of view at least, it is the finest and the most complete I have ever seen. Wisely it has been entrusted to Serge Grigorieff, who was Diaghileff's stage manager from the beginning. He graduated from the Imperial School in 1900, and performed for twelve years at the Maryinsky as dancer-mime. For four years he learned dramatic technique from Davidoff and Sanine. Then he worked for Fokine in private performances, and joined Diaghileff in 1909, finally severing his connection with Russia in 1912 after two years' leave. No critic has ever given full credit to Grigorieff for his immense work and experience. The smooth running of each performance, with its correct lighting and complicated cues, is due to him. He carries the entire old repertoire in his head. Grigorieff is a strict disciplinarian, even a martinet at times, but he never loses a grim sense of humour. He represents tradition.

His wife, the beautiful Tchernicheva, takes the classes, and there is a young Grigorieff, Vsevolod, educated at an

English university, ready to carry on the tradition and to cope with the worries. It is the most difficult and thankless task of all.

It is only in the Monte Carlo Ballet that Woizikovski, still another Polish dancer[1] and a pillar of the old régime, has truly revealed himself in a succession of strong rôles. Previously it had always been his misfortune to assume, like a younger brother, the cast-off rôles created by others, to assume them with brilliance as a dancer but with the inevitable sacrifice of personality. He inherited *Prince Igor* from Bolm, *L'Après-midi d'un Faune*, *Petrouchka* and *Carnaval* from Massine. These were his outstanding Diaghileff performances, in dancing, no whit inferior to the originals. His vitality and clean work have always been the signal for enthusiastic applause, but till recently Woizikovski has been undiscovered. The first rôle, which he could call his own, was in *Matelots*, and then, in the last Diaghileff creation and Lifar's first, *Le Renard*, he carried the entire weight on his shoulders. After that a long and sad interruption. One of my most painful memories is of seeing him with Pavlova's company after her death, dancing as brilliantly as ever, but completely lost. One sat waiting for a climax that never came ; and suddenly realised more vividly than ever the death of the two gigantic figures.

Then at a loose end, Woizikovski gave some of his knowledge to the English dance, by putting on *Carnaval* and *L'Après-midi d'un Faune* for the Ballet Club, and dancing with them for a season.

Woizikovski is the most essentially sane of all the dancers. " It may be fashionable for dancers to go mad," I have heard him say, " but I have not the slightest intention of doing so." Perhaps just because he is so reliable, and does

[1] In the Ballet School at Warsaw he led the Cotillon with Pola Negri.—A. L. H.

not " play at madness," he has never had his real due, save from the applause of the moment. His memory is prodigious. It is thanks to him that many of the ballets we see are alive to-day.

From the very beginning of the Monte Carlo Ballet he comes into his own. In *Cotillon* as the Master of Ceremonies, in *Concurrence* as the lousy, unwashed Beggar, in *Présages* as the centrepiece, Fate, in *Scuola di Ballo* as the Master; always the strong and experienced dancer in a young and talented company, but never snatching his effect by over-emphasis. Technically a good classical dancer, he is by temperament a " baritone " with an extraordinary range that allows him to go from the delicate *Commedia dell' Arte* of *Scuola di Ballo* to the vigorous national dancing of Spain and Russia. A company that is fortunate enough to possess Woizikovski, has in him five strong dancers and five fine artists.

The next " old timer " is Alexandra Danilova, last *ballerina* of the Diaghileff company. Young as she is, and now in her prime as a dancer, she just belongs to the old tradition in Russia. She is especially brilliant in light mischievous rôles as in *Le Beau Danube*, but she is by no means limited to these. Her classical work has real nobility. Danilova is a dancer of such a type that the performance she gives is, as a whole, far more brilliant than the details that go to its making. The better her audience, the better her dancing. To see Danilova at a gala performance, a first or last night, is to see her at her very best, when there are few who can equal her to-day. The outstanding feature of her work is the tautness of her magnificently straight knees, a natural foundation that is rare indeed. This alone makes her *Lac des Cygnes*, a ballet where every line i revealed, into an outstanding performance. Danilova stan almost alone, amongst the already experienced dancers, who could have fitted so happily into this brilliant young group. She is still supple enough to make progress, and to accept the challenge that they offer her.

Those fine artists, Natalia Branitska, pure classical stylist, L. Obidennia, Tatiana Chamié, Jan Hoyer and Maryan Ladre, make up the survivors from Diaghileff. In these early days their responsibility has been heavy. Perhaps at times they sigh for the old days, and think sadly of " Big Serge," but they have been loyal to the new.

The Russian emigration of great *ballerinas* from the Maryinsky Theatre has now lasted long enough to take effect on the generation born during the first years of the revolution. Whether the Russians are physically or temperamentally better suited to make dancers than other nationalities is an interesting but unsatisfactory subject for discussion. From experience, I believe that they are, and I have put it to the test, on more than one occasion, by picking out two or three of the best pupils from a crowded classroom, without exception always Russians. I cannot explain the reason either to my own satisfaction or anyone else's.

Too much may easily be made of the youth of the new dancers, especially in England, where we are apt to take to our hearts those foreign artists who are long past their prime and no longer welcome at home. It must also be remembered that when we saw Russian dancers for the first time in Western Europe, young as they were, they had already appeared sufficiently long on the Imperial stage to be thoroughly established. This is our first real opportunity of watching the actual creation of the *ballerina*. These dancers are at the most three years younger than usual, and they have had an experience of life that was denied to their carefully cloistered predecessors. Although the older dancers have a *school* and a finish missing in these children, youth is a quality in dancing that has been too rarely seen. The dancer is at her prime between twenty-five and thirty, and these years of formation, which we are now privileged to see, are the most absorbing of all, especially treasured by the Russian *balletomane*. Now, we too can emulate Valerian Svetloff, doyen of critics, who once wrote that a small débutante, Anna Pavlova by name, seemed destined for very great things.

It is also argued, by those who exaggerate this whole question of youth, that the young dancer is easily spoilt by too much praise, applause and critical attention. Rubbish, complete and utter ; by the lack of it perhaps. Praise can never change the genuine artist. At the most my remarks will cause a *mauvais quart d'heure* to my poor friend de Basil. He and Madame Tchernicheva, at her morning class, will soon readjust things. With daily classes there can be no conceited dancer—exception made for a few males.

A few depressing souls, of the type of my elderly Russian gentleman, say, "That is all very well, but this is no return to the old days : they are not classical, the big rôle would lose them." That is not so. At present they are mainly concentrating on the new repertoire, and the emphasis is there. Equally careful guidance in the old would produce great results in people who have already brought *Les Sylphides* back from the dead. Once again I deny the inferiority of the modern dancer, and the dancers of yesterday are solidly on my side.

As I saw the company at work and enjoyed their success, I became jealous and frightened for Tamara. This was so clearly her home, and the Savoy was playing to empty houses. We went together to a performance one day, and

I

it was infinitely sad to see her rôles being danced by others. She was brave, but I regretted having brought her. Then, when her own company disbanded, she went back to Paris to work, and to get thin. I received constant bulletins of the progress : " J'ai perdu 9 kilos ! Mais je ne danse pas et je suis triste." So daily I pestered the good-natured de Basil. " Without Tamara you are incomplete. She and Irina must be in the same company. With both of them you will conquer the world." " Peut-être; nous verrons," and the smile, but he did not commit himself. At last I received an excited letter : " J'arrive Mardi," and on the next afternoon she was dancing as if she had never been away, but it was only later that I saw the perfect Toumanova, thinner, lighter, more certain and restrained.

Her real " come back," the creation in *Choreartium*, was an exciting event, routine at the beginning with the endless long rehearsals—and then the first night. If she was nervous, I was terrified. It is always an agony for me to watch the first performance of anyone of whom I am especially fond, and whose reactions and difficulties I can follow through the smile, the make-up and the costume. Almost from the first I could see that she was in pain, although she danced superbly, making her entrance like " a big black sun." When I went round afterwards her foot was swollen, and she could scarcely walk. She had been dropped three or four feet on her toes !

The next morning I took her round to a famous bone-setter, promising her immediate and miraculous results— " just a click and you will be dancing again "—but he shook his head and would not touch it without an X-ray examination. We waited impatiently, going over the whole occurrence, each one with a different diagnosis, more cheerful than we really felt. He came in looking grim. " I am afraid there is a fracture in a small but important bone. It will come all right, but it is a nasty business: two months at least." Tamara and her mother cried, while I was completely sick, and, like Diaghileff on another occasion, felt like saying, " It was all too beautiful to last." He bound it up in plaster of Paris, and told us to come back the next day.

However upset we may have felt, that next day started as a farce. The doctor's room was completely invaded by an excited, sympathetic crowd ; Delarova, Massine, de Basil, all asking questions in Russian, calming poor Tamara, and at the same time happy and excited by the fine reception of *Choreartium*. I imagine that the doctor will long remember this. He took another series of X-rays,[1] and Madame Toumanova, completely out of control, against all orders followed him into the developing-room. She returned in a few minutes laughing hysterically, and tried to tell us something. We were frightened. Then the doctor followed her. " I have never before been so ashamed of myself. There is no fracture at all, but a small supplementary bone of most unusual shape, that I have only seen now that I compare the two feet. You have torn some ligaments and will be well within a week. Here are the photos. Every dancer should be X-rayed in a normal state." Tamara slid off the bench on to both feet, without noticing the pain, and we proceeded to dance round the doctor, who unexpectedly found himself a principal in a strange, very Russian, ballet.

After the excitement I took a giggling and very happy schoolgirl, hopping on one foot, home to the calm of nursery tea.

There can be no escape from the fact that the wh

[1] See plate.

story of Toumanova, in essence the story of all the *émigré* dancers, is extremely sentimental. Let us revel in it, there is no escape.

The daughter of a Russian colonel and a young Caucasian girl, she was born in a cattle-waggon, occupied by seventeen officers, during the cold and hardship of a retreat into Siberia. Her father had been badly wounded in the civil war, and her mother also had suffered a fractured jaw. After many wanderings they settled in Shanghai, where the colonel found work of a sort. Then Anna Pavlova came on tour, and upset the plans of the whole family, as she habitually upset family plans. Little Tamara had always been fond of acting her own tragedies in front of the mirror, and warning off any grown-up who interrupted, with a " Go away, you don't understand." Once she had seen Pavlova she determined to become a dancer, and even wrote a letter to God, asking Him to make her one, and quickly, too. Shanghai offered no opportunities, but the family had found security there, and it was difficult to move. The mother believed so strongly in her child that finally she persuaded her husband to risk the great adventure of Paris, staking everything on Tamara's wish and her faith. They went straight to Olga Preobrajenska. They could just pay for the first few lessons, and then it became increasingly difficult, but the great *ballerina* realised that here was exceptional material, and helped them to live. Tamara quickly developed, and was equally brilliant in her lessons and at the piano, but soon she had to devote all her energies to dancing.

Pavlova came to the school, saw Tamara, and was moved to tears, and this is one of the rare cases, of the many that are reported, where she predicted a brilliant future. Tamara made her début with Pavlova at the Trocadéro

I remember the occasion well. Not because she danced brilliantly, and made me into a successful prophet, but because her first appearance was greeted with laughter and applause. She was the smallest person I have ever seen in ballet skirts, and, to accentuate this, her hair was done up in an enormous top-heavy bow. Everyone in the entire theatre became intensely maternal, and to my shame I remarked, " Much too young. She ought to have been in bed long ago." After the performance she was handed over the footlights, embraced and fed with chocolates. I did not see her again till the Savoy.

Meanwhile she began to work hard to pay the rent and food bills. With private parties and receptions her reputation grew, the fashion in baby dancers started, and young Russians flocked to the studios. An offer from the Casino de Paris at a dazzling salary was refused, and she even felt a little hurt. Critics praised her, and then wrote gravely about cruelty and exploitation. It was natural, but it amuses me now that I know of her parents' loving tenderness and their attitude throughout. At the age of eleven she appeared as a guest artist at the Paris Opéra in *L'Eventail de Jeanne*, the joint work of Ravel, Ferroud, Ibert, Manuel, Roussel, Milhaud, Poulenc, Auric, Schmitt ; nearly a composer for each year of her age !

Then, after a further period of recitals, when she was thirteen, Balanchine, who was recruiting the Ballets Russes de Monte Carlo, saw her and she became a star. He created for her *Cotillon* and *Concurrence*, and she danced in the revivals of *Petrouchka*, *Le Lac des Cygnes* and *Les Sylphides*.

André Levinson, always grudging in his praise where the classics were concerned, wrote of her :

" Tamara, qui porte le même prénom que son illustre
ainée, Karsavina, partage avec elle une certaine langeur
orientale et ce don poétique si rare, pénétrant chaque
mouvement d'un fluide lyrisme élégiaque. Mais les
airs penchés, les mines dolentes que les chorégraphe
s'accordent pour attribuer à la suave Caucasienne avec
son teint mat et ses grands yeux pleins d'un étonnement
mélancholique, cache un méchanisme d'une vigueur et
d'une perfection que ne possédait aucune des Sylphides
' Impériales ' de 1909."[1]

This great critic, whose word could make a reputation,
had acclaimed a thirteen-year-old dancer without reserve.
Tamara had "arrived." Her struggle had been intense but
concentrated. In another form it still continues, in that
quest for perfection which it has been my greatest joy
to watch.

This unusual beauty, technique, dramatic and musical
ability in one person are attributes that spell *Giselle*, and
if she can last the pace, always a debatable question with
that type of temperament, she may well be the greatest
Giselle in history ; then so may Baronova. They are reaching greatness from different angles. At present Tamara is
Act I, Irina Act II.

Irina Baronova too, to-day my ideal classical dancer, from
the same school, had the privilege of Levinson's seal, unfortunately for every dancer and *balletomane* now a thing
of the past, at her very first performance in *Orphée* at the
Mogador :

" Mais ce fut une variation du ballet des Nymphes
qui nous réserva la surprise sensationelle de la soirée.

[1] *Candide*, June 16th, 1932.

Elle mit en vedette Mlle Baronova, toute jeune fillette, qui enleva son galop, culminant en un tourbillon vertigineux avec un naturel ingénu et une sûreté magistrale. . . ."

What a pleasure it is to quote from Levinson. How many dancers will live again through his writings. A *Russian* ballet and art critic, pupil of Volyinsky, after the revolution he became one of the leading *French* writers on music, painting, literature and the drama, and a superb stylist in the language of Voltaire. On ballet he stood supreme.

I have already written of the first vivid impression Baronova's beautiful artistry made upon me.

Each one is fortunate in her only rival. I was right, when I told de Basil that together they would conquer the world.

The third prodigy is Tatiana Riabouchinska, daughter of a dancer and a wealthy Moscow merchant, patron of the arts. She possesses a lightness that I have rarely seen equalled, and an elevation that the others have yet to discover. At present her field seems restricted to the composer's lighter moods, to the third movements of Tchaikovsky's Fifth Symphony and of Brahms' Fourth. She has a quiet personality and charm that grows on one, and a strongly developed sense of atmosphere, without being a great actress. Her finest rôle is that of the Child in *Jeux d'Enfants*, with its gawkish movements that must never be overstressed, a perfect synthesis of character. There is also that feylike quality that makes of her the ideal Sylphide, bu* greatest of all gifts are her arms, a present from her teach* Kchessinska. They make everything that she undertakes i* poetry, and they will make a complicated Russian name * a household word for those who understand the danc*

Nina Verchinina, more than anyone, carries in her the new symphonic conception of the dance, and it was only natural that Massine should discover her at the very beginning of his new departure, and make full use of her in the first two ballets.

She starts with an unusually sensitive understanding of symphonic music, which she feels plastically rather than in the rigid classicism of her upbringing. She has at her command a strength usually denied the plastic dancer, so that her supple movements are under the most perfect control. Verchinina, as used by Massine, is the union of the essentials of ballet and Duncanism. Who can forget her entrance in *Les Présages* ? In it she reconciles so many seeming opposites : points with the plastic dance, enormous strength with fluid movement. What so many others have stressed in the past, she conceals. Her second movement in *Choreartium* gives the instant effect of simplicity with energy in reserve. It is never redundant, always immediately effective. Without such a dancer as Verchinina one might well say that some symphonic movements cannot be danced. The union in her of these mental and physical attributes coming so directly through music, something different and more abstract than the ability to mime, that we have discussed, shows the enormous range that ballet, when properly understood, can possess.

To delve deeper into those riches : there is Hélène Kirsova, the compatriot of Genée, so many of whose gifts she shares, elusive in personality, flawless in technique, with her back of finely tempered steel ; Tarakanova, from a picture by Botticelli ; the beautiful Rostova of the lovely arabesque ; Delarova, one of the finest light mimes of to-day, who adds distinction to rôles as small as a nurse in *Petrouchka* as large as the Bad Pupil in *Scuola di Ballo* ; the witty

Simeonova ; tall, distinctive Sidorenko with her keen musical ear ; the irresponsible Morosova, straight out of *Carnaval* ; and others, each a distinct personality.

Among the men David Lichine is outstanding, a new type of male dancer, whose virility can never be questioned. He is fiery, dominating, irresistible. Sketchy in detail, he excels in some striking climax—the leap over the box in *Cotillon*, the struggle and victory in *Présages*, the dive off-stage in *Plage*. He is not a classical dancer nor definitely a character dancer, but a *jeune premier* with character and personality, and the first of his kind. The choregrapher is the most important member of a company, and Lichine is, as yet, the only one of the new generation to show real promise in that line. His début with *Nocturne* paralleled both his gifts and faults as a dancer: it was untidy, ill organised, yet strong in climax. He understood his own body remarkably well, and created the finest dance, Puck, for himself, always a weakness in the inexperienced ; not a sign of conceit, but the very natural result of conceiving movement in terms of the thing one knows the best, one's own body. This strong dance was near to the Faun in spirit, but always just different. When we discount what was derivative, and the novice's desire for movement just for the sake of movement, something big in hope remains. Already in his second work, *Les Imaginaires*, there is more discipline, and one complete success in the *adagio*. In this ballet again there is the conflict between his fine original idea and something romantic and personal. His whole attitude and approach is sound. He will certainly achieve big things—in time.

There is Yurek Shabelevsky, maintaining the Polish tradition, a beautifully finished dancer in every field, and André Eglevsky, truly classical *premier danseur* of the immediate future. He is large, ungainly, all hands and feet in repose, but in movement long in line and graceful, with a strong technique and the gift of turning slowly and deliberately that I have never seen equalled. He takes everything with astonishing ease. When the young colt—he is sixteen years old—grows up he will surely be a record-breaking racehorse. The male dancer takes longer to mature, and unfortunately lasts but half as long.

In Vania Psota we have a magnificent dancer-buffoon, traditional funny man of ballet, a figure from the Italian Comedy but able to create fresh rôles and keep pace with the new.

Special mention must be made of three non-Russian members of the company; Paul Petroff, a Dane, who has lately revealed himself as an accomplished classical dancer and supplied strength in the one direction where it was lacking; our own fleet-footed Edna Tresahar and that fine character dancer, Algeranoff, who shows his full powers as the Kostchei in *L'Oiseau de Feu*. He is the first English dancer of that essentially Russian type.

Nothing would give me greater pleasure than to portray the whole *corps de ballet*, all of whom are individual artists, if only for the subsequent satisfaction of saying, " I told you so." With Massine in charge, always free from preconceived ideas, anyone may suddenly be taken up to create a leading rôle.

From within that company, as it is now composed, should come the important work of the next twenty-five years. My future has been assured. I am at home once again.

CHAPTER XIII

TO AMERICA WITH THE BALLET

" The Triumph of a Generation."

S. Hurok Presents
Monte Carlo
Ballet Russe

W. DE BASIL, *Director-General*.

PLAYBILL

IT WAS IN BOURNEMOUTH after the final performance, and all the excitement of the fire that had so nearly ended in tragedy, that I announced to my friends in the company that this was my hundredth performance.

" But of course you are coming to America with us," said Delarova, and, without a moment's thought, I replied, " Of course. When exactly are you leaving, and on what boat ? " No one was in the slightest bit surprised. Here my *obsession* was normal, and perfectly understood by those who had given their whole lives to dancing. There could be nothing strange in someone willing to give up his evenings, and part of his mornings and afternoons too, in watching them and receiving what they gave.

I have realised from the very first, without making any plans, that it would be quite impossible, now that I was safely " at home " once again, to leave it all behind for a number of months, especially during the most exciting adventure of all. I had followed them to Golders Green

Streatham Hill and Bournemouth ; America was not so
far away ! By now I was a definite part of the company,
their travelling audience and friend, and the hundred
performances had far from satisfied me, for there was
always some improvement to look forward to, in this history
of rapid artistic development. On tour, too, I had just
begun to know individuals, and to get interested in them.
I was absolutely starved after all these years. I wanted to
talk of ballet, live in its atmosphere and to go on learning.
I wanted especially to witness the amazement of an
audience who had known no true ballet since 1916 and the
disastrous Nijinsky venture.

I left for London, going straight to Thomas Cook's from
the station. The decision was taken, but it was distinctly
difficult to explain. My wife, of course, understood, and
urged me to go from the first, with the plea that it was so
rare that anyone got such positive joy from anything in
life that it would be foolish to miss the opportunity. Most
people, however, pitied her demonstratively and thought
me completely mad, though they themselves were always
willing to set a few weeks aside every year to go to winter
sports and the like. An elderly relative prided himself on
his deep knowledge of human nature at having discovered
the true reason. " There's a woman in the case of course."
(He probably said, " Cherchez la femme.") " There always
is, and he's following her to America. It's perfectly simple.
He's in love." It was too simple. He was so very nearly
right. I was in love, but with an art, and an entire company. I am sure that he is still quite unconvinced, still the
clever man of the world, who found out the true reason.

I left for Plymouth to see the final performances. The
company had made it like Monte Carlo in atmosphere.
At every street corner there were animated conversations

in Russian, Woolworths was the great shopping centre for the little *ballerinas*, and the whole town had become ballet conscious. Surely small girls were worrying their mothers to let them dance, mothers were worrying their husbands, and all were dreaming dreams. Thank heavens that so many will be walking out or married before they can put it to the test.

It was the beginning of the cold snap, and the theatre was like an ice-box. " I see that *Aladdin*'s the next performance," Algeranoff told the stage manager. " If you don't get the theatre warmer the oil will freeze in his lamp." Many London friends had come down to see us off; the excitement and confusion were amazing. Some of the girls were terrified at the prospect, convinced that the ship would sink, while one had mislaid her mother and no one seemed to know whether she would join the ship in England or in France, if at all. Young Grigorieff, a chip of the old block, must have had an especially difficult task in tracing them all, since in the majority of cases stage names differed from those on the passports, and came as a revelation even to their owners. Who is Khacidovitch? Why, Tamara Toumanova. Ellen Wittrup? Kirsova, of course.

No one was lost. We got on board at midnight, and were ushered into the dining-room. Immediately it was obvious that everything was ballet, and the ship belonged to us. One unfortunate gentleman, a total stranger with a Russian name, was almost forcibly detained in our party until final orders were given by Grigorieff, amazed why he could not go quietly to bed. The missing mother had been sighted from the tender, and was greeted with loud and startling cries of " Mama " by the entire company.

It was rough from the first day out, and many of the company disappeared and were seen no more. De Basil

made daily tours of the cabins and shouted words of encouragement. Sometimes he went into the wrong ones, but
it did not seem to worry him at all ; just a smile. "Eh bien,
comment ça va—oh, pardon." Finally he decided that no
one in his company should be allowed to be sick any
longer, and together we carried Verchinina and Kirsova,
the worst offenders, on deck, very much against their will,
followed by the reproaches of a fat and intensely motherly
stewardess. But de Basil was right ; they were cured within
a few hours, and playing deck games the next morning.
There was one unfortunate relapse, when, during a talking
film, the music of *Présages* was played. Its suggestion of
violent movement was too much for many.

I had proved myself abundantly. I could still believe that
girls, whom I had seen with hair bedraggled, a wild look in
their eyes, being very unpoetical in sound and look, were
truly sylphs. Crossings may have wrecked honeymoons ;
they could not disturb the *balletomane*.

Soon a routine was established ; Massine worked daily
in his cabin, Dorati memorised musical scores and played
Hungarian melodies for us by the hour, Toumanova and
Baronova found fresh rivalry at deck tennis, de Basil sent
cablegrams, Algeranoff and Tresahar told of their travels
in out-of-the-way places with Pavlova, and Grigorieff
marched the deck, for once not captain.

One night, in mid-Atlantic, Tarakanova came of age,
and we celebrated the event. Twenty-one ; the Ballets
Russes de Monte Carlo are growing up! There were three
christenings too. Our Ballet Club girls became Russian ;
Prudence Hyman as Polina Strogova ; Betty Cuff, Olga
Nelidova ; Elizabeth Ruxton, Leza Serova. The names soon
passed into common usage and only their owners were still
a little dazed from time to time. Then there was the ship's

concert, a grand *Gala des Ballets Russes* followed by a supper and dance. The ship rolled badly, in spite of engines especially stopped; outside there was a regular blizzard. I have seen better performances of *Les Sylphides*, but never under more curious circumstances.

I had many long talks with de Basil.

" Sometimes I feel like giving this all up; truly the strain isn't worth it. I have been through the war, so that I know what strain means. It's those mothers. I have to take them along to look after the children, but instead of providing a good home atmosphere, they provide nothing but trouble, putting all sorts of ideas into their daughters' heads. Every small event is immediately magnified into a conspiracy. Why can't they see that their interests and mine are identical ? Success is the common aim. Of course, if the girls themselves were not naturally jealous, they wouldn't care enough to be artists ; there is always that consolation. I have received letters from aggrieved fathers too. I can even understand that, but when I receive a letter from a sister-in-law the limit has been reached. Look at this."

Once, I think, I have seen something extra in his usual smile, almost a wink. He has just been to visit a very sick and sorry mother, one of the most troublesome.

I sympathise with him, also I think that he enjoys it. It is all a game, the same game that is played in every girls' school. Nothing goes very deep; the bitter enemies of half an hour ago are soon friends again. It livens existence to see plots everywhere, and at heart to know that it is just a game.

Blessed jealousy, constructive jealousy, a virtue in all dancers ! Each one performs the better for knowing tha' her rival in the wings is watching every movement, an will dance the rôle better, if she can, at the very next performance. It is an incentive, the certain great inspiration. What has killed so much talent in England is that fine public school attempt to stamp it out. "Jane came to the school first; she must have the leading rôle at the school performance." Heavens, if Jane is no good and Jill, the newcomer, is brilliant, can there be any doubt? Jane's feelings in seeing Jill dance may stir up that something in her. Once a *maître de ballet* told me with pride, "There is no jealousy here, we are all one big happy family," and I believed it at once, for I had just seen the performance. A dancer need no longer be jealous only when she has bought her very last pair of shoes, or settled down to a comfortable suburban existence. Till then long live jealousy, say I, and its results. Only the outsider, who knows but one dancer in a company, and does not yet fully understand the game, must watch his step, or he will easily believe the worst of everyone, and so many illusions will be speedily shattered.

Just when we had settled down into a comfortable routine, made doubly so by the French ship's company, whose honoured guests we had felt from the very start, the journey ended. Journalists besieged the ship, and the great adventure had begun.

"Say, is the great Dye-aghileff with you?" someone asked. "Dead; no, you don't say that? Well, if it isn't just too bad, and he was the greatest dancer ever."

"Now, girls, bunch up together, show plenty of leg; you're dancers, aren't you? Well, what are you waiting for? Hey, you, you're a good looker; step right in front and smile; that's right."

This lasted for some two hours. A paternal-looking man, ur impresario, Hurok, came on board, followed by two men holding out bread and salt—a beautiful old Russian ceremony of welcome, cheapened by its obvious publicity use, and the careful photographic poses. If it served its purpose, well and good.

At last we get off the ship. It is pouring, and the famous skyline has come out blurred but still impressive. Americana is my sole hobby, and it gives me a tremendous thrill. At the customs we get a really bad reception from a crowd of ill-mannered, quarrelsome petty officials, who must give many a traveller a totally false impression of the warmth of American hospitality. There is immediate trouble about the ballet shoes found in every trunk. "Six pairs; you'll have to pay on those." Everyone shouts at once. I translate for a little group. "These shoes are already darned and ready for use. They are purely personal property, and without them the dancers could not perform. At the most they will last ten days, and then they will all buy American shoes." "I don't know anything about that. You come along with me, and pay up quick." I do not attempt to translate further; no one could possibly hear me. The bewildered official is now surrounded by four furious and voluble mothers (they have their uses now); all speak in Russian together, their anxious daughters chirping in from time to time. "Say, they're plum crazy, that's what they are. I'll leave them to cool down a bit." Just as he is walking away, a more important official turns up. "Let 'em all through." With relief he scribbles on the baggage. First great and complete victory for the mothers, how complete I only learned later. The English girls, with an unquestioning belief in law and order, had paid the sum demanded after a little polite argument. Their money was promptly and apologetically refunded. With such tactics free trade would soon be an established fact. We have been given lists of hotels, and go off in groups. The seventeen-year-old Riabouchinska, who has been here before with Balieff, constitutes herself our guide. We greatly admire her knowledge, as she points out, " This is Broadway; that's the Roxy; there's a cafeteria," and excitedly, " There's Woolworths," which makes us feel at home. We know that we are completely safe in her hands.

A brief visit to our theatre, and surprisingly enough we are free for what remains of the day to unpack and find our equilibrium. Some of the girls are a little scared. A few days before we had seen a James Cagney roughneck picture, with plenty of shootings and beatings up, and Dolotine, a hundred per cent disguised American, had told them that it was a pretty accurate picture of daily life in New York, especially around Broadway. The happenings at the customs had not helped to dispel the illusion.

The following day is given over entirely to rehearsal. Everyone has recovered, and there is immense joy at being back at work once again. Dancers resent an enforced holiday. Also, a good sign, there is a revival of some feuds temporarily suspended. In the Green Room, Madame Karinska is in complete control, trying on costumes and superintending a whole company of little Jewish tailors. I feel that she should be on the stage and not under it ; as beautiful as any of our dancers, during the journey she earned the name " Princess." No matter how rough, there was " The Princess " at eleven each morning, walking up and down the deck as calm and elegant as if she had been in the Bois. This business-woman-artist from Russia has stormed the city of dressmakers and won. The work of the great decorative artists of the day is entrusted to her ; they admire her beauty, enjoy the wit of her conversation, and trust her completely.

A charming friend, who travelled with us, Mrs. de Mille, mother of Agnes, had asked me to tea with some of the leading dancers of New York, among them Martha Graham, most famous exponent of the modern dance, whose link with ballet had been a performance of *Sacre du Printemps*, directed by Massine. The account of an angry debate with Fokine had greatly prejudiced me against her. On first sight I found her a plain, earnest, rather grim-looking person, who, apart from her expressive hands, might have been a New England " school marm." She was different from any dancer I had ever seen, but as she talked and became animated I discovered in her a real beauty and a quiet, pleasing strength. She was so entirely reasonable, too, as I immediately and tactlessly questioned her on the famous debate and on her attitude towards ballet in general. She did not deny ballet, she had studied it and realised that it was not for her; also she had no intense admiration for German dancing, which she found too cerebral. She was sorry that her views had been so misrepresented. She never said that only Pavlova's bow was interesting, but the very opposite, that with such a dancer as Pavlova *even* her bow was interesting. I must see her if possible, though it was more than likely that I would not approve. To my regret the opportunity never came. I was left with the impression of an utterly sincere artist of strong personality, who can, when her interest is aroused, *make* herself beautiful.

I still do not know why the exponents of the " modern dance " despise feminine frills and fashions. Not one of them has ever given me the idea that any man has ever waited for her at the stage-door. It may well be a reaction against artificiality, but it is in itself terrifyingly artificial. There is nothing more natural than for a woman, and an actress, to appear at her most beautiful. When she becomes a missionary for a new cause, a rabid enthusiast, then her cause would be all the more rapidly advanced by a little propaganda off the stage. Without resorting to the extremes of the " show a little leg, girls " of our reporter friend, a fine appearance off the stage is at any rate a guarantee that something beautiful will be seen on the stage. This first denial of beauty is in itself the sign, not of revolt, as they imagine, but of something utterly out of contact with the realities of life, the very charge that is so often ignorantly made about ballet. It is part of the dancer's education to know how to wear the costume of all periods becomingly. It should be second nature. Only when one is a Lydia Lopokova, with an amazing record of beautiful creation, can one afford to be seen walking down Bond Street in Wellington boots and a knitted tam-o'-shanter—and even that seems a pity.

There too I met John Martin, the leading dance critic of America. We disagreed on many points, and found little common ground that first meeting, but we belonged to the same party, only to different branches, which made our quarrel a family affair. Martin has done big things for the dance in America, the most important being the difficult task of driving home the fact that it is an art and not a light entertainment. Like every conscientious critic, he has troubled to learn himself, so that his standards are high. For the rest, we both think each other a little misguided, a trifle narrow-minded, and enjoy the friendly rows that ensue.

The first night was almost a repetition of London—the same crowded house, the same shouts and applause, but *Concurrence* and then *Beau Danube* drew it all, and *Présages*, the ballet that had kept the company for so long in London, the meat of the performance, was obviously not greatly liked.

The Americans were exactly in the same position as Western Europe before 1909, only prejudiced against the very name " *ballet*," and no wonder. Mr. Roxy's efforts at entertainment under that sacred name were sufficient to bewilder any intelligent person with a sense of the theatre. He provided girls by the hundred, pretty ones too, elephants whenever possible, dazzling lights and costumes ; and all that on a stage the size of Waterloo Station. Personality was out of the question; even sex-appeal, America's gift to the theatre, was not strong enough to break through these methods of the wholesaler in his warehouse. It is a current joke that a man up from the country, seeing elephants in one of these ballets, turned to his neighbour and said, " I never did like performing mice." To make matters worse, these " ballets " were given the names of standard works, so that to-day *Scheherazade* means elephants and girls instead of the pantherine leaps of Nijinsky. It is true that Massine worked there for two years, but, while he could make the pattern richer, he could not do the impossible and create a weekly masterpiece. Also this had undoubtedly damaged his prestige. It was all that they knew of him. The rest was hearsay, and New York takes nothing on trust.

Against that was the memory of the one creative American dancer, Isadora Duncan, who had made her reputation in Europe. If ballet meant Roxy, then she was clearly justified in all that she said against it. Her sayings were cherished, even more than the memory of her performances. At some time she had said that it was not possible to dance to symphonic music, although she did so herself. The ballet, then, could enjoy success when it did the lighter

things, but it must not attempt to be too serious; that was
the province of the concert dancer. Also it was unforgivable
for those serious things to be demonstrated by young and
very pretty girls. Against all advice, de Basil took another
big decision, persisted with *Présages*, and so made the final
triumph possible. The Americans, sensibly enough, were
not prepared to take European success as a hall-mark.
They were less *au courant* of ballet than we, but all the more
critical. It was a magnificent test for the dancers, and it
matured them. They saw in it a challenge and excelled
themselves. Never had Toumanova given more significance
to *Concurrence*, Baronova more poetry to *Les Sylphides* or
Lichine danced with greater fire. And they won handsomely, so that Europe will be the poorer for several months
a year.

This victory has now made it possible too for America
to use her own dancers. Hundreds are trained every year,
the schools are popular, but then they disappear, absorbed
into the dance factories and films. There is Harriet Hoctor,
light as a feather, with a dignity that triumphs over surroundings and audience; Patricia Bowman, superb tech-
nician, who has worked with Massine, but not long enough
to be " discovered "; and Paul Haakon, worthy pupil of
Fokine, all being used as trick machines in vaudeville.
Under Russian guidance they can bring a new contribution to ballet, the American spirit of the sheer, effortless
joy of movement. The Camargo Society had already revealed a fine talent in Anna Ludmila (of Chicago), the
perfect blend of classicism and American sex-appeal. They
can regenerate the name of ballet and expose the untheatrical and anæmic group concerts that have been
forced into prominence *faute de mieux*. Curiously enough,
the forms of dancing that are indigenous do not come

straight from Duncan, in spite of the power of her name, but from Ruth St. Denis and Ted Shawn, veritable dance chameleons, who have dabbled in the dances of the entire world. I saw some of the groups arranged by their most successful pupil, Charles Weidman. To me, they were weak and unconvincing. " Art comes to the cabaret," wrote the critics, but a form of art was already there, awaiting their interest. Fred Astaire is an American artist, the troupes of girls express a phase of life—as a machine, it is true—and such negroes as Bill Robinson provide a quality that is unique. There is all that wealth awaiting artistic development, and that can be added to the ballet movement and expression of the future. There is a richness of theme, legend, history and daily life that could inspire all those limbs to beauty, if it takes a Frenchman to conceive of it as a school, and a Russian to set it in motion.[1]

One day on my way to rehearsal I took a taxi.

" St. James's Theatre."

" Where's that ? Oh, I know ; 44th and Broadway. What's on there now ? Russian Ballet. Well, you're lucky, I'll say you are. You'll see real women, not little painted dolls with platinum blonde tops to them. There's nothing to touch Russian women ; real flesh and blood, plenty of temperament. I must go to that show; haven't seen a Russian ballet for years; ah, the good old days. I speak with feeling ? You bet I do. Was born in Russia, Tobolsk, forty-five years ago." So spoke my hundred per cent American driver. He was irresistible, and naturally I treated him to the show.

Before I left, the scenery and costumes of the Diaghileff Ballet were once more with their rightful owners ; the Polovtsian warriors seemed more savage in Roerich's fine

[1] A start has been made with the Russo-American *Union Pacific*.

setting, the Russian crowd more animated in Benois' original décor. The link with tradition too meant something to these young dancers, thrilled at discovering a historic name in a faded blouse. *Le Chapeau Tricorne* was in active rehearsal. As I saw Toumanova learning, with Tchernicheva, Massine and Woizikovski stamping in a corner, Picasso's bridge, and the twinkling stars, I thought of the tragedy connected with its first presentation. As it has so often been used in various fantastic ways against Diaghileff, and linked to the tragedy of Nijinsky, I will tell the true story.

When in Spain, Diaghileff, ever on the look-out for unusual talent, discovered a cabaret dancer, a foundling and thorough rough diamond, Felix by name, who was exceptionally gifted in the dances of his country. Sokolova remembers going with a party to see the gypsy dancers of Seville. One after another performed in intense rivalry, Felix, who was seated at their table, growing paler and paler, more and more anxious, until finally Diaghileff told him, "Now you show us what you can do." No one will ever forget how he danced that night; he excelled them all.

With *Le Chapeau Tricorne* in view, Felix was taken on to teach Massine, Woizikovski, Sokolova, and later Karsavina, his native dances. He was always a little strange, being known by his friends at home as " Felix loco," but in London he became stranger still. He imagined that he was to be launched as a great dancer, and that *Tricorne* and all the preparations were for him. He was haunted too by the rhythm of his native dance. When friends visited him in his lodgings, they found him in front of a metronome, tic-tac-tic-tac, taking mouthfuls of food to the rhythm, finally chewing his fork in a feverish endeavour to keep up with it . . . tic-tac-tic-tac-tic-tac. Then one day the truth dawned on him, and he disappeared from the theatre and was lost.

A few days after, a policeman on his beat heard strange noises in a church—tic-tac-tic-tac. He entered, and there was a man dancing, leaping, stamping on the altar, a modern *jongleur de Notre Dame* performing his greatest rôle before his invisible audience.

The body of Felix is still alive to-day, well cared for in an asylum near London. Part of him lives in the work I saw in preparation, the Spanish dance that had haunted him.

.   .   .   .

Meanwhile in the present, on Broadway, the crowds came to the box-office ; they had discovered the ballet for themselves.

CHAPTER XIV

CONTRASTS

" The gifts divine are theirs, music and laughter ;
All other things, however great, come after."

CLAUDE MCKAY

" Vo doh dee oh do "
" 'It 'im—Kill 'im "
" Bravo, Torero "
" Allez-oop."

TRIBAL CALLS

IT IS NECESSARY for a time both for the dancer and
the choreographer to get away from the atmosphere
of the classroom and the stage in their search for
perfection. Noverre, centuries ago, urged the choreographer
to study nature closely. "Watch the jealous man, observe
the shades and differences of expression on his face." The
old-fashioned *maître de ballet* had stayed too long in the
school, if " ballet is nature embellished with all the charms
of art," he had forgotten the meaning of nature, and could
only put into his ballets, steps, steps, and yet more steps.
Massine in his Spanish travels had brought from the
cabarets and *corridas* movement that has enriched the
whole of the dance.

I too found that it was profitable to tear myself away
from the theatre to investigate movement by which I
could measure the truth of choreography, lest by sitting
there night after night I came to attach too great importance to the actual execution of the *pirouette*, lose myself in

its technical enchantments and, by forgetting the whole, reduce myself to the condition of the crossword-puzzle fiend.

It may well be this whole question of outside experience that has given the young dancer of to-day her particular qualities and her early development. Where the Imperial school gives an academic and technical knowledge, the life of the *émigré* with its wanderings, hardships and vivid contrasts provides a depth of feeling to draw upon. In New York, city of contrasts, I learned three such lessons in ballet.

I. NIGGER HEAVEN

A favourite haunt of mine after the ballet was Harlem, and in particular the Savoy in Lenox Avenue. It provided a powerful contrast to the classicism I had just seen, and gave me a greater pleasure in each. There could really be seen the American contribution to the popular dance and music of the world. The latest steps performed in the smartest restaurants and music-halls of London and Paris, both by the Duchess and her *gigolo*, the orchestra to which they danced, and the greatest rage of all, the " crooner," have all originated in some such place in Lenox Avenue. The Pullman porter and bell hop are blissfully unaware of this, and perform purely for their own pleasure, so that here at its actual source it is full of meaning, but by the time it has been commercialised and canned, and has had all the native taken away from it, it is anæmic and empty as a spectacle.

So few of those who hate jazz, or make a fetish of it, have ever seen the real thing.

One Tuesday night—the best for it is the meeting of the Four Hundred Club—daringly I took Lubov Tchernichev and Grigorieff to show them something absolutely new dancing. They were sceptical, and it takes something really new to impress Sergei Leoniditch, who has seen so many generations of dancers, but from the moment we entered I could see that I had succeeded. They were dancing the *Lindy Hop*, but it was not ordinary ballroom dancing in the sense that we understand it. There was a strong feeling of rivalry amongst the couples, and each one was not a self-contained unit of gloom. They improvised and separated, men and women performing intricate steps in front of one another and then coming together again. But such was the bond between dancers and orchestra, like one big heart beating for them all, that there was no impression of separate couples, but of one huge Afro-American ballet, danced by some five hundred principals, or *corps de ballet*, as you will. I saw couples twenty feet or more apart, dancing in unison, as if controlled by invisible wires. All were grinning, their eyes rolling, just as I had noticed in a religious revival ceremony in New Orleans : that was the very apotheosis of Jazz. Now New York, Pullman cars and elevators were completely forgotten. They had, too, an extraordinary feeling for décor ; a semi-darkened room arranged like some Southern grove, with lighting effects of angry thunder-clouds rolling by ; a scene that became convincingly real, just because they believed in it, but that a bright light or a lack of sympathy could have destroyed in an instant. No Parisian artist could have improved upon their sense of style. If they were physically grotesque, then they accentuated that grotesquerie up to a point when it became beautiful. Squat, fat, thick-lipped women wore diminutive Paris hats, perched at an angle on op of their fuzzy African heads, till all that could be seen as a hat, a hank of hair and a broad toothy grin. If they re beautiful—and many were—they gave that beauty a

worthy setting. I shall never forget one tall slim nigger
Venus, coal black, in a low-cut white satin *robe de style*, with
long white open-work gloves. It was perhaps obvious, but
no one else there had thought of it, and she was the certain
envy of all, her nearest rival wearing a canary yellow
jumper with a high rolled round collar. They improvised
on the fashion, never becoming slaves to it, and obviously
gave it the greatest thought. The rhythm of colour is
highly developed in them ; negro Baksts, they blend the
impossible and create beauty.

On this night new members were initiated into the club
with all the horseplay of the elderly stockbroker becoming
an Elk and a great deal less self-consciousness. First there
is a parade of all the members around the hall—an excellent
opportunity to watch types and costumes. They walk
magnificently, lightly caressing the floor, and take an
obvious pride in their footwear, the men in patent leather
with cream cloth tops, the women in the very highest of
Louis heels. The parade over, intending members remain
on the floor. The men form a long line, while the initiate
must run rapidly through their legs, receiving a good hard
hit as he passes. With the women it is a kind of dervish
dance. Each one is given a small stick, which she must
point downwards at the floor ; then she is spun around it by
three strong men, the audience chanting the number of
her turns. When she has done some fifteen she either falls,
amidst laughter, with a loud crash to the ground, or staggers
drunkenly across the floor to hand her stick to the M.C.

Then follows the " floor show," the same type of thing
as in the ordinary cabaret, but performed before an audience each one of whom is an expert, to a loud commentary
of approval or otherwise. Gradually, as the evening wears
on, the excitement grows greater and greater. When th

band plays some slow sad blues, they surrender themselves
to the point of tears; when gay, they swing in and out
dervish fashion with never a collision. That night a man
lightly touched the white-gowned Venus. Like a flash her
partner hit him on the jaw and sent him spinning. The
women disappeared from the centre of the floor and a
running fight followed, as clean and beautiful as the dance.
(Razors are getting out of date in the North.) It is all a
part of the ballet, a little masterpiece of unconscious
choregraphy, a male *pas d'huit* centre stage, with a gesticulating, shouting chorus, and an accompaniment of drums
and trombone. One or two are knocked down, only to get
up and bolt into the crowd like rabbits. The fight ceases,
the *pas d'huit* is swallowed among the whirling, dazzling,
dancing darkies, and there is nothing to tell it has not been
a dream, for, fighting or dancing, there is no pause, no
change of tempo. The whole evening has an extraordinary
dreamlike quality. Then, as morning comes, the dancers
creep home to the drudgery of elevators and dustbins, to
exist until the glorious freedom of the following Tuesday
night, when each one can be drugged by the ritual of the
dance once again.

.   .   .   .

Whether we can call negro dancing an art or not depends
very much on our definition of art. If we belong to those who
associate creation with the free play of the child, then the
negro dance is at any rate the stuff of which art is made.

> " *And what would I do in heaven, pray,*
> *Me with my dancing feet*
> *And limbs like apple boughs that sway*
> *When the gusty rain winds beat?* "

asks the little coloured girl.

It is the most interesting thing by far that can be seen in dancing in America to-day, and America is foremost in its creation. It is far more expressive of the rhythm of the country than the dreary, self-conscious groups of dancers influenced by German post-war neuroses.

During the past twenty years or more Harlem influence upon all branches of art and life has been as great as the Diaghileff influence, and has been felt even in the ballet, stronghold of tradition itself. *The Blackbirds* was one of the most important manifestations of theatrical art we have ever seen in London. London enjoyed it thoroughly, but Paris realised it more consciously and made capital from it. The French, with their essentially logical outlook, invariably make a school out of every individual manifestation, and in a few years naturalise it. The negro entered the ballet first through the plastic arts. Picasso, Derain, Vlaminck and Modigliani, backed up by the poet Apollinaire, and the entire *fauve* school has looked to primitive negro sculpture, just as its immediate predecessor was influenced by the Japanese colour print. Then the man of letters justified this and glorified the negro, who was as unconscious of this art of his ancestors as any suburban dweller in England.

The entire modern school, who looked upon Blaise Cendrar's *Anthologie Nègre* as a divine revelation, have been swayed and almost dominated by the negro. The same, but to a very much lesser degree, is noticeable in the theatre with the success of such plays as *Porgy*, *The Emperor Jones*, *All God's Chillun* and *Green Pastures*.

Such influence has been developed consciously by th astute colonial officials in France, where it serves excellent colonial propaganda ; and its climax was reac at the time of the Colonial Exhibition. If the Americ unwilling to admit indebtedness to the negro, the French have no such scruples, and what the black man under the French flag produces all goes to the greater glory of France. There are two manners of regarding this ; the one draws a strong artistic colour line, and deplores the fact that the white races should owe anything to " savages," whose ancestors were " anthropophagi and men whose heads do grow beneath their shoulders," while the other welcomes any new blood, says that the white man is over-civilised, artistically sterile, and that Greek culture has been worked to death. Both are very wide of the mark. People in talking of the negro always lose all sense of proportion.

It is important to know what is this *Jazz* that the negro has given us, as a blessing or a curse.

We are told that poverty compelled the music-loving negro to evolve instruments of his own, and, for reasons practical as well as atavistic, these instruments were chiefly percussion, bones and the like. One C. W. Handy, unknown to-day, but whose influence is felt more than that of Wagner or any other Aryan composer, brought up in this atmosphere of improvised sound, wrote the first piece of music proper, *Memphis Blues*, which was performed by a coloured Chicago cabaret artist, Jasbo Brown, who owed his popularity to some startling discoveries. He found that by placing his bowler hat over his trombone he could make it laugh and cry. Already something more complex to add to the simple background of percussion. " More Jasbo, More Jasbo, More Jas'," his listeners yelled, and so jazz was born, the results of a necessity for rhythm, poverty and invention. Once the drums were throbbing the trombone bleating—wah—wah—wah—the dance could not remain behind, so Shelton Brooks, a negro comedian, popularised a new strut, "Walkin' the dog," and added his name to those of Handy and Brown to the classics of this new "art"; and it is perhaps just at that point that it becomes an art, if ever it does. Previously it had been purely improvised and unconscious. The step-dance came from the cotton buyers of Lancashire imported into the South, and with its new home underwent a change, and was superimposed upon the dances of Africa, though for how much Africa is in all this one can only wonder. It is faster, gayer; it has banished much of the feeling of witch doctory and fear. Also there is still another element, the missionary and *Hymns A. and M.* Gradually the life of America is shutting out the jungle. The motor-horn is more strident than the tom-tom, the revivalist's hallelujah more blatant than the mumbo jumbo of the medicine man.

The Lancashire man regarded his dance more as a sport for a wake or special occasion, while the negro promptly attached it to his everyday life. He would dance when washing, dance when cleaning boots, and every movement had a real significance, which to this day marks the entire difference between the step-dance of the white man and the black. Where with the white it is a complicated technical exercise, that means precisely nothing at all, because both musically and plastically it is barren, with the negro it is a means of conveying joy or sadness, with all the endless different shades of meaning in between. It has become a living and growing folk dance. The true negro dance obeys one of Fokine's fundamental laws; it is closely related to life itself. It is that reason, and not so much the fact of the special physique of the negro and his markedly finer sense of rhythm, that makes his dance quite meaning-less when performed by the white. The white man in-variably draws attention to its difficulties, while the whol*

K

basis of negro dancing is the fact that it is natural and not acrobatic : it is free, an expression of the feelings of a certain person at a certain moment. Frederick Ashton, who has had the unique experience, amongst serious choreographers, of working with negro dancers, tells me that if they do not approve of a certain movement they will all rub it away imperceptibly during rehearsal, and revert to what seems really natural to them.

Its essence lies in its artlessness ; but both music and dance have followed the usual path of folk music and dancing to a more sophisticated form of expression. The " Jazz " of the modern composer is something very different, sentimentalised beyond recognition. The majority of these composers are Jews, far too sophisticated ever to collaborate with the negro, their very opposite in every respect, and they have brought into it entirely new elements. The " mammy singer," too, is a Jew, and he is clearly thinking of a " Yiddisher momma." Gerschwin alone approaches the real thing at times. Paul Whiteman's band is different ; Duke Ellington's is far removed, but of the same kind as Jasbo Brown's. Serious composers, in Paris of course, Auric, Milhaud, Satie and others, have understood this far more clearly than the writers of popular music. The negro is sensual. He is not all the time wanting to go back to some place or other. He revels in a glorious mixture of sex and religion, without any false sense of shame ; once shame is imported it becomes disgusting. The negro revivalist and Aimée Semple Mac-Pherson are poles apart. The white has tried to clean it all up, put it on a European basis, and has succeeded in making it into a highly paying proposition. All this material for creation is still awaiting someone who can translate it into our own conception of music and dancing, and make use of it as all folk movement has been utilised : to translate it just as the negro translated clog dances and the hymn-book, and not imitate it.

The negro himself, through social reasons, is a grave offender in that respect. The first " negro " song and dance act to gain popularity was our old friend the nigger minstrel, still surviving on the halls with a new lease of life on the wireless—a white man with a cork-blackened face, dressed to ape the negro. He would use the negro dialect more or less correctly, but his voice and his movements were different, and he raised his laughs through the attitude, " I'll show you how darn funny these niggers can be. They're a rum lot—yes, sir." Then followed the first coloured entertainers, but in this very same tradition. It was a proved success and was expected of them. It would have been lacking in respect and business acumen to do anything else. The white man must be made to feel his superiority the entire time. So the negro imitated the white man imitating the negro, and laughed *at* the negro instead of *with* him. He didn't cry at all. It would never have done to be so human. To this day that attitude has persisted with a large number of coloured artists.

The fascinating Josephine Baker, who for so long has been amusing Paris, is to my mind very far from expressing anything real. She is by now as fully Parisian as Mistinguett or the Dolly Sisters—" They want a Zulu with a bunch of bananas sticking out behind. Well, I'll give it to them and how. Just watch me," she seems to me to say, and proceeds to give it to them with sophistication and a deep calculation of the current rate of the franc. It was different with the late Florence Mills, who was at all times a very great artist, with much to express about herself and her people, and with fine technical means at hand. She expressed this spirit of childish fun and its opposite of sensuality, but with none of the offensiveness of the pseudo-negro performer. After seeing her, one understood their problems; she carried on the propaganda of a Booker Washington in a far more telling manner. She knew it too, and was fully conscious of a mission. To-day the greatest coloured pantomimist, Bill Robinson, is the finest dancing clown I have ever seen, just because he is never bluffing or cringing in his attitude. The whole negro is revealed in his act.

If we look at Jazz other than historically, and try to find its universal meaning rather than its local and national interpretation, we can immediately see how difficult it is to transpose into choregraphy, which is the ordered orchestration of dancing. Jazz is the very opposite: spontaneity; David dancing before the Ark; the revolutionary *Carmagnole*; a Jewish Wedding Dance. It implies noise, lack of restraint, anarchy, escape.

Balanchine, now on the spot, with his extraordinary feeling for musical rhythm, and his sympathy with vivid contrasts, may be the first to achieve a real success in this fascinating field.

All this becomes clear, not so much through a visit to the music-halls and cabarets, in spite of such a superb dancer as Bill Robinson, who certainly improvises, for I have never seen a dance of his repeated identically, but through those visits to the negro ball. Once one has seen that, it is impossible to applaud imitation. It is the great unconscious ballet with music, décor, lighting, all a perfect unity—the natural result of some four hundred people all out for a good time.

'Tis best to sit and gaze ; my heart then dances
To the lithe bodies gliding slowly by,
The amorous and inimitable glances
That subtly pass from roguish eye to eye,
The laughter gay like sounding silver ringing,
That fills the whole wide room from floor to ceiling—
A rush of rapture to my tired soul bringing—
The deathless spirit of a race revealing.
Not one false step, no note that rings not true !
Unconscious even of the higher worth
Of their great art, they serpent-wise glide through
The syncopated waltz. Dead to the earth
And her unkindly ways of toil and strife,
For them the dance is the true joy of life.[1]

II. IDEALS OF MASCULINITY

One night, again in pursuit of contrasts, I left the theatre after the first ballet, *Les Sylphides*, and went to Madison Square Gardens to watch a wrestling match, billed as for the World's Championship. Immediately I found my contrast, for in the ring were two misshapen, sweating, grunting men, sprawling on the floor in an embrace, one of them sitting on the other, clutching tightly on to his thumb and bending it back until his unfortunate victim yelled out in pain. Finally he managed to break loose, get up, seize his opponent by the hips and throw him over his shoulder, so that he landed on his cannon-ball head with a loud thud. This was repeated four times in quick succession, the man-missile growing dizzier until his legs crumpled under him, and he collapsed, cross-eyed, in a heap on the

[1] Verse from " Negro Dancers," by Claude McKay, the coloured poet.

floor. It was by no means over yet; more sprawling, hugs and yells, with an occasional cuff on the side of the head. This sorry performance lasted for an hour and a half, watched by eager thousands, who would scorn the *corrida* as a degrading spectacle. My neighbour seemed to be echoing my thoughts :

" Disgusting I call it, disgusting. Why, in Dallas, where I come from, they wouldn't stand for this ; no, sir, they'd have 'em right out of that ring in a jiffy. . . . Hi, lay off, you big pansy. . . . Sissy stuff, that's what I call it ; there's no action at all. They're not trying. Why, in Dallas I've seen 'em gouge eyes out, and we don't even have top-liners."

In disgust and boredom I left. Afterwards those in the know told me that my horror was wasted, as this was all as carefully rehearsed as the ballet itself. At any rate it had made me enjoy *Les Sylphides* all the more in retrospect, and this, together with an experience I had had in Spain, also in search of contrasts, taught me a great deal about the functions and quality of the male dancer.

I had gone to my first *corrida* with Markova and Dolin. There from the first mad entrance of that superb character dancer, the bull, we understood what we were seeing and our natural repugnance was overcome by our interest. Here was a ballet and not a sport, for the outcome was inevitable—a twenty-minute religious ballet in three acts ; the parade, various forms of the dance, cloak play, entrée comique of the picadors, the pure classicism of the banderilleros and the grand *pas de sacrifice* as a climax, where the matador is the complete dancer and never a butcher. *Religious* and *sacrifice* are the exact words, for, when St. Theresa was canonised, three hundred bulls were worked in her honour. There is a definite choregraphy, varied only lightly in each particular case by the exigencies of the one unconscious dancer, the bull. There are also distinct schools of tauromachy ; the classical, the romantic and the modern. The great Juan Belmonte, Fokine of the *corrida*, had imposed his methods throughout the bull-ring. It is entirely from this, our dancer's angle, that the Spanish crowd approaches the *corrida*, a running of bulls mistranslated as a fight. The *afficionado* is blood brother to the *balletomane*. His first interest is in the beauty of the " dancing," and of the execution of such definite steps and moves as the *veronica*, *navarra* or *mariposa*. He will criticise it in detail right up to the final bow, when the matador is receiving the plaudits of the crowd, which is a definite part of the whole ballet.[1]

Théophile Gautier, *balletomane*, who has left us so many exquisite impressions of contemporary dancers, noted this attitude. He says in his *Voyages en Espagne* :

" Because they behold, unmoved, scenes of carnage which would cause our sensitive Parisian beauties to faint, it must not be inferred that they are cruel or deficient in tenderness of soul. . . . The sanguinary side of a bull fight, which is what strikes foreigners the most forcibly, is exactly what least interests Spaniards, who devote their whole attention to the amount of address. . . ."

Courage the *afficionado* will admire, also a clean quick kill, but reckless courage will be condemned if it is too showy and obvious, and the kill must be done according to strict rules. Even the bull is criticised as if he were a conscious protagonist and his footwork carefully noted. A bull

---

[1] " X is too much the clown. His bows to the applauding arena are lacking in the dignity that is the first essential of the serious artist."—Account of *corrida* in *La Petite Gironde*, August 1932.

who will not do the orthodox thing is called *criminal*. Costume, too, plays an important rôle and is subject to criticism.

Martial Lalanda was one of the finest and most classical dancers we had ever seen. In writing an article for the Spanish Press I fell quite naturally into the point of view and even the jargon of the *afficionado*, naturally without being able to go at all deeply into detail.

The wrestler and the matador, two different ideals of masculinity; more vivid still, the wrestler and the male dancer.

To those who hold that the unpleasant and witless display in Madison Square Gardens is a glorification of masculinity, the *torero* and more especially the male dancer in *Les Sylphides*, with his long hair, white tights and velvet jacket, must certainly appear effeminate. The two conceptions are far apart ; they have as their respective champions the fist and the sword. D'Artagnan, for all his grace as a fencer—and grace means reasoned movement— his long hair and his ornate costume is surely very much more the ideal of manhood than a Primo Carnera or the sweating monstrosities of the wrestling ring ? It is a sad confusion of ideas, not man against effeminate man, but stupid primitive man against sophisticated man. Also it is a confusion between what is effeminate and what belongs to a romantic period. In truth the effeminate dancer—and there are many, especially in England to-day—is without exception a worthless dancer. The very *raison d'être* of the male in ballet is to stand as a strong mental and physical contrast to the woman. His body is different, his movements are different. One of the great beauties of the classical system lies in the fact that it can bring out the characteristics of both man and woman. When the man apes the woman that whole contrast is lost, and he has no longer any place in ballet. It is for this reason, the need for the mature male, that we do not hear of many men " infant prodigies " in ballet. A striking example of such contrast occurred in Nijinska's *Fâcheux*, where Anton Dolin was given a dance on the points, a technique that is by tradition exclusively reserved for women, though very many male dancers are able to perform it quite naturally. There was an immediate protest from the audience. It looked all wrong, and was æsthetically, although in this case there was a very sound literary reason for it. Dolin was representing a fop, *L'Élégant*, and it was an essential part of the character. The public however had felt the truth, that this natural balance was lacking.

In his use of one man in *Les Sylphides*, Fokine gave a striking example of his genius. The man has little actual dancing to do, but one cannot conceive of the ballet without him. Not only does he lift his partner, but his contrasting line is indispensable to the design, and his presence to the whole idea and atmosphere of the ballet. He brings into it a definite feeling of love (the word is too strong for anything so ethereal) : an idea that is stressed at the very last moment, where he leaps into the final pose at the Sylph's beckoning. When the man is effeminate there can be no climax at all.

Le Spectre de la Rose is another example of the effect that is gained by the orchestration of male and female movement and personality. The idea of the spirit of a rose is in itself banal. Thousands of producers would have adopted it, thought no further and used a woman ; unconscious Lesbianism to their mind being safer than the experiment of a male rose.

The whole conception of the effeminacy of the male dancer has arisen through Nijinsky in these rôles. In

Le Spectre de la Rose he was not there to exploit his masculinity, for he succeeded in conveying the sexless spirit
itself, but had he been in any sense effeminate, acting
opposite Karsavina's young girl, the very essence of
femininity, the ballet would have been an unpleasant
failure from the first. In *Scheherazade* there was the embodiment of masculinity, expressed with so little restraint that
it shocked many by its brutality, while the Faun was the
excited male animal itself. The whole notion of Nijinsky's
effeminacy, even admitted by some of his most fervent
admirers, with a pathetic, "But then he was so beautiful,"
is utterly absurd. The classical dancer must be a far finer
athlete than anyone in the world of sport. Remember the
mighty feats of elevation in *Le Spectre de la Rose* and *Scheherazade*, records perhaps in height, certainly in the beauty
that disguised their prowess.

The *danseur noble*, in his self-effacing rôle as a partner, is
displaying perfect gallantry, formerly recognised as a male
characteristic. He is the eternal Raleigh, making easier the
passage of his queen. If he sweated and groaned when
carrying his *ballerina* around the stage, instead of showing
how very light she was, he would immediately be proclaimed the hundred per cent male—a revolting creature, if
he exists outside the films, for it is through the films, where
every man worth his salt must throw the villain down a
flight of stairs before the climax, that such an ideal has
been most advertised.

In Samoa the gallantry of the male dancer is carried to
such extremes that the men appearing with a girl of real
merit will assume grotesque and clumsy postures to under-
line her grace.

The male dancer is the lover in every movement, a conception of masculinity that may be difficult to understand

in countries where, by a strange paradox, it is considered so essentially masculine for men to be happiest in the company of their own sex.

The male dancer in the Russian Ballet was the first feature that astounded Paris in 1909, not merely for the reason that they had never seen such virtuosity, but because without such strong contrast they had never seen perfect ballet, and could not measure their own *ballerinas*. Diaghileff, because of his particular outlook, gave a greater importance to the male than had been done previously, though this has been exaggerated, since *Les Sylphides* was created before his reign, but he never could tolerate the effeminate man. A Fokine, Bolm or Nijinsky not only made their own reputations; they enhanced those of Pavlova and Karsavina.

It is so often said as a recognised fact that all male dancers are perverts that this must be contradicted at once. The obvious freaks, who flocked to the ballet at a certain period, were attracted by the dancer in exactly the same way as the gallery girl by the matinée idol. One of my friends receives several letters a day from amorous men, usually signed in full. He throws away this potential fortune in blackmail in amused disgust. No man can be held responsible for his admirers. Of the outstanding male dancers that I know, and I know them all, not one is effeminate in manner, and very few indeed are not thoroughly normal.

" But you must be wrong. It is so unnatural for a man to be graceful at all," says the respectable married woman, hankering after a little dirt, and thinking of her husband, the table he knocked over in the drawing-room, and his old golfing shoes.

But why, I cannot see. Grace means efficiency, it is an

attribute of both sexes, and *she* has no monopoly there.
The runner is graceful, the tennis player is graceful, and
so is her husband, in his rôle as a golfer, if he is any good
at all.

III

On my very last night in New York came my third contrast, a totally unpremeditated one this time, and most
vivid of all.

With Massine I went to Carnegie Hall to see the Maryinsky Soviet dancers, Veceslova and Chabukani, in their
programme of dances from the *new* Soviet ballets : *Corsair*,
Don Quixote, *Le Petit Cheval Bossu* ! This phrasing alone was
sufficient to convict them of active anti-revolutionary propaganda, but they enjoyed a very big reputation in Russia,
and their teachers were the same as my friends'. Danilova
could remember the little Veceslova as a promising pupil.

From the very first dance, an acrobatic waltz of cabaret
type, we knew that we should see no revolutionary fire, no
carmagnole, but the oldest of dances to the cheap " ballet
music " of our friend Minkus, performed in a manner so
vulgar, the usual permanent smirk with behind sticking
out, and an acrobatic approach so deliberate and insistent
that it could not dazzle anyone who knew the art of a
Trefilova or Pavlova in these selfsame dances. It seemed
aimed as a direct appeal to everything that was most bour-
geois, smug and self-satisfied. It was as crudely applause-
inviting as the sentimental singer who removes his hat
and pauses as the last note of his song fades away.

" There," said Massine, " you have the worst of the pre-
Fokine ballet, and danced without any of the nobility of
the pre-Fokine *ballerina*, yet the man is perfect in build and

a wonderful performer. A few months' work could transform him completely. That is the tragedy."

It was a step into the past, the result of a whole generation who knew neither Fokine nor Massine, who had forgotten Kchessinska, save in a political sense. The reactionaries had won in the end, and this was the measure of their victory.

The famous *Red Poppy*, from the excerpts I have seen, is nothing more than a conventional and well-arranged series of exercises that might have come from Petipa at his least inspired. Judging from this couple and the Messerers, who were on much the same level, Russia is continuing to produce good, even brilliant material, and is now waiting for a revolutionary leader—strange paradox. Balanchine, who might have filled the rôle, was forced to leave at the very height of the revolution in order to find the freedom to produce his revolutionary ideas, just as twenty years before, under the Tsarist régime, Fokine had left the Maryinsky to make a name abroad.

Choregraphy apart, the very spirit of Russian dancing, with its large free movements, had vanished. I am taking a risk in generalising from these few examples, and in judging a whole well-organised school, but it is justifiable from the very fact that these are the dancers who have been chosen to come abroad, and who have been so widely advertised as from the Maryinsky.

Hurriedly we returned to the theatre, each one to our respective jobs—Massine to dance in *Le Beau Danube* and I to watch him. As I saw once again the exquisite finish of this ballet to old-fashioned music and an old-fashioned theme, apparently as counter-revolutionary as the doings at Carnegie Hall, I lived in one evening the whole of the ballet development of the last thirty years. I needed no such extreme contrasts as *Le Sacre du Printemps* or *Le Pas d'Acier*. In thirty years, from virtuosity to art.

There was Baronova doing the same *fouettés* as Veceslova, but they had a real meaning both musically and dramatically. They were an expression of the joy of living of the little Viennese *soubrette*, and she performed them with exactly the same simplicity and apparent ease as that mimed flirtation scene where she is having her portrait painted—one of her many little masterpieces. There was an absolute lack of tension, or rather the illusion of it, for I have watched her prepare in the wings, and knew perfectly well what she felt; only she left all that strain in the wings. The Soviet dancers had given one a constant feeling of actual physical discomfort, so that there was never a climax, repose then excitement, the constant device of such a choregrapher as Balanchine. There too was Massine moving his audience more by standing still, his arm raised, than could Chabukani in spinning through the air. " No artist," people say, " but a fine technique, nevertheless." Not at all, for it is Massine who has the fine technique. With the Maryinsky couple every *préparation* was made visibly on the stage, this obvious bracing up for an effort. The negro is actually spontaneous; the technique of the Massine type of artist is to appear so. Both give pleasure. *Only when one movement blends into the other does dancing begin and acrobacy cease.*

The margin between the two is very small indeed, lying first in the intention. *Acrobacy is the making of a movement for the sake of the movement itself, the solution of a problem ; dancing, the making of a movement, it may be the identical one, for what it can express.* Nine out of ten so-called acrobatic dancers are not dancers at all. It is only when the impression received has nothing to do with the danger involved or the difficulty of the trick, when neither are signalled out by obvious preparation or underlined by special music, when the movement expresses the music, that they can be called dancers, and then the word acrobatic has no meaning at all.

The supporters of Greek and natural movement claim that all ballet is acrobatic. They themselves illogically make an enormous sacrifice to convention by using, because they are forced to, music that has nothing whatsoever to do with Greek civilisation. Like us, they can only hint at Greece, and convey the atmosphere as best they can. If either succeed, it is not a proof of authenticity, but because the audience too does not know the music of Greece. Where they generally fail is through being untrue to the laws of the sequence of movement. Their original source, the vase or sarcophagus, is dead, and they themselves must devise the transition from one pose that they know to the next; that transition and not the pose is the dancing.

The late Cecil Sharp, a real expert and enthusiast on his own subject of folk dancing, once made the ridiculous statement that dancing *sur les pointes* was laborious to acquire, exceedingly painful and not without danger even. This is of course quite inaccurate. To many it comes perfectly naturally, as soon as the rudiments of movement have been learned; by most it is acquired in a few months. Dolin, for instance, was able to dance on his points without a single lesson. It is painful perhaps for a very short time, as all unaccustomed movement— riding, swimming or running—till the bones and muscles are properly educated ; dangerous never, unless imposed by an idiot teacher on a child with an unusual toe formation, just in the same way as a voice can be ruined by incompetence. It is no more *unnatural* than Cecil Sharp's folk dancing, now that it has been resurrected by learned professors, dressed up and brought, with pomp and ceremony, from where the village green once stood to the Royal Albert Hall.

The " point " is mistakenly considered the mainstay of ballet, hence the term " toe dancing," the sure betrayal of the complete tyro. Actually this " toe dancing " only occupies some ten minutes of an hour's class. Its æsthetic justification is the impression of lightness that it creates—a bird about to leave the ground. Its mechanical justification is the facility that it gives in turning. Actually it only develops an inch more of the foot than is used by the " naturalists " themselves. Another objection to the use of " points " is on the grounds of the block shoes, but the male dancer, who does not dance on his toes at all, also requires slippers, for the friction of a series of turns would tear the feet to pieces. Isadora Duncan uses the misleading argument, " Shoes on a dancer are as ridiculous as gloves on a pianist." But Isadora, from her own magnificent work, clearly realised that the feet alone are not the dancer's instrument, but the whole body. To be thoroughly consistent, why wear clothes at all? In any case the piano analogy is an unfortunate one to advance in an argument for naturalism. Is it *natural* for a man in dress clothes to sit down at an instrument manufactured in a factory, of wood, ivory and wire, and to hit the ivories with his fingers, bang the pedals with his feet in an attempt to reproduce something that is in itself the result of a highly complex and artificial system ? " Dancing is an art because it is subject to rules," said Voltaire, the French *balletomane*, in an anticipatory reply.

I am not in the slightest interested in the health and curative effects of dancing, but, since they are always stressed by the other side, it is worth mentioning that Alicia Markova, who has legs and feet that any " natural

dancer " might envy, originally took up dancing to cure
a bad case of knock-knees. Nemchinova's bare feet are the
most beautiful that I have seen, naturally so, but embellished by their fine training.[1] " The ballet dancer's back
is rigid," said one " naturalist," in a controversy we had.
Perhaps she had never seen the astonishing back bend in the
last few bars of *Les Sylphides* or the dance of the odalisques
in *Scheherazade*, where rigid backs would have snapped in
an instant. " But ballet is remote from life, an exotic,
a luxury." She had forgotten the moving tragedy of
Petrouchka, that is the tragedy of us all, or the vast primitive
Sacre du Printemps, that is the infancy of us all. In any case
this whole stressing of the word *natural* is a fallacy that has
gained ground through laziness and *dilettantism*. It can
only ever be used in a very qualified sense, modified by the
theatrical convention, as the *ballet-naturalism* of Noverre
and Fokine. Little that we do to-day is natural : poetry is
unnatural, so are music and painting, while the films spend
much time and vast sums of money daily to give, by the
most unnatural mechanical methods, the natural impression
of a man walking down the street, in itself a most unnatural
thing.

Yet all these things are a logical development of the
natural resources in man, and the doing of them alone
distinguishes him from the monkey, who knows not the
use of fire or instruments.

Isadora Duncan tells of how she was watching a small
child dancing on the sea-shore in perfect unconscious tune
with the waves and the clouds, the sun and the shadows.
She thought, as all people of the theatre should, of how to
transport on to the stage, not only the unaffected grace of
the child, but also the suggestion of the harmony with the

[1] See plate.

waves and the clouds, the sun and the shadows. As a great artist she must have solved the problem for herself; she certainly realised that to put the child on the stage behind the footlights and proscenium was no solution, and that even her own grace would be lost and appear unnatural, for in order to appear natural a definite translation is necessary. Diaghileff illustrated this vividly when he turned his great mind to the problem. In *Contes Russes* there arose the question of bringing a horse on to the stage. Once there, he discovered what is now a theatrical truism, that away from its own surroundings the horse looked grotesque, not like a horse at all. It was necessary to find its stage equivalent—in this case a painted wooden horse.

This seems far away from an evening of dancing at Carnegie Hall, but, if ballet does not provoke such an investigation, then the Greeks were wrong in assigning it a muse. It is as an art that it must be seen and studied, and not as something that is good or bad for the health, natural or unnatural. I have never understood why of all arts dancing should be considered thus. Singing, also a natural gift, is never subjected to such cant.

. . . .

On my way home in the boat, by contrast, I learned still a further lesson, one that I really knew all along : for me, life without ballet was really not worth living. Every minute I was being carried further and further away from the small group of inspiring artists, my friends. The sea was calm, the company deadly, and I felt sick—at heart.

CHAPTER XV

THE ARTISTIC BACKGROUND OF BALLET

" Ballet to-day is the last stronghold of theatrical art. Everywhere else, even in opera, the search for realism has degenerated into a sacrifice of theatrical convention."

GONTCHAROVA

" Costume and décor create both the material aspect and the psychological atmosphere of the scene, before ever the actor has made a movement."

GONTCHAROVA

" When devising a period costume, it is necessary, not to copy conscientiously and accurately, but to create original results, as if one were actually working in the period."

LARIONOV

IN Moscow one night, thirty years ago, after a concert given in honour of Debussy, Diaghileff met young Michael Larionov leaving the hall, and asked to be shown some works by Natalia Gontcharova, whose painting had caused a sensation in various group exhibitions. It was late, but both men were enthusiasts, and Diaghileff's visits were brief, almost a halt between two train journeys, with discoveries to be made and contacts taken up. Diaghileff refused a lift in Debussy's smart car ; he was timid of new inventions, unless they were artistic, and took the usual cab that followed him around—carefully closed, of course, so that he could catch no sort of infection from the horse ; even such slow travelling had its hidden dangers. The studio was in complete darkness, and with the aid of a candle they examined canvas after canvas.[1] Diaghileff was at once excited, exclaimed that it was the painting of a genius, and commissioned an important décor, his first by a young artist with a career unmade. And so, the following year in Paris, the curtain went up on the *Coq d'Or*, the audience gasped, and a whole new school of decorative art was born, distinct from that of Leon Bakst —to my mind, more characteristically Russian.

The audience gasped, because they felt the brilliance and the novelty, but without quite knowing how to situate it or where it was leading.

Most of us have been content to accept and to enjoy the decorative art that the Ballet has shown us, without any curiosity as to its origins. Like the audience that night, we have applauded from the first moment the curtain rose, but what we have seen has been either something brilliant and entertaining on its own, or a background for our favourite dancers. The loss is ours, for it illuminates the whole genesis of the Russian Ballet, and shows it quite clearly to be, not an isolated theatrical undertaking, but something that has been given life, by the finest minds of a whole nation, at a time of unparalleled artistic renaissance. The Russian artist has interested himself in the theatre, the music and the literature of his period. It is characteristic that the portraits that predominate in the work of such great artists as Serov, son of the famous composer, are not of society beauties, provincial officials or even wealthy patrons, but of brother artists. Moreover, books were not illustrated by a special caste of hack-workers, termed " book illustrators," but were decorated by the finest

[1] Some of the pictures that they saw that night are in my own collection. Their variety is extraordinary, ranging from impressionism to *surréalisme* ; and the date 1904 !—A. L. H.

creative minds, and the covers of musical scores, even, were rich in fine designs.

The fame of Russian art has suffered through our lack of curiosity. It does not consist of ikons, Repine and then straight on to Bakst, painted peasant dolls, and the artists made known through the *Chauve Souris*,[1] who mistakenly appear to so many to be its standard-bearers. It is more complete and more logical.

The whole history of the Ballet is so closely bound up with the social and artistic movements of the last century in Russia, that it is essential to give a brief sketch of them, in order to understand why the Russian artist was so eager to welcome ballet as a medium, and in that sense give a lead to the modern French masters, who finally took his place. The whole development has been so rapid that I have been able to meet and talk with many of its leading protagonists in each successive stage.

The nineteenth century in Russian art is summed up by the successful assaults of two groups on official academism, the decay of the first and the emergence of the second into world importance, led by Serge Diaghileff, Alexandre Benois and others.

The first group was foreshadowed in 1855 by an important manifesto of Tchernichevsky's, *The Relationship between Art and Reality*, in which he denies " art as an end in itself " and sees in it " an instrument for popular education " ; the professed attitude of a modern cinema Tsar at his most hypocritical, only Tchernichevsky was in deadly earnest. This was the period immediately before the freedom of the serfs,[2] and agitation was at its height. Many

---

[1] I have the greatest admiration for Balieff's *Chauve Souris*, but to talk of it as an important artistic manifestation, alongside of the Russian Ballet, is preposterous. It is valuable, not because it has discovered a new art, but because it has brought the current artistic ideas to the cabaret, and produced them with taste and wit.—A. L. H.

[2] 1861.

of the artists were themselves serfs, and active sympathy with democracy, reality and popular education was only natural. Politics have always played a bigger rôle in art history than many will allow ; in Russia the expression of this was cruder, more sudden and more evident.

In 1863 came the actual secession from the Academy in what is known as the *Revolt of the Thirteen Competitors*, who refused to participate in the subject set for examination, *Odin in Valhalla*, as being too non-Russian and remote from reality. Out of this was born the *Perejvidniki* movement, seven years later. The name, which means *The Ambulants*, outlines an entire programme. They stood for the representation of something national and not for St. Petersburg alone. As all the important commissions were in the hands of the official world, the artists had at first to live a communistic life, pooling their resources, but they soon found their Mæcenas in the Moscow millionaire collector, Tretiakov, and their victory was then speedy and complete. The subject triumphed over technique, and many acres of pictures were turned out with a sound moral and an appropriate historical background. It was the great era of advertising democracy, with " Every picture tells a story " for a slogan. The dominating figure was Ilya Repine, with his grandiose and often inspiring illustrations, but obviously its most interesting legacy is its crude and vigorous portraits, and the reaction away from it. *The Ambulants* were extremely hostile to the great movement that was going on in France, and Repine himself wrote deploring the high prices fetched by Degas and Delacroix in public sales and extolling certain tenth-rate German rtists.

It did not take long for the new movement to become solidly and immovably academic. It had reached the furthest point from what we know of Russian art. The swing of the pendulum brought the whole school of art associated with the ballet. It was centred round *The World of Art* (*Mir Isskoustva*), a magazine of which Diaghileff was the editor; and if his story ended there, in the early thirties, he would already have created history. It must be stressed that he did not merely bring the work of others to Western Europe, as any brilliant opportunist might have done, but the fruits of his own inspiration.

The World of Art threw aside the mediocrities of German painting, and welcomed wholeheartedly an alliance with France. It was recruited too for the most part from a higher social class, from those with more leisure, who had travelled and were conscious of other cultures. Alexandre Benois, its most articulate member, helped by his pen as much as by his brush. His ancestry gave him a leaning both towards France and the theatre. He had been impressed with Versailles and could see St. Petersburg in a new light. It was just at this period that the beauties of Russian *rococo* and *Empire* were beginning to be understood, as against the more Oriental glamour of Moscow.

The whole difference in outlook between the two great cities is important. It can only be traced here in the widest possible manner, as there are so many other influences at work. St. Petersburg was more formal, Moscow experimental, so that where the first city viewed the ikon archæologically, the second saw in it an important phase of art that could have a living message to the artist. St. Petersburg turned to the French eighteenth century; Moscow, with its rich independent Moscow merchant collectors of peasant stock, to contemporary France, and recognised the *Fauves* almost before Paris itself. In ballet, St. Petersburg

was well ahead, rich in great dancers, but, when the
time came for a new note to be struck, it was a Moscow
dancer, Leonide Massine, who took the lead, and that
perhaps is typical of the relationship between the cities.
Benois in his orientation is definitely St. Petersburg.

There are many reasons, apart from Benois' tastes, that
turned this group to ballet, and made theatrical decoration
to them what the fresco was to the Italian of the *Quatro-
cento* ; reasons psychological and economic. The Russian
liked the immediate and glamorous effect of this medium,
and there was at the time a dearth of Russian collectors of
Russian pictures ; the fashion was solidly for French. Here
in their midst was this wonderful institution, the ballet. It
was only natural therefore to embellish it, and to let it
carry their names across the world. Prince Serge Wolkonsky and his successor, Teliakovsky, were responsible for
bringing *Mir Isskoustva* to the theatre. For the first time
in history, Russian art became international, revolutionising
not only the entire conception of stage decoration, but
fashions, fabrics, shop displays and furnishing. I remember
Diaghileff's excitement at the Paris Exhibition of Decorative Arts, when this was so obvious in the pavilions of every
nation that it was commented on by the entire Press.

The great figure behind the reform of theatrical décor
was M. A. Wroubel ; painter, sculptor, architect and
designer. He was at once the most complete, yet the most
incomplete and tragic figure in the whole history of
Russian art ; a giant, the result of whose labours has
reached us nightly since 1909, but who is completely
unknown outside Russia. Always he was bitterly disappointed at his own impotence. " Is there anything," he
wrote in his youth, " more tragic than to feel the infinite
beauty around one, to see God everywhere, and to

feel one's incapacity to express the great things?" That was the refrain of his life, as he struggled with the Demon. He died a madman, but the glowing visions of colour that he left behind him were seized upon by Bakst and others, and given to us. It is time the world acknowledged this truly remarkable man.

Bakst's fame is world-wide, and deservedly so, but he must not be allowed to eclipse the other artists; he is but a brilliant colour in a complex, glowing scheme. It was an essential policy of Diaghileff's to change his artists before the public had an opportunity to weary of them. It was consistent after Bakst to leave the "Oriental" style for the logical of cubism, to avoid direct comparison at all costs. Diaghileff brought the French easel artists, Braque, Derain, Matisse and others, into the theatre. They were a direct continuation of the Russian school from whom they learned their *métier*, but although they created masterpieces, they have always lacked the inventiveness of their predecessors. In the later days painters such as Rouault, Utrillo and Chirico produced typical fine Rouaults, Utrillos and Chiricos on a large scale, but they can never be said to have added one jot to theatrical art, which is so much more than the enlargement of a canvas. Of the non-Russians, Picasso alone has pointed a new direction in *Le Chapeau Tricorne* and *Pulcinella*, which was closely seized upon by Pruna and others. Where Bakst exploited colour, Picasso showed the effectiveness of angles.

Only two artists, Russians—Gontcharova and Larionov—have made the whole journey with Diaghileff, from the first days of Massine till the very end.

Larionov is the biggest of all Diaghileff's artist-collaborators: where Bakst represents emotion, Benois erudition, Larionov is the perfect blend of both. His success in ballet lies in the fact that he conceives choreographically from the start, sees his costumes, shapes and colours in movement. He can initiate ideas and collaborate with the dancers. He is a master of the grotesque—not the morbid German importation, but the buffoonery that has its origins in the people. His own education makes an interesting story that covers this whole period of Russian art.

He was born in 1881 in Tiraspol, a small village near Odessa. His father was the local chemist, and his earliest memories are of eating cough candy and lozenges in the store. From the first he drew every scene that interested him. Then the family moved to Moscow. It was intended to make of him an explosives chemist, but he took the law into his own hands and, instead of sitting for the chemical examinations, unknown to his parents presented himself before the Moscow Academy of Arts. There were one hundred and sixty competititors and twenty-eight places. He came out thirty-first, through never having drawn from casts. Fortunately three of the candidates were rejected for other subjects, and he was received, the last. There among his professors were Serov, Levitan and my friend Korovin.

The actual school did not interest him a great deal. He was fonder of discussing art in the common-room, on occasions so heatedly that they came to blows over a canvas of Levitan's.

He exhibited some landscapes with the *Perejvidniki*, and at the school exhibition some erotic illustrations to the *Arabian Nights* that did not pass the censor. When the *Mir Isskoustva* started he threw himself wholeheartedly into the movement.

A minor artistic scandal saw him rusticated for a year, during which he painted a landscape which Serov bought for the Tretiakov collection. On his return, Makovsky, a mediocre genre painter on the governing body, maintained that his work was so poor that he must be sent away for good. Serov took his part, and agreed to a compromise. He must either win the annual gold medal or leave. He won the medal.

This entitled him to a shorter term of army service, but the army was a turning-point in his career. Its vivid contrasts—the brutality of the soldiers, the dandyism of the officers—interested him, and he was attracted by what he calls " the water-closet school of art," a form of *surréalisme*, and the only place where the soldier could express himself.[1]

Free of the army, he became president of the annual school exhibition, changed its whole character, and devoted a room to the works of a young animal sculptor, Natalie Gontcharova. Diaghileff was immediately attracted by him, and he was sent to Paris with Diaghileff's first continental venture, the Exhibition of Russian Art in the Grand Palais.

Immediately he became a wholehearted propagandist for French art, though he stayed only for a fortnight, having spent all his grant buying books and prints. The pictures that he bought were presented to the Schtoukine collection, where they are at present. Amused and understanding, Diaghileff advanced him the money to return home. Moscow never seemed more gloomy than after " la ville lumière," but he organised a whole series of exhibitions, that turned Russian art in a new direction. Once, when a critic accused him of deliberate *épatisme* and said, " What will your next medium be—grass ? " Larionov answered, " No, my face," and went through the crowded

[1] Stravinsky's *Tale of a Soldier* owes something to Larionov's army experiences. —A. L. H.

Moscow streets with a facial fresco. But he had learned a lesson, and his next exhibition was entirely anonymous.

He asked himself, "Why should certain pictures be called art and placed in museums, while others, such as signboards, are not taken seriously?" He could not answer the question, and turned more and more to popular subjects and freer methods. It was in this mood that he met Diaghileff again. Can it be wondered at that the great " discoverer " valued this man, and turned to him for advice and, later, active help?

The first result was Gontcharova's *Coq d'Or*, with Larionov in Paris once again, as Diaghileff's guest.

We have left the curtain up on *Coq d'Or*,[1] with the effect made all the more dazzling by what was then a new theatrical device of Gontcharova's, its raising during a black-out, so that the whole set could be seen at once.

In *Le Coq d'Or*, Gontcharova went to popular Russian art for her inspiration. The subject lent itself to that treatment, and the singers were grouped on stairs at the side of the stage, in a manner suggested by religious paintings, but that was at the same time intensely practical, leaving freedom for action.

This method led to immediate trouble, and illustrates Diaghileff's manner of working throughout his whole career. No one, save he and the artist, realised what the finished result would be. Each actor knew his own small rôle. If there were any disappointments, Diaghileff preferred them at the very last moment. A leading operasinger asked Gontcharova what the astrologer's costume would be like, and she, thinking of the costume for the dancer's rôle, gave him a glowing description. Imagine

[1] The Empress Eugénie was in the audience and later presented on the stage. It was the only occasion after the fall of the Second Empire that she visited a French theatre, easy in her conscience because this was a Russian spectacle.—A. L. H.

his rage when he was issued with a cerise cloak, the same as all the other singers ! He flatly refused to sing, but, after a short talk with Diaghileff, changed his mind.

" That was genius," says Larionov, and Diaghileff truly was a genius at avoiding last-moment difficulties. On one occasion when Nijinsky, dissatisfied with his shoes, refused to appear half an hour before a performance, Diaghileff entered the dressing-room and came out shortly afterwards with his hat bashed over his head, in a very dishevelled state. What exactly happened no one knew, but Nijinsky danced.

The popular style of *Coq d'Or* gave birth to that whole pseudo-folk-school of the *Chauve Souris* ; Gontcharova herself abandoned it for the religious motives of *Liturgie* and the mysticism of *Noces*. Later an exhibition in Berlin led to the " Caligari style," and a whole series of new film angles. That too she abandoned as soon as it became popular. Like Diaghileff, she was eager for exploration.

The war cut short the partnership. Larionov served for a fortnight on the Russian front, was wounded, spent six months in hospital and was invalided out. Diaghileff in Italy bombarded him with telegrams,[1] and he and Gontcharova left for Florence, where Diaghileff was living in a house that was so small that, when more than three persons sat down to dine, it was necessary to open the door. He was served by an amiable rascal, Beppe, about whom he said, " I know he is dishonest, but I like dishonest people at times. You don't have to be particular about what you ask them to do." Shortly afterwards Beppe decamped with whatever he could lay hands on. Fokine, the last link with

---

[1] Diaghileff wired almost daily. He loathed letter-writing, and on occasions paid a first-class return fare from Russia to Paris to discuss a matter that another might have settled by post.—A. L. H.

the old Russia, had left; Massine was being formed along with the real Diaghileff Ballet.

The first work to be devised was *Chout*, with music by Prokofief. Larionov himself undertook the choregraphy, with Slavinsky as a technical aid. He had greatly wished to start Sokolova as choregrapher and felt certain that she had the gift, but Sergei Pavlovitch did not then like the idea of a woman in charge, and it came to nothing. Woizikovski was his next choice, but the idea did not appeal to him. Then Diaghileff urged Larionov himself to dance, but he suffered from stage fright and refused.

For this ballet he found many innovations, not all of which were adopted at once; objects not in actual use were painted on the cloth, tables were slanted at an angle and the objects hooked on to them. This was a crazy house, the home of buffoons. Many of the constructivist ideas, popular in the modern Soviet theatre, were first conceived here. The work, however, proved too complex for hurried presentation and was given years later. In the meantime Larionov prepared *Le Soleil de Minuit*, Massine's first work, and a photograph from that time bears the inscription, " Your grateful pupil."

At this time also Respighi, a pupil of Rimsky-Korsakov, proposed to Larionov a ballet made up of those small pieces of Rossini that were composed for the entertainment of his guests. Massine and Diaghileff were enchanted with the idea, and Larionov prepared a series of designs. He thought of it in an impressionistic manner, the scene laid in a country fair. However he did not progress any further, and suggested Bakst, who also made designs. Finally Diaghileff proposed it to Derain, who was greatly impressed by a recently published history of playing-cards, and saw it as a game of cards. It was rediscussed with

Larionov, and the ballet that we know and love is an amalgamation of these ideas, which is typical of ballet creation.

At the same time, in Italy, Massine created *Les Dames de Bonne Humeur*, influenced by Hogarth at the instance of Bakst, Jacques Callot at the instance of Larionov. Massine's unique ability at assimilating plastic knowledge is the foundation of his great career. More than anyone he has profited from the Diaghileff circle.

The Larionov-Massine *Contes Russes* is in many respects the most truly Russian of all the repertoire, an attempt to see folklore, not through the eyes of the professor or even the poet, but as the people see it; for that reason the most moving, living fairy-tale ever presented on the stage ; Kikimova, Baba Yaga and the rest, grotesques that are bigger than life. This is not a children's fairy-tale, but the tale of a primitive people, and it is in that original angle that its genius lies.

The two versions of *Le Renard* further illustrate Larionov's original approach; they are entirely conceived by him, an expression of the army experience that moved him so deeply. Enchanting colours are left behind, replaced by harsh browns and reds, ornamented by scribbles instead of arabesques.

In the first version the Cock is a dashing hussar, the Fox a *ballerina* in nun's clothing, while the other farm-yard characters are yokels ; it is however the second version, Lifar's first choregraphic essay and Diaghileff's swan-song, that has survived in the memory. Here Larionov's passion for popular art and the circus gave him the idea of exploiting dance and acrobatic movement simultaneously, with a double caste of similarly costumed characters. Its execution was difficult. The first troupe of

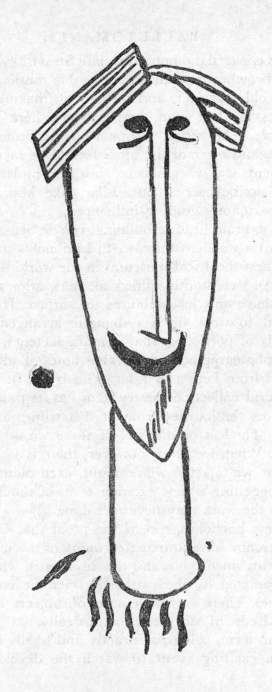

acrobats engaged did not appreciate Stravinsky, and would not be browbeaten into accepting his music. They, too, had an old tradition, and insisted on making their preparations in their own tempo, which here was clearly impossible. The actual troupe who performed was less brilliant, and some of the ideas had to be sacrificed. The experiment was magnificent, but incomplete, and still remains to be carried out. Lifar, like Massine, started under Larionov's guiding influence.

To-day, in an historic building, rue de Seine, four cruel flights up a wooden staircase, in Larionov's studio, is one of the finest theatrical museums in the world, kept in such disorder, so constantly added to, that, after several long visits, I have only just skimmed the surface. It is my great ambition to work on a systematic arrangement of the hundreds of portfolios, that contain sketches, maquettes, letters, photographs, and working notes of all the choreographers from Petipa to Lifar. This is not in any sense a sentimental collection ; every item has its practical value that traces the journey from St. Petersburg and Moscow to Paris. The loss or disposal of these works would be a tragedy. When we meet, however, there is so much to be said that we talk the whole night, each picture or document suggesting a new exciting train of thought, so that perhaps the work may never get done.

In these portfolios, too, is the proof that Gontcharova and Larionov have anticipated many of the major artistic movements since 1900, and the disorder in which they lie is contradicted by the extremely scientific nature of the researches. There are whole series of subjects, each treated in hundreds of drawings, realistically, as caricatures, studies in form, colour, abstractly and finally theatrically. It is an exciting event to watch the development and variations of a theme, if and when Larionov can find the right portfolio. They are carried out in every type of medium, painted and drawn on papers, from thick parchment, rare Japanese vellum, to a brand of toilet paper, the possibilities of which delighted him. Larionov realises their value as documentation. He is continually increasing his knowledge, but he makes little effort to make himself more generally known as an easel painter, in a city where it is necessary to help genius by an ocasional shout.

He is fully accepted by a small group of brother artists, and has been acclaimed by the two finest critical minds of his generation, Diaghileff and Apollinaire. His ultimate fame is certain, but probably he will never enjoy it. He does not complain, but I do. It is largely his own doing that he is not as universally recognised as Picasso, whom he has influenced, as he influenced the whole Diaghileff circle, and whose equal he is, at any rate as an artist-investigator.

Perhaps one afternoon he had a very narrow escape from prosperity. Paul Guillaume brought the Philadelphia collector, Albert Barnes, to visit him with a view to the purchase of some of his works and Gontcharova's. Barnes eagerly selected various pictures, and was prepared to pay a good price for them, but Larionov refused to sell those particular ones. He had given them to Gontcharova, and she was attached to them. The millionaire, cheque-book in hand, was disgruntled and amazed. He walked out, missing the opportunity of adding some further masterpieces to his collection and of " discovering " an artist of world importance, and Larionov lost the material benefits of such a " discovery." He was most certainly amused by the whole affair, and soon consoled by the discovery of some dancing print on the quays.

Some day I must, however, make that catalogue.

GONTCHAROVA ON THE ESSENCE OF
THEATRE COSTUME

" When an artist says to one of his friends : ' I have created dresses for such a firm,' or ' I have created costumes for such a play,' the reply will always be the same. ' It is very interesting (thrilling) to create dresses (in the first case), costumes (in the second).'

" For the friend, dresses and costumes are identical.

" Perhaps there is no difference ; perhaps the theatrical costumier is only more *decorative*. There is another word with no clear meaning.

" The everyday dress is conceived to cover, decorate, hide, embellish, to keep warm ; in fact to make life bearable and even agreeable amongst one's fellow creatures. Everyday wear dresses a person !

" The reason and aims of the theatrical costume seem to me to be different. While they, too, cover the actor, they create the impression of an imaginary person, his character and type. When a dress serves this purpose in everyday life, it is theatrical, destined to give the illusion of an imaginary person conceived by the wearer—fancy dress, wedding dress and the like."

CHAPTER XVI

THE END IS THE BEGINNING

"Wolkonsky, by his remarks, made us depend on the understanding
of a principle of acting and not merely on copying a demonstrated
exercise."

"Matilda Kchessinska—brilliant to audacity"

"Preobrajenska, witty and accomplished, the darling of the audience."

TAMARA KARSAVINA, in *Theatre Street*

I WAS introduced to La Kchessinska, most famous of
all Russian dancers, by Diaghileff in Monte Carlo,
while he was making every effort to induce her to
return to the stage. He failed, and the loss was enormous.
Kchessinska would have dazzled us then, just as she could
dazzle us to-day. She thought otherwise, and would not
risk the memories of those days, when she stood, more than
Pavlova even, for the Imperial Russian Ballet and its great
traditions. I still feel sore at having lost that season ;
without it, my collection of memories is sadly incomplete.

By way of compensation, I was taken to visit her, in her
school, by Prince Serge Wolkonsky, former director of the
Imperial Theatres, a fact that greatly pleased me, for it
was through her that he had lost his difficult post in one of
the greatest balletic comedies in history, and the happy
ending was artistically correct in this case.

To-day, Prince Wolkonsky is a leading critic on all
branches of the theatre, and an expert on dramatic declamation. Handsome, with the face of a sane Don Quixote,

he is the very opposite of my " elderly Russian gentleman."
However much he may regret the things of the past,
joyfully he welcomes the present and the future.

" I am seventy, the reference books say so, but I don't
believe it. I have never lost my zest for the theatre, and,
when the curtain rises, I still get the old thrill of expecta-
tion. How wonderful to see the perfection of these young
dancers to-day."

He has gone much further than I have in his welcome of
to-day. He has even become an enthusiastic " film fan,"
and has made a close study of the technique, relating it to
his knowledge of the great actresses of the past. All memory
of his struggles in the theatre has vanished. Now he is a
staunch admirer of Sergei Pavlovitch, and there is no one
more welcome in Kchessinska's studio, where the pupils
dance especially well for his benefit. His brief reign in
Russia was a stormy one.

At the very beginning of his régime he had trouble,
through his official recognition of Diaghileff, then beginning to be known as the revolutionary editor of the *World
of Art*. He was entrusted by Wolkonsky with the editorship
of the *Annual of the Imperial Theatres*, hitherto a dull official
publication. He made of it " an era in Russian book
production . . . the first of a whole series of works that
mark an epoch for the Russian book."

But Diaghileff had a genius for raising opposition, and
his sponsor suffered. However, Wolkonsky had the greatest
faith in Diaghileff, and entrusted to him a new production
of *Sylvia*. The " die hards " would not stand for this ; a
year book was one thing, but a production by an upstart
on those sacred boards ! The order was retracted, and
Diaghileff resigned. The very same people, who had first
fought against him, turned on the unfortunate director,

and by devious routes the case reached the Tsar, who confirmed Wolkonsky in his action. That was the beginning, but there was never a set fair. The middle period was stormy, the climax a gale.

Prince Wolkonsky has described the episode in his memoirs, under the appropriate title of "Farthingales."[1]

Kchessinska was to dance in a revival of the celebrated ballet, *Camargo*, and for the Russian dance[2] a special costume was designed, the counterpart of one worn by Catherine the Great, at a ball she gave in honour of the Emperor Joseph II.

"About two weeks before the performance I heard rumours that Kchessinska did not want to wear the farthingale. The nearer the day approached the more persistent the rumours became. At that time society was very much interested in all questions connected with the ballet; they were even capable of agitating it. Every trifling occurrence behind the scenes became the subject of town gossip, and, as by an electric wire, the excitement was transmitted from place to place. . . . The question of the farthingale assumed the proportions of something great and important.

"The day of the performance arrived. The theatre was filled to the last place, and quite half the audience was occupied with the question : ' Well, what will it be ? In a farthingale or without a farthingale ? . . .'

"The curtain rose, and to the sounds of the Russian dance Kchessinska appeared—without the farthingale. The next day there was published in the journal of the

---

[1] The farthingale, cause of all the trouble, is a wire basket, worn under the petticoats and on the hips, to make the skirts billow. Not an ideal dress to dance in. One can sympathise with the great *ballerina*.—A. L. H.

[2] A Russian dance was inserted into every ballet, wherever the action lay ; a point that I might have used in my argument with the elderly Russian gentleman.—A. L. H

directorate the following order : ' The Director of the Imperial Theatres has imposed a fine on the *ballerina*, Kchessinska, for wilfully changing the appointed costume in the ballet *Camargo*.' . . ."

This was the beginning of a costume comedy that had nearly as far-reaching effects as Nijinsky's refusal to wear tights in *Giselle*, only with the reverse ending : the director left. Strings were pulled energetically, the whole Court was interested, and, one morning early, Wolkonsky was summoned by a Minister, who requested him to remit the fine. He decided to do nothing of the kind, and, delighted with the pretext, resigned from his complicated post. To have held it longer might have killed that zest in the theatre. In his place I could never have stuck so determinedly to my resolve. Duty, principles and the rest are small things beside Kchessinska's incomparable charm. I have yet to meet a more remarkable woman. I cannot say if she is beautiful ; on reflection, I doubt it. But there is about her a harmony that is enhanced by something exciting—charm, intelligence, character—that breaks up the monotony of harmony, and makes her perfect, the complete artist. Kchessinska is the artist in life as well as on the stage. To watch her at ease, let alone dancing in her classroom, is to learn something new about the possibilities of movement. Beside her the word *graceful*, that we so often use, has absolutely no meaning.

It is useless ; I am completely defeated, I cannot translate Kchessinska into words. A small pupil in her class recently paid her a greater, simpler tribute.

For two weeks the new arrival, an eight-year-old, would not attempt to make a movement or to join in with the others. She stood apart and watched. Then one day, coming up to the great *ballerina*, she said : " I like your dancing.

Now I will try." And she tried, with conspicuous success.

The class is one of the finest I have ever seen : very personal, stimulating and a definite artistic experience. Kchessinska has given herself to the work with intense enthusiasm, working and dancing with her pupils, sometimes for eight hours a day.

YESTERDAY AND TO-DAY

A. L. H. : How do the dancers of your time compare with the young people to-day ? No one can give more valuable information on that point.

Kchessinska : It is a curious thing, when I think over the great reputations of the past, first those of my schooldays. Many, who were greatly applauded, through their whole style would make one laugh to-day. Gerdt, for instance, was a great dancer, but I cannot for a moment imagine him on the stage now. There are others, however, who could triumph, to-day just as yesterday. Virginia Zucchi, for instance, was one of the greatest artists I have ever seen. There are some dancers whose performance excites you at the time, but who leave you with nothing. After all these years I can still see Zucchi.

The dancers of this time are technically very far advanced, more so than even Legnani, whose name at one time stood for technique. In the development of the artistic personality it is a different, more complicated matter.

A. L. H. : Can artistry be learned ?

Kchessinska : Up to a point, it can be developed. The innate artistry of our great Anna Pavlova is a different matter, but I can think of many notable dancers who learned to be artists gradually.

The time factor is the important thing in answering all
these questions. This works in many directions. We learned
longer before tackling difficult rôles, and though technique
to-day justifies a shorter apprenticeship, the mind is not
yet always ready. It is in watching great artists that we can
become great artists ourselves, in time. In those days we
had plenty of time to watch. I remember, when I was
twenty, asking Petipa to let me dance *Esmeralda*. " Not
yet," he told me, " you are not sufficiently ripe." And he
was right. Those old ballets may have had many ridiculous
features, but to interpret them emotionally was an enormous test. I felt *Esmeralda* so strongly when finally I did dance
it, that often I had to fight with tears before I went on.
Here again time plays a part. These ballets were long and
sustained. One could develop a rôle or learn by watching
its development.

I am amazed at these young artists, but I often ask
myself, Will they last as long as we have done? Will they be
as fresh as Anna Pavlova in middle age? It is the time
factor again. They dance nightly, we only at intervals. It
is impossible to be in the right mood every night, and to
force one's inclinations may be dangerous for the young ;
but time again will show.

A. L. H. : Your class differs from any that I have seen
in many respects. Have you any special method of teaching?

Kchessinska : I try to make every class new and exciting.
I want to teach dancing as well as the isolated movement
that is part of it. I try to place the orthodox, routine steps
into a context that will stimulate the imagination. In this
way the dancers will, when the time comes, be able to
assimilate choregraphy rapidly. You will notice that I
never count aloud. It ruins a class as much as it does a
performance. Before beginning to dance the pupils must

get the rhythm into their heads. It is useless to begin until then.

A. L. H.: How do you prevent them becoming small imitation Kchessinskas ?

Kchessinska: By studying them as individuals. While each one must learn the general technique, when they are sufficiently advanced, I give them exercises to which they are especially well suited.

I do not believe in Cecchetti's methods for a long period of training. I find they stifle the imagination by making the class too stereotyped, where it should be an artistic adventure. It is admirable to develop strength and confidence in someone already trained. He taught me the *fouetté*, and I shall always be grateful for what he did for me. It is Johannsen whom I consider the greatest of all teachers, and the creator of the Russian *ballerina*. He was one of the very few men who could teach a woman how to dance.

I agree with you, in spite of these small reservations, that the ballet to-day is remarkable, and anyhow the dancers will continue to develop on the stage. In my own case complete mastery came at about the age of thirty. How easy it was to dance then, quite effortless. Before then, and after, one had sometimes to make a little effort to be in the right mood. Now, maturity will come early. The three little girls, Riabouchinska, Toumanova and Baronova, should play a very big rôle in the future history of our art. They have also ensured the supremacy for Russians, for some time to come.

. . . .

The first Russian dancer to gain supremacy for Russia over the Italian school, Kchessinska, is teaching those who

will maintain the Russian name. These ideas have already
produced Riabouchinska, Rostova, Simeonova, Tarakanova, Lichine and others. That is a proof of their
wisdom. When you applaud them, you applaud her.

My final pilgrimage is to the class of Olga Preobrajenska,
great Maryinsky dancer, famed for her wit ; and it is my
final pilgrimage, for there Toumanova and Baronova received their first lessons. The Ballet is in Paris, and they
are back once again under Preobrajenska's eagle eye.
What the audiences of Paris, London and New York have
applauded, she will appraise critically ; the faults they
have missed she will correct. Mesdemoiselles Toumanova
and Baronova are no more, only the two small pupils—
Tamara and Irina.

It is a curious thing, although I have now been with
the Company a year, it was not until on our return from
America, when I started attending classes with regularity,
that I noticed Irina Baronova's outstanding technique, to
me the most *complete* that can be found at the present day.
I knew from the first that she shared with Spessiva alone
those movements that flow one into the other, and that
nobility of line that seems to reach into infinity. I knew
that she was an exceptional mime, able to render the most
subtle shades of expression with a range that extended from
the passionate drama of *Présages* to the jealousy of the Top
in *Jeux d'Enfants* and the fine light comedy of *Le Beau
Danube* and *Scuola di Ballo*.[1] All these things I knew well,
but somehow I had never thought of her as a technical

[1] She is, in my opinion, the only artist of recent years who has fully understood the
difficult rôle of the Dancer in *Petrouchka*, and who has been able to solve the problem
of balance involved ; " how much doll, how much woman ? "—A. L. H.

dancer, and that is her triumph. It also explains so many things about English dancing, and perhaps finally answers the troublesome question of the reason for the marked superiority of Russian dancers. It is, of course, possible for us to produce Baronova's technical equal, but in that case both the dancer and we, her public, would be so very excited about it, that we would cry out loudly in our triumph, and forget all those other things that turn the dancer from the acrobat into the artist. The Russians talk less about technique than we do. They work for it hard in class and then leave it at that. Actually their standards are far more exacting. They have had so many years in which to grow accustomed to technical prowess, while we, as newcomers, are still too thrilled with the possibilities of technical achievement. It all comes back, then, to the question of tradition with which I started this book. Added to this the Russian has by nature a deep humility, not modesty, that is a social attribute, but a humility in front of the immensity of art itself, so that he will never imagine that a flawless *pirouette* in itself means attainment. Karsavina in her praise of our superb Sokolova stresses that : " religious fervour gave her the same attitude towards our work as we had."

Baronova possesses to the very highest degree all those qualities that distinguish the Russian classical dancer. Since Pavlova no one has moved me in quite the same way, there is a similar almost frightening transformation from the person one knows to the stage personality, and to-day the difference between them is one of quantity and not of quality. I am amazed at the manner in which she takes applause. When the music ends she becomes almost completely the little girl at the school show, pleased, then a little frightened, as if wondering what all the fuss is about. A fine intelligence and a serene nature rob all prophecies as to her future career of their dangers. These are bold words, but then this opinion is the result of over 200 consecutive performances, and not a sudden seasonal enthusiasm.

I have also this season been taking lessons in make-up from Baronova, in return for some English lessons. Like all dancers she turns up at the theatre at seven o'clock for nine, one hour in advance would be considered running things dangerously close. Gifted with an exceedingly mobile and plastic face, she has experimented in the one short year since she has been making-up by herself until she can perform wonders. Now she has with infinite patience given herself a new nose. The charming little Russian snub becomes Grecian, the schoolgirl looks more completely the loving heroine of *Présages*, or the film-vamp, Lady Gay of *Union Pacific* ; then, with three minutes work and some cold cream she is ready to go on again as the soubrette in *Beau Danube*, where the snub is so completely a part of the picture. Like Karsavina she too finds inspiration in the make-up box, bringing one plastic art to the aid of the other in her quest for perfection. Yet in spite of all this conscious effort, this intelligent prelude to success, I believe that it was an accident that played the biggest part in turning a great dancer into a great artist with such rapidity. Playing in the snow at St. Louis, Irina fractured a small bone in her leg. For a few days she took it lightheartedly, until one day in bed she plugged on the wireless. It played Tchaikovsky's Fifth Symphony, the music of her very own *Présages*, that she should have been dancing at that moment. She broke down and cried for hours. Then two months later, when she could dance again, we saw Baronova, the incomparable, of whom I have been writing.

There are others in that same studio to-day, waiting to challenge my favourites, a nurseryful and more; a mischievous, apple-cheeked Russian girl, T. Stepanova, who in five years' time may delight us. Already Massine has his eye on her. Perhaps some of them feel as Tamara did (" I think we had better leave at once, mummy ") when *Madame* shouts at them. Doubtless, too, like her they are sensible, and stay. A wiser, more devoted friend they will not find.

THE END

is the beginning of a new story. I will stay to learn.

APPENDIX I

SOME IMPORTANT DATES IN THE DEVELOPMENT OF BALLET

JUST BECAUSE it has not been my intention to deal with the ballet historically, this list of key dates may be of interest as background to a story that is very much a part of the great tradition, though it deals mainly with the events of the present century.

1661 Louis XIV, the first ballet dancer of importance, establishes L'Académie Royale de la Danse.

1681 The first appearance of women in ballet, in Lully's *Le Triomphe de l'Amour*. The first dancers were Mlle de Poitiers, Mme de Sévigné and other ladies of the Court.

1721 First appearance of La Camargo, who scandalises many of her contemporaries by shortening the skirt a few inches, thus paving the way for " modern " ballet and allowing it to develop vertically as well as horizontally. Marie Sallé, her great rival, also made considerable dress reforms.

1735 The Empress Anne founds a ballet school in Russia.

1759 Beginning of the letters of the great *maître de ballet* and choreographer, Noverre, the principles of which still govern the art. Already, in its short life, ballet has become old-fashioned and full of artificialities against which he writes.

1766 Heinel of Stuttgart makes her Paris début, and amazes her audience by a new step—the *pirouette*.

1801 Didelot, a French *maître de ballet* and dancer, comes to St. Petersburg, and begins to develop native Russian talent. Great Russian dancers of the period are Istomina, celebrated in verse by Pouschkine, and later Andreyanova, the first Russian to dance *Giselle*. Didelot is followed by other leading French choreographers.

At the beginning of this century Maillot, costumier at the Paris opera, perfects tights, if he does not actually invent them, and in French they still bear his name.

1820 Carlo Blasis' *Treatise on the Dance* is published. This lays down many technical rules, and stresses the value of the feet being turned out at an angle of ninety degrees ! The birth of the classical ballet.

1821 Début of La Taglioni. The ballet comes into the great romantic movement.

Taglioni's costume for *La Sylphide*, her greatest success, designed by the French painter, Eugène Lamy, becomes the accepted *ballerina* dress that with variations we know so well to-day.

From here onwards the great period of Grahn, Grisi, Cerito, Duvernay, etc., begins, ballet becomes less formal and more of a living art moulded by individuals of rare talent.

1841 Carlotta Grisi creates the rôle of Giselle.

1847 Marius Petipa arrives in Russia as *premier danseur*.

1858 He is appointed *maître de Ballet*.

1862 He causes a sensation by his five-act ballet *La Fille de Pharaon*. This marks the beginning of a reign that lasts for nearly fifty years, till his death in 1910. Technique is developed enormously and the great *ballerinas* that we know—Kchessinska, Trefilova, Preobrajenska, Pavlova, Karsavina—are born in this, the Russian classical school.

Petipa's surviving works are *Le Lac des Cygnes* and *The Sleeping Princess*, both in abbreviated versions.

1904 Beginnings of the new ballet with Fokine's *Dying Swan*. (See text, page 138).

1907 Isadora Duncan makes her début in St. Petersburg. (See text, page 135.)

1908 Fokine's ballet, *Eunice,* is produced at the Maryinsky and the Greek tunic is worn for the first time on that stage. A great controversy rages between classicists and "moderns." This work marks the transition period between the old and the new.

1909 First Diaghileff season in Paris, and the beginning of the great Western European revival. There had been a lean period after the days of Taglioni and her peers.

1910 Publication of Fokine's letter in *The Times*. (See text, page 137.) Anna Pavlova forms her company.

1912–13 An interlude during which Nijinsky produces *L'Après-midi d'un Faune*, *Jeux* and *Le Sacre du Printemps*, and further enriches the repertoire of movement in a direction contrary to classicism.

1914 Between 1909 and this date Fokine's most important works are danced in Western Europe : *Les Sylphides*, *Petrouchka*, *L'Oiseau de Feu*, *Sheherazade*, *Le Spectre de la Rose*, *Narcisse*, *Daphnis et Chloé*, *Thamar*, *Le Coq d'Or*.

The majority of these ballets still survive in the repertoire of companies all over the world.

1917 Massine creates his first major work, *Les Dames de Bonne Humeur*, which up to the time of writing has been followed by a whole series of the most important ballets of our day. On many occasions one might have said that his period of creation was ended, but the important symphonic works *Les Présages* and *Choreartium* prove that a fresh period has started, both in his own evolution and that of the ballet. (See text, page 149.)

1921 From this date onwards Nijinska and then Balanchine (1925) create ballets for Diaghileff and establish themselves as choregraphers.

1929 Death of Serge Diaghileff.

1931 Death of Anna Pavlova.

Formation of Les Ballets Russes de Monte Carlo under the direction of Colonel W. de Basil, introducing the era of the young *ballerinas*, Baronova, Riabouchinska and Toumanova, who will influence the whole future of ballet.

1932 The first symphonic ballet, *Les Présages*. (See text, page 248.)

1933 *Première* in London of *Choreartium*. (See text, page 250.)

APPENDIX II

[COPIE]

LE MYTHE DE LA STRATOSPHÈRE

Ballet fantastique en 2 Tableaux à la gloire de tous ceux qui, morts et
vivants, ont franchi les frontières stratosphériques
de
SERGE LIFAR
Maître de Ballet de l'Opéra

———

Dédié à M. Jacques Rouché

———

Les habitants de la planète " Vénus " se font une idée fantastique de
la vie sur la terre. Notre image physique leur demeure aussi mystérieuse
que la leur nous est inconnue.

. . . .

Iᵉʳ TABLEAU

Deux jeunes hommes ont traversé la stratosphère. Ils sortent de leur
ballon d'acier ayant atterri sur la planète Vénus ou toutes les mesures
et toutes les dimensions leur sont étrangères.

La joie les exalte, mais rompus par la fatigue et grisés d'un air in-
habituel, ils s'étendent pour se reposer.

Leur arrivée soudaine à laquelle a assisté Vénus elle-même rendue
inquiète par les avertissements des oracles de son temple, suscite chez
la déesse une épouvante ; elle découvre des visages et des formes plas-
tiques qu'elle ignore, car les habitants de la planète *n'ont pas de visage*.

Curieuse et enchantée, Vénus s'empêtre dans des fils électriques, ce
qui produit un court circuit et une explosion. Le ballon est détruit.
Mais, oh miracle, Vénus est complètement métamorphosée par cette
force nouvelle pour elle : l'électricité. Elle s'identifie à la plus belle des
statues grecques de l'antiquité.

Des monstres sortent de leurs antres, des serpents, deux s'entredévorent, des êtres fantastiques, des géants poursuivent Vénus au secours de qui s'élancent les deux jeunes humains. Vénus comprend alors qu'élle n'appartient plus à cette planète. Elle va du côté des héros harassés et les emmène tous les deux vers son temple.

2ème TABLEAU

Un temple où siègent les neuf muses ; à l'entrée des jeunes héros, Uranie, muse de l'Astronomie, qui agonisait lentement depuis que les jeunes gens avaient quitté la terre, meurt et disparait comme un météore. Les huit autres muses, qui ne savent pas marcher, continuent de servir Vénus sans quitter leur piédestal.

Sous un ciel nocturne, où les astres et les planètes attirent le regard par leur éclat, et leur promiscuité, Erato, muse de la poèsie érotique, lance ses fluides sur Vénus qui sent bientôt les feux de l'amour la pénétrer et s'abandonne dans les bras du conquérant.

Vénus présente ses muses et le deuxième héros s'approchant de Terpsychore la soulève de son piédestal. A ce contact humain, le corps se dessine, les jambes et les bras naissent. Alors un rayon extraordinaire qui vient de la terre touche la muse et la transforme en un être humain.

SERGE LIFAR
Maître de Ballet
Premier Danseur
du Théâtre National de l'Opéra.

1er Mars 1934.
3me Copie
pour Arnold Haskell
Amicalement
S. L.

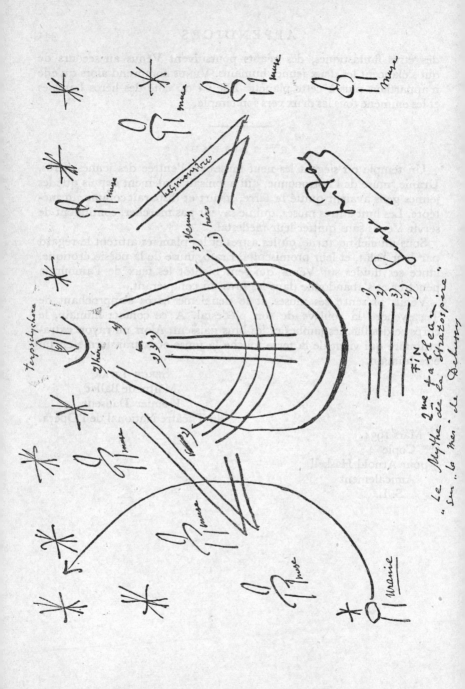

INDEX

BALLETS

Acis and Galatea, 135
Adam and Eve, 208
Anna-Anna 232,
Après-midi d'un Faune, L', 122, 139, 174, 214, 254
Atalanta of the East, 214
Audition, 221
Autumn Leaves, 96
Apollon, 140
A Willow grows aslant a Brook, 208–209

Bacchanal, 34, 98
Bal, Le, 53
Barabau, 153
Bataille de la Marne, La, 227
Beau Danube, Le, 65, 147, 150, 157, 183, 228, 239, 247, 255, 276, 301, 332, 334
Biches, Les, 84–85, 223
Blue Bird. (See *L'Oiseau Bleu*)
Bolero, 217
Boutique Fantasque, La, 45, 75, 77, 161, 176, 182, 183, 185, 223, 247
Boxing, Le, 215
Burghermaster's Bransle, 222

PERSONS

ADDISON, ERROL, 57
Alanova, 220
Algeranoff, H., 266, 269, 270
Andreeff, D., 104
Andreyanoff, 152
Apollinaire, G., 287, 323
Argentina, 218
Argyle, Pearl, 211, 213, 215
Ashton, Frederick, 100, 188, 206–208, 217, 290
Astafieva, Seraphine, 37 *et seq.*, 76, 91
Astaire, Fred, 279
Astruc, Gabriel, 124
Auric, Georges, 17, 77, 121, 290

BAKER, JOSEPHINE, 291
Bakst, Leon, 43, 62, 160, 308, 313, 319
Balanchine, Georges, 41, 100, 104, 131, 151–156, 184, 208, 229 *et seq.*, 244 *et seq.*, 261, 301
Baldina, 173
Barnes, A., 323
Baronova, Irina, 17, 18, 42, 64, 65, 68, 70, 158, 223, 228, 237–239, 244, 262, 270, 278, 302, 331 *et seq.*
Beaumont, Cyril, 195–196
Becheharoff, 173
Belmonte, J., 295
Benois, Alexandre, 89, 118–119, 141, 158, 309, 311
Berners, Lord, 225
Bernhardt, Sarah, 99*n*
Blasis, Carlo, 29
Bolm, Adolf, 254, 299
Bowman, Patricia, 142, 278
Branitska, Natalia, 256
Braque, G., 82, 313
Brianza, Carlotta, 55, 57
Bridge, Frank, 209
Briggs, Hedley, 210
Brigitta, 194
Brooks, Shelton, 288
Brown, Jasbo, 288
Brussel, R., 159
Burra, Edward, 208
Butsova, Hilda, 169